FAIRY TALE ROMANCE

FAIRY TALE ROMANCE

The Grimms, Basile, and Perrault

JAMES M. McGLATHERY

UNIVERSITY OF ILLINOIS PRESS
Urbana and Chicago

Publication of this work was supported in part by an Arnold O. Beckman Award from the Research Board of the University of Illinois at Urbana-Champaign.

This book is printed on acid-free paper.

Library of Congress Cataloging-in-Publication Data

McGlathery, James M., 1936–
    Fairy tale romance : the Grimms, Basile, and Perrault / James M.
McGlathery.
        p.   cm.
    Includes bibliographical references and index.
    ISBN 0-252-01741-2 (alk. paper)
    1. Fairy tales—History and criticism. 2. Love in literature.
3. Grimm, Jacob, 1785–1863—Criticism and interpretation. 4. Grimm,
Wilhelm, 1786–1859—Criticism and interpretation. 5. Perrault,
Charles, 1628–1703—Criticism and interpretation. 6. Basile,
Giambattista, ca. 1575–1632—Criticism and interpretation.
7. Literature and folklore. I. Title.
PN3437.M34 1990   90–11032
398.2'09—dc20   CIP

For Ernst Alfred Philippson and Henri Stegemeier

Contents

Preface

Some two hundred years have passed since the births of the Brothers Grimm, through whose efforts the European folktale was to become a popular delight the world over. Still today, there are few who will not be entertained by stories such as those in the Grimms' *Children's and Household Tales.* It remains an open question, though, how these tales are to be understood, and in what spirit they were invented.

A vague familiarity with certain of these stories is common to most of us, even if only through the visual media of television and film. My own acquaintance with fairy tales as a child, like that of many, came through Walt Disney's films, and additionally from a Saturday morning children's program, *Let's Pretend,* which those who experienced radio's golden days in the 1930s and 1940s will remember. I had long since forgotten about fairy tales, however, until I began to study E. T. A. Hoffmann's fantastic tales—he wrote the Nutcracker story on which Tchaikovsky's ballet ultimately is based—and similar works by his and the Grimms' Romantic contemporaries. These investigations made me eager to learn more of folktale, as the relatively artless ancestor of such sophisticated artistic creations as those of Hoffmann.

Almost without exception, the fantastic tales of the German Romantics were stories of love. Since these *Liebesmärchen* were the object of my particular fascination, I was especially eager to investigate how love was handled in folktale. As I read the stories, I began to notice that relationships between brothers and sisters, fathers and daughters, older women and young maidens, brides and bridegrooms, and suitors and their bachelor friends tended to be of certain characteristic types.

Popular and scholarly interest in folktale has been rising over the past decade. This is surely one of many manifestations of widespread longing for the simpler life of earlier times, in reaction to the tides of change that characterized the 1960s. The appearance of Bruno Bettelheim's *The Uses of Enchantment: The Meaning and Importance of Fairy Tales* in 1976 was timely, coming near the start of the present wave of enthusiasm. It is hard to think of another book interpreting fairy tales that has managed to enter the public consciousness to any comparable degree. Bettelheim succeeded in winning new readers for fairy tales, and in sparking debate as to whether these stories carry symbolic messages and, if so, what they are.

Bettelheim's study impressed me particularly with its identification of certain symbolic representations of matters relating to sexuality. His point of departure, however, is child psychology, while mine is the study of literature per se. Bettelheim's basic question is what folktale shows about growing to maturity and what lessons about this process the stories hold. By contrast, I wish to ask in what spirit folktale portrays the effects of erotic passion, especially with regard to its awakening. To explain my differences with Bettelheim another way, he wishes, as a psychoanalyst, to believe that folktales are conceived with an eye to having a therapeutic effect on children, while I, being a literary scholar, am interested in whether many of the more popular stories, including most of those discussed in Bettelheim's book, are meant to be entertaining depictions of the power of desire—a major theme in much great and popular literature.

As my subtitle indicates, the tales I shall discuss are from three of the best-known literary collections. I have used the following editions: Jacob and Wilhelm Grimm, *Kinder- und Hausmärchen: Ausgabe letzter Hand mit den Originalanmerkungen der Brüder Grimm [und] mit einem Anhang sämtlicher, nicht in allen Auflagen veröffentlichter Märchen und Herkunftsnachweisen*, edited by Heinz Rölleke (3 vols., Reclams Universal-Bibliothek, 3191–93 [Stuttgart: Reclam, 1980]); Giambattista Basile, *Il Pentamerone ossia la fiaba delle fiabe: Tradotta dell'antico dialetto napoletano e corredata di note storiche*, edited and translated by Benedetto Croce (1925; reprint, Bari: Laterza, n.d. [1957]); and Charles Perrault, *Contes: Textes établis, avec introduction, sommaire biographique, bibliographie, notices, relevé de variantes, notes et glossaire*, edited by Gilbert Rouger (1967; reprint, Paris: Garnier, 1972). All translations from these editions, and from other sources, are my own, except where otherwise indicated. In discussing Basile's tales, I have depended on Croce's translation of them into modern Italian rather than on the Neapolitan original. For an edition of the collection in the original, see Giambattista Basile, *Lo cunto de li cunti: overo, Lo trattenemiento de peccerille; Le Muse napoletane et le Lettere*, ed. Mario Petrini (Scrittori d'Italia, 260 [Bari: Laterza, 1976]); and for comment on the faithfulness of Croce's translation see Ester Zago, "Note alla traduzione di Benedetto Croce del Pentamerone di Giambattista Basile" (*Merveilles et contes*, 1, no. 2 [1987], 119–25).

Among the more readily accessible English translations of these three classic literary collections of folktales are *Grimm's Fairy Tales: Complete*

Edition, translated by Margaret Hunt, revised by James Stern, and with an introduction by Padraic Collum and afterword by Joseph Campbell (New York: Pantheon, 1944); *The Grimms' German Folktales,* translated by Francis P. Magoun, Jr., and Alexander H. Krappe (Carbondale: Southern Illinois University Press, 1960); *The Complete Fairy Tales of the Brothers Grimm,* edited and translated by Jack Zipes (New York: Bantam, 1987); *Il Pentamerone: or The Tale of Tales,* translated by Richard Burton (New York: Boni & Liveright, 1927); *The Pentamerone of Giambattista Basile: Translated from the Italian of Benedetto Croce,* edited by N. M. Penzer (London: Bodley Head; New York: E. P. Dutton, 1932); *The Fairy Tales of Charles Perrault,* translated with an introduction by Geoffrey Brereton (Edinburgh: Penguin Books, 1957); and *The Fairy Tales of Charles Perrault,* edited and translated by Angela Carter (London: Gollancz, 1977).

The tales discussed in this study are listed in the Appendix in the order of the corresponding number assigned to them in *The Types of the Folktale: A Classification and Bibliography: Antti Aarne's Verzeichnis der Märchentypen (Folklore Fellows Communications, No. 3), Translated and Enlarged by Stith Thompson* (2d rev. ed. [Helsinki: Suomalainen Tiedeakatemia, 1961]). The tales for which no such "AT-number" was found are given at the end of the list in alphabetical order by the English title used in this study. The numbers the Grimms assigned to the tales in their seventh and last edition of the collection (1857) are given in the text itself in parentheses following the abbreviation of the German title, e.g., "Hansel and Gretel" (*KHM* 1); similarly, the identification of Basile's tales by chapter and number is given in the text after those titles, e.g., "The Myrtle" (I, 2). For easy reference, in the appendices a list is additionally provided of the Grimm and Basile tales in the order of these numbers, followed by a list of the Perrault tales alphabetically by the English title used in this study (and in each case with the corresponding AT-number, if any, in parentheses). Finally, the tales are listed in the index by the English titles used in this study, with cross references to other commonly used English titles, as well as to the titles in the German, Neapolitan, and French originals and to the titles of Basile's tales in Croce's modern Italian translation.

Most information about secondary sources, and especially about those pertaining to the interpretation of the stories, is given in the notes. To simplify the presentation, remarks about versions of the tales known to the Grimms which they chose not to include in their collection proper have been relegated almost entirely to the notes as well. These remarks, however, should not be overlooked by the reader, since they are of considerable relevance for the discussion.

I am grateful to the interlibrary loan service of the University of Illinois Library for locating items not available in the library, and to Ann Michels for helping me secure all of the secondary sources consulted, as well as to the Research Board of the Graduate College of the University of Illinois for a grant to make her service as my research assistant possible, and also for a publication subsidy. I wish to thank Sheila Auer, too, for typing the original version of the manuscript. I am indebted, moreover, to Judith McCulloh, executive editor of the University of Illinois Press, for her interest in this project, and to Patricia Hollahan of the Press for her excellent suggestions at the copyediting stage. Finally, to the students in my course on the Grimms' tales I owe a debt of gratitude for their views and comments that helped me to develop my ideas about the stories.

Introduction

I

At the mention of the term *fairy tale,* speakers of English think first of
magical stories about beautiful princesses finding and marrying handsome
princes. Much the same happens with Germans on hearing their equivalent
term *Märchen,* with the French in thinking of *contes des fées,* and Italians
in hearing mention of *fiabe* or *conti popolari.* It is of course mistaken to
believe that everything we call fairy tale is a story of magical romance. On
second thought, one remembers that Little Red Riding Hood, Hansel and
Gretel, Jack and the Beanstalk, the Three Little Pigs, Goldilocks and the
Three Bears, and the Bremen Town Musicians have no princes and princesses, no brides and bridegrooms. Yet fairy tales about love and marriage
hold a particular fascination. Walt Disney's film versions of Snow White
and Cinderella, for example, have proven highly popular throughout the
world.

Our English name *fairy tale* bears an especially close relationship to
magical romance, historically speaking. The term was suggested surely by
the titles of French works such as Marie d'Aulnoy's *Contes des Fées,* a
collection of tales in which the author appropriated motifs from folktale to
create magical stories of love. Prior to that work's publication, folktales
were referred to in France either as *contes de ma mère l'Oye* ("Tales of
Mother Goose"), to which the frontispiece of Charles Perrault's *Histoires
ou contes du temps passé* of 1697 alluded, or simply by the name of one such
tale, "Peau d'âne" ("Donkey Skin"), that Perrault had retold in verse.[1]
In the eighteenth century, during the course of which Madame d'Aulnoy's
tales and similar stories became widely popular throughout Europe, great
distinction was not yet made between so-called old wives' tales transmitted
orally among the folk and stories that, like hers, were creations of a known
author.[2] The broad appeal of d'Aulnoy's wondrous love stories and others

like them contributed immensely to the association of folktales with magical romance in the public mind.[3]

The currency of *fairy tale* in English referring to stories like those about Cinderella, Snow White, and Hansel and Gretel is unfortunate in that it suggests that the genre is limited to, or especially characterized by, tales in which fairies play a role. As Stith Thompson complained, "*Fairy Tale* seems to imply the presence of fairies; but the great majority of such tales have no fairies." Thompson favored using the German term *Märchen* instead, and offered the following definition: "A Märchen is a tale of some length involving a succession of motifs or episodes. It moves in an unreal world without definite locality or definite characters and is filled with the marvelous. In this never-never land, humble heroes kill adversaries, succeed to kingdoms, and marry princesses."[4] While the genre characterized by Thompson's definition is the subject of the present study, for the benefit of those readers who are not academic folklorists, we shall use the popular term *fairy tale*. Moreover, we shall not entirely omit from our study tales that may lack the element of the marvelous, in the sense of magical or supernatural occurrences; nor shall we attempt to exclude completely the related genre known as the novella. Thompson observed, "the distinction between *novella* and *Märchen* is not always drawn," and explained the relationship this way: "Near to the *Märchen* in general structure is the *novella*. Literary examples of this form may be seen in the *Arabian Nights* or Boccaccio, but such stories are also told by the unlettered, especially by the peoples of the Near East. The action occurs in a real world with definite time and place, and though marvels do appear, they are such as apparently call for the hearer's belief in a way that the *Märchen* does not. The adventures of Sinbad the Sailor form such a *novella*."[5] For the present study it will suffice that a story that may perhaps be more properly considered a novella has nonetheless been included in a classic collection of stories that predominantly display the qualities of *Märchen* as defined by Thompson.

A special feature of folktale is the—pretended—naive or innocent manner of narration. Usually little or no comment is given about the emotional experiences the central figures undergo, much less about the sense or significance of these experiences. Were the creators and transmitters of these stories oblivious to the meaning of the action? Are there indications that this discretion is, on the contrary, a conscious aim, this silence an artistic device? Is the story told as though the teller were unaware of veiled or secret imports in order to hint precisely at the opposite? Are we dealing here with narrative irony, as a reflection of folk humor?

Were we investigating oral narratives as actually performed, the issue of irony would perhaps be easier to decide. The oral storyteller may indicate through timing, tempo, inflection, and gesture how the tale should be understood and received by the audience. Strategies of communication between storyteller and audience have recently come under closer scrutiny. A leading scholar in this area observed that "the concept of performance has begun to assume central importance in the orientation of increasing numbers of folklorists and others interested in verbal art. . . . the term 'performance' has been used to convey a dual sense of artistic action—the doing of folklore—and artistic event—the performance situation, involving performer, art form, audience, and setting—both of which are basic to the developing performance approach."[6] Regarding the question of how the audience receives performances of oral narrative, the same scholar has commented, "I understand performance as a mode of communication, a way of speaking, the essence of which resides in the assumption of responsibility to an audience for a display of communicative skill, highlighting the way communication is carried out, above and beyond its referential content."[7]

Moreover, the study of oral narrative as performance has emphasized the individual artistry of the tellers, including their skill at tailoring the presentation to the particular audience: "A further noticeable consequence of our deeper awareness of the artfulness of oral literature and the radical importance of performance as constitutive of verbal art has been the restoration of the work of oral literature to the creative individuality of the performer's accomplishment."[8] Tellers of ironic folktales may easily tip their hand without adding anything that would find its way into a transcription of their words. This possibility is denied to the storyteller in written narration. In the literized folktales that form the object of study for the present investigation, we are essentially limited to examination of the text alone in deciding whether the stories are to be understood straightforwardly or ironically.

Observance of the genre's requirement of silence about the action's meaning is especially noticeable when magic is involved. The story's quality as fairy tale can only be preserved if the point or significance of the strange happenings remains mysterious, unexplained, and unrevealed by narrative comment. The hearer, or reader, must accept the magic at face value lest the primary and immediate delight in fantasy be lost. We are led to join the storyteller and the figures in the tale in suspension of disbelief. Or, to put it differently, we are encouraged to identify with the naiveté of the characters and become like them, for the moment at least. As one critic recently put it, "the supernatural is accepted as part and parcel of everyday reality. The appearance of witches, gnomes, or seven-headed dragons may arouse fear, dread or curiosity, but it never evokes the slightest degree of surprise or astonishment. Not a single fairy-tale character marvels at the marvelous."[9] Just as the characters do not reflect on, or even notice, the wondrousness of their adventures, the listener or reader must not do so either—at least until the tale has been told. One enters a matter-of-fact world of fantasy where things happen quite differently. Allusion is being made indirectly, though, to aspects of life that are extremely familiar indeed.

Erotic passion and its effects are the side of life in folktale on which this study focuses, as its title indicates. Earlier in this century, two German scholars went so far as to declare flatly that *Märchen* or fairy tales, in the narrower sense, are distinguishable from other types of folktale chiefly in that they are love stories.[10] The question is how folktale, as represented in the collections of the Brothers Grimm, Charles Perrault, and Giambattista Basile, deals with this subject. Whether romantic involvements are important in folktale is of course not at issue. As Stith Thompson observed, in his classic folkloristic presentation of the genre, "In a very considerable number of stories . . . the winning of a wife or husband or the recovery of a mate after some disaster forms the central motivation of the whole."[11] What we are investigating is rather whether, considering the need for innocence in narrative tone and perspective in folktale, erotic feeling can be indicated in these stories. In particular, what role if any does magic play in suggesting veiled erotic meanings?[12]

A possible approach to our subject would be to attempt to identify which folktales are love stories and which are not, and then to confine our attention to the former. For this purpose, we would seek to determine in which plots erotic desire is the chief motivating factor, with hindrances to its fulfillment providing the dramatic complication. The difficulty with this approach is that, as we have seen, in marked contrast to romantic stories as we usually think of them, fairy tales do not dwell on, or even indicate, the nature of the characters' feelings and emotions. The title of this study is thus somewhat misleading, and is indeed meant to be ironic. When the princess meets her charming prince, in the stereotypical fairy tale situation, there is almost never much romantic about it, in the way of lovers' talk or description of their reactions. The characters typically appear almost not to feel, only to act. The lovers meet; external obstacles to their union are overcome; and they marry—all rather prosaic, except for the magical realm in which the action may be imagined to take place. In view of the difficulties just described, instead of focusing on genre it has seemed better to approach the question of desire's role in folktale by including reference to all stories in which marriage is an important aim and culmination, as distinguished from those tales in which it is clearly and simply just a prize won or virtue's reward.

II

While we may be justified in saying that a distinguishable mode of story-telling we call folktale existed in early modern Europe, it is a different matter if we ask ourselves just what is or is not an authentic folktale.[13] We would like to know how these stories were actually told in homes or public places in those times. But to discover that, covert electronic listening devices (and even hidden video cameras) would have had to be positioned at the proper places. In those days, of course, no such technology existed; and perhaps no one would have thought to put the technology to this use if it had. Even assuming that simple tape recorders had been available, the manner in which the stories were told, and what was told or not told, would have been altered by the tellers' awareness that their voices were being recorded. Essentially the same problem presented itself with literal transcription when it was eventually undertaken.[14] Such attempts were begun only in the course of the nineteenth century, at a time when storytelling had long since come to be influenced by published collections of folktales that were not authentic in any strict sense. As a leading folklorist has observed,

> We cannot speak of authenticity in our sense before the 1940s. The general public did not distinguish between oral narrator and tale writer and regarded published stories as common property free for anyone to change. Scholarly recording of oral tales from the folk, at the same time, meant notation of a skeleton content of stories judged to be genuine. Style editing along the lines of existing models then embellished the tales to reflect more of the style of the collector than of the raconteur. Texts the scholars regarded as folk-alien, nonauthentic, corrupt, or retold from a book were omitted. Small wonder that most published collections reflect the wishful thinking of folklorists, not the real folk repertoire . . . [which was and is] an oral tradition of miscellaneous provenience.[15]

Folktale as known through literal recording of oral tales thus dates from our modern period, when the custom of storytelling was already in marked decline.

For contemporary records of what folktales were like in early modern Europe, we are thus entirely dependent on versions of these stories that were preserved by literary—or at least highly literate—persons who were not folklorists or pure recorders of tales in today's sense. Moreover, the tales that have become world classics are based on stories as narrated by authors who were very much a part of the literary life of their respective times. The solution to this problem of authenticity which folklorists have preferred has been to attempt to reconstruct the stories in what may have been their original form, and to do so by studying all known versions of a given tale and favoring those preserved in oral tradition.

The present inquiry into the nature and meaning of folktale will approach the problem of authenticity differently. The literary transmitters of folktale possessed sufficient understanding of the genre's requirements to make it seem that the stories they were offering their readers were actual popular tales. Being literary authors, they of course could not resist improving on a tale as they saw fit, making it more charming and entertaining and tailoring it to the literary, moral, and cultural tastes of their time. Occasionally they deliberately altered the point or meaning of a story. More often, surely, they interpreted the tale in their versions according to what they believed the story was meant to depict. To this extent, at least, attempting to fathom how literary transmitters of folktale appear to have understood these stories may not be wholly irrelevant to the question of what the tales may have meant as told orally in early modern Europe. In any case, as one scholar put it, "For no folktale can we name an author. . . . we must substitute the last teller in place of the unknown author."[16] For the purposes of this study, we shall investigate the stories involving love and marriage contained in three collections—those by the Grimms, Perrault, and Basile—that have come to be considered the early and still essential classics.[17] This approach recommends itself, too, in view of the attention increasingly paid by folklorists to the interdependence of oral and literary tradition in the transmission of folktale. To be sure, in their investigations folklorists continue to give primacy to the oral tale. As a leading exponent of this method puts it, "The folkloristic approach to fairy tale begins with the oral tale—with literary versions being considered derivative and secondary. It includes a comparative treatment of any particular tale, using the resources of numerous publications and the holdings of folklore archives."[18] Yet there is substantial agreement that oral tradition was influenced by literary tradition and vice versa. As one of the editors of the *Enzyklopädie des Märchens* (Encyclopedia of Fairy Tale) has observed, work on that project has indicated anew that "countless tale types and motifs were drawn from the treasure trove of medieval epics and lives of the saints, from Renaissance novellas and humanist compilations, from Baroque sermons and Enlightenment doctoral dissertations, from almanacs and chapbooks. We have read far too little of the vast amount of these 'lower' literary genres to be able to maintain that some form of 'oral' tradition was not written down or printed and read or read aloud and thereby transported further along, either shortly before or at most two generations before the storytelling act."[19]

A related question is, indeed, whether fairy tale, in its recognizable early modern European form, began as an oral or a literary genre. As another folklorist has commented:

It is an irony that the documents from which folklorists infer the primacy of an oral tradition come from fixed literary and artistic versions. The themes can be traced back to literary documents of early simple narration, and there is little unanimity concerning when the oral genre *Märchen* emerged. Wesselski cautiously marks the beginning of the *Märchen* as a distinct genre with Straparola's nights, or even later with Basile and Perrault, whereas Schenda points out that the *Märchen*, earlier far less popular than jokes, became the literary fashion of high society only as late as the eighteenth century.[20]

Concerning the sources on which Basile and Perrault actually drew for their stories, little is known. It is not unthinkable that in one case or the other they invented a tale, though as a rule they surely confined themselves to giving artistic form to stories they had heard or had found in manuscript or printed sources. Basile and Perrault were interested in injecting folktale into the literary life of their times, as Boccaccio had done centuries before with the type of short fiction that since the *Decamerone* came to be known as the novella. The Grimms, however, being among the founders of the modern science of folklore, rather differently wished to convey an image of the range of possibilities in popular storytelling. They therefore provided notes on the individual stories, especially commentary that reported on, or pointed to, other versions with which they were familiar. We thereby learn that they often faced a choice as to which form of a story should be considered preferable. Most important, we are made aware that a given tale can be told in a number of quite different ways.

The Grimms, though, were not entirely candid about their informants. They did indicate in their notes which tales they had taken or adapted from published material, but they did not identify or accurately characterize their informants for the stories that came to them by way of oral tradition. In the case of such tales, they reported simply that the story was one that was told in this or that region of the German-speaking countries, thereby creating the impression that the informant was a typical teller of popular tales from that area. We have since learned that the number of the Grimms' informants for stories from oral tradition was rather small. Moreover, these informants were almost invariably from the middle or upper classes. Indeed, most of the Grimms' more important informants were personal friends or persons known to them through literary circles. In some cases, the informants were culturally as much French as German, being of Huguenot descent.[21]

The authenticity of the Grimms' tales is likewise diminished by the brothers' treatment of their sources. In giving form to their stories, they were guided by notions of how folktales should be told to achieve the greatest interest and effect, and what shape the stories may have had originally. They therefore added language, both dialogue and narrative elements, as they saw fit, and substituted situations and action taken from other versions or sources—or even material of their own invention. The result is often a composite tale drawn from more than one source, much embellished and with other changes, as dictated by the Grimms' prefer-ences and by the literary tastes and moral culture of their day.[22] Again, the Grimms were not fully candid with their readers about the extent of such changes.[23]

Under the circumstances, it is just as well for purposes of interpretation to accept the texts as the Grimms published them—as one must necessarily do in the case of the earlier collections by Basile and Perrault, in view of the complete lack of information about their direct sources. The Grimms discarded or destroyed the papers from which they worked in preparing their stories for the printer. Only by chance has a copy of a manuscript survived that contains most of the tales they had collected by 1810, two years before the first volume of the *Kinder- und Hausmärchen* appeared.[24] Even this manuscript cannot be considered a transcription of what the Grimms or their informants may actually have heard from their sources. What the manuscript does show is the considerable extent to which the Grimms expanded or otherwise altered the tales between this stage and their publication shortly thereafter. The task for the interpreter of the stories is further complicated by the fact that the Grimms introduced other changes in the course of the collection's subsequent editions, especially between the first and second. In the later editions, moreover, certain tales were dropped, and many more added. For scholarly interpretation in the strict sense, then, each tale must be studied individually with regard both to its fate in the series of editions and to its relatively direct sources, as far as they can be known. The leading scholarly investigator of the Grimms' tales has outlined the requirements of this process:

> a serious and comprehensive philological investigation of *Grimms' Fairy Tales* would have to consist of some 240 individual studies, since that many tales play a part in the printing history and sources of this work. There were 211 texts in the edition of 1857, the last during the Grimms' lifetime, and thirty texts that were eliminated along the way in the course of the previous editions, not to mention many numerous parallel versions, about which the Grimms reported in their scholarly commentary on the stories. For each text, one would need to describe its history before the Grimms, to uncover the form in which the Grimms became familiar with the tale, through hearing or reading it; and to document and interpret the changes made, whether as a result of misunderstanding, for reasons of stylistic improvement, motivation, embellishment, or abridgement, or above all as the result of manifold con-tamination. And this must be done not only for the first edition of 1812–15, but for all seventeen editions of the collection (seven of the full versions,

and ten of the shorter version), taking into account, of course, the manuscript material in the form of inscribed notations and textual changes.[25]

For purposes of the present discussion, however, we will deal with *Grimm's Fairy Tales* almost solely as they exist in the last edition done by the brothers, that is, in the form in which their work has become fixed as a world literary classic. Comment on other versions that were known to have been familiar to the Grimms will only occasionally be introduced, or given in the notes.

No attempt will be made here to discover the Grimms' intentions in telling the stories the way that they did. We will let the texts speak for themselves. That is to say, we will restrict ourselves to what these stories, taken collectively, may suggest to us regarding underlying patterns and meanings. This is not to argue, of course, that the Grimms did not exhibit particular tendencies in handling the stories that involve love and marriage. On the contrary, this subject itself would make another book, in which a careful study of the Grimms' sources for each individual tale would need to be made, together with consideration of all versions of a given story known to have been at their disposal and of all changes they made over the course of their editions of the collection.[26]

It needs to be pointed out, too, that while the Grimms sometimes had a large hand in shaping a tale, often they changed very little if anything, as can be ascertained in the case of stories they took from published sources. In such instances, one of course can hardly speak of the Grimms' intentions at all, except as regards their editorial decision to include the tale in the collection. One would have to examine these texts with an eye to the life and works of the author or editor of the published source. Then there is the further question of how these writers or publishers may have altered the story as they found it. Quickly, it becomes clear that this type of critical and interpretive investigation, based on study of the sources, proves as difficult and time-consuming as it is important and potentially fascinating.

The present investigation can only suggest avenues for further study of the underlying role of erotic desire in stories about love and marriage in the collections by the Grimms, Basile, and Perrault, and by extension, in folktale generally. As folklorists rightly insist, interpretation of a single text must not be confused with interpretation of stories as types: "When one studies the Perrault or the Grimm Text of a fairy tale, one is studying a single text. This may be appropriate for literary scholars who are wont to think in terms of unique, distinctive, individual texts written down by a known author or poet. But it is totally inappropriate for the study of folklore wherein there is no such thing as *the* text. There are only texts."[27] The point is put forth, too, that the Grimm and Perrault collections have too often been uncritically accepted as the canonical standards: "Literary scholars, accustomed as they are to working with 'the' text rather than with 'a' text, have simply taken the Grimm (or if of French persuasion, the Perrault) text as 'the' text for analysis. Psychoanalysts have done much the same."[28] We can, however, attempt to discover patterns of depiction in these collections that may not be merely the invention of a particular storyteller or transmitter but more broadly typical of popular narrative. It is not because incomparably more is known about the Grimms' collection and its sources that most of our attention will be directed to that work, but because it is much larger, numbering 210 tales in the final edition (or 211, since a second no. 151 was added in that edition), as against fifty in Basile's *Pentamerone* and only eleven in Perrault's *Contes de ma mère l'Oye* and *Contes ou histoires du temps passé* taken together. A leading folklorist has recently commented on the special place of the Grimms' collection in that scholarly discipline:

> Any folklorist who wishes to define the Märchen in its historic development and current existence will somehow relate it to the *Kinder- und Hausmärchen* of the Grimm brothers. This collection is a landmark, deeply rooted in sociocultural conditions of nineteenth-century Germany. But, at the same time, it is also a source for the scrutiny of the previous history of the European folktale, and a point of departure for the study of its worldwide dissemination. The *KHM* was the most complete, representative collection of miscellaneous narratives chosen from literary and oral tradition in and outside of diverse social contexts.[29]

In particular, over sixty of the Grimms' stories involve love and marriage in ways that suggest indirect depiction of desire and its effects, against some two dozen of Basile's and a half-dozen of Perrault's. To be sure, Basile's collection contains a higher percentage of tales revolving around love and marriage, reflecting its closeness historically and culturally to the Boccaccian novella, especially as represented by latter-day examples like the *Piacevoli notti* (1550–53) of Gian Francesco Straparola. Yet the Grimms' stories depict desire and its effects in a far less open and robust manner than the Neapolitan author's tales, thereby rendering the meaning mysterious, thus more fascinating as well. The Grimms' tales, that is to say, tend to be more enigmatic than Basile's, and present greater challenges to our interpretive imagination. Perrault's tales, meanwhile, lie somewhere in between, as may be expected from their chronological location between early seventeenth-century Italy and early nineteenth-century Germany. His late seventeenth-century French stories increase the association between magic and love already found in Basile, yet he comes close to providing answers to the riddles thus posed, if not in the texts themselves, then in the—albeit often ironic—morals he appends to the stories.

Since the Grimm tales involving love and marriage often are later developments of types already represented in earlier collections, the examples from Basile and Perrault may offer evidence about the meaning of stories in the Grimms' collection that might otherwise escape our notice. It is useful and enlightening for historical perspective, in any case, to see what has become of motifs or whole stories over the course of one to two centuries. For example, the tendency away from an earthy and matter-of-fact attitude about sexual desire to veiled or indirect depiction from Basile to Perrault and Perrault to the Grimms parallels shifts in sensibilities from the Renaissance by way of the Enlightenment to Romanticism. At the same time, these differences may also reflect longer-standing cultural preferences and proclivities in Italy, France, and Germany, respectively. It is not the aim of this study, however, to investigate the tales as products of the historical period in which they were generated. The approach here is essentially ahistorical.[30] Our concern will be how the different treatments of similar narrative material help provide perspective on the underlying role of sexual desire in these literary retellings or adaptations of folktale.

III

Among the various general approaches to folktale, the best established is that of the folklorists.[31] As the name of this scholarly field implies, a chief concern of such research is, as for the philologist, the gathering and preserving of as many texts as possible. Like the botanist, though, the folklorist is interested also in identifying variety and diversity in popular storytelling and in classifying tales according to type, chiefly on the basis of a large number of commonly recurring story lines or plots.[32] Also like the botanist, the folklorist wishes to determine the native habitat of a given tale, to trace its migration to other geographical areas, and to discover the mutations that it has thereby undergone. And, some folklorists believe, as the Grimms did, that a tale's chief constituent elements, or at least certain motifs, are quite ancient and derive from myth as a form of primitive theology or cosmology.

A second general approach to folktale is anthropological, ethnological, or sociological. As anthropology, this type of investigation has much in common with the folklorist's interest in popular storytelling as possibly preserving elements of prehistoric myth. The anthropologist, however, is concerned with the larger question of the structure of values and norms of behavior in the culture as they may be reflected in folktale. The stories may be studied as representative of the cultural period that is actually depicted or in which the teller lived; but more often the anthropologist focuses on elements that are survivals, perhaps, from earlier, more primitive times.[33] The ethnologist or sociologist, meanwhile, endeavors to discover information about the structure and organization of the society actually depicted or reflected in the tale.[34] In particular, the sociological critic is interested in indications of social tensions, especially lower-class attitudes toward the upper or ruling classes.[35]

Psychoanalysts, too, have contributed to the study of folktale, going back virtually to the beginnings of that psychiatric theory around the turn of this century. Psychoanalytic criticism of folktale differs from both the folkloristic and the anthropological or sociological approaches in its focus on the characters' mental and emotional development as suggested by the action and symbolism of the plot. For the psychoanalyst, the social and cultural setting or origin of the tale is of relatively minor importance. The emotional situation depicted or symbolized is viewed as more or less universally present and valid, at all times and places in human history. Moreover, the tale's inventor and its transmitters are implicitly assumed to have unconsciously intuited and anticipated the tenets of psychoanalytic theory. For those who assume the omnipresence of the Freudian Oedipal complex or the Jungian collective unconscious, it follows that these psychic phenomena have manifested themselves not only in life but in literary and artistic depictions.[36]

Psychoanalysts, folklorists, anthropologists, and sociologists most often have been attracted by popular storytelling partly because they view it as an unconscious—or not especially self-conscious—art. For much the same reason, literary historians, on the whole, have ignored popular stories as an object of interpretive study. Folktale, as such, has been considered a subliterary genre. Scholars studying German literature have, to be sure, been concerned with the history of the Grimms' interest in folktale, and with their activity in collecting, editing, and publishing their popular stories. Scholars have also addressed such questions as the Grimms' immediate sources for their tales and the existence of earlier versions of a given tale in older publications or manuscripts. There has also been a great interest in attempting to define the characteristics of popular tales as distinguished from artistic fairy tales, or *Kunstmärchen*, and in setting apart the fairy tale, or *Märchen*, from other forms of popular narrative.[37] What literary scholars have hardly begun to do is to subject tales such as those in Basile, Perrault, and the Grimms to the interpretive analysis they regularly undertake with other fiction. One reason for this is that they are accustomed to dealing with works by known authors, or at least with anonymous works that can be assumed to be the work of a single author (exceptions include large epics like those attributed to Homer or, in German literature, the *Nibelungenlied*, where the questions of authorship and of the work's origins in oral tradition form fields of scholarly inquiry in themselves). The authorship and origins of the individual folktale are complex and shrouded in mystery. The philologist feels a need to have answers to those questions before proceeding to probe the meaning of a text. This concern is of course justified. How can we ask about meaning when the text is the work of so many hands? Another reason for literary scholars' reticence in interpreting folktale, however, is a belief, deriving from romantic notions about popular culture, that these stories are products of a naive imagination incapable of conceiving hidden or deeper meanings of the sort that critics discover in other types of text.

The present study will challenge this belief in the innocence of folktale as regards the depiction of matters pertaining to sexual desire. In contrast to psychoanalytic critics, we will not assume that portrayals of psychic processes were produced unconsciously by the stories' creators, nor that the storytellers were forerunners of modern psychoanalysts. Since the approach will be a literary one, we will instead make the contrary assumption that, while the invention of the story may have occurred more or less in the unconscious, its creator understood its meaning and expected its audience—at least some members of it—to understand its import very much within the specific cultural framework of the time. We thus are asking whether the creators or adapters of these stories were interested in the depiction of desire and its effects and, if so, how they went about indicating this. Also, we shall want to discover which aspects of desire's effects interested the tales' transmitters most especially or most broadly, and which not at all.

An analysis of the role of desire in early modern European literature, and the attitudes toward it reflected therein, lies outside the scope of this investigation. It will be accepted by anyone familiar with the literature of the Renaissance—and of the Middle Ages and antiquity—that depiction of sexual matters was not only common but a major subject for mirth and delight and a chief object of wit and humor. One needs only to think of Boccaccio and Chaucer, Cervantes and Shakespeare—for earlier times, Homer and Ovid. With specific regard to the collections of Basile, Perrault, and the Grimms, they were done during the period—early seventeenth to early nineteenth centuries—that saw the rise to theatrical hegemony and then the decline of the *commedia dell'arte*, in which the plot typically concerned the fulfillment of a young couple's desire despite the machinations of an old fool, usually the girl's uncle or guardian or both, who falls in love with the maiden himself. It might be objected that these examples are from the literary, as opposed to the popular, culture of the times; but the burden of proof that popular culture in early modern Europe did not participate in such mirth about sexuality rests squarely with the doubters.

Comic depiction of sexual love in early modern Europe often employed traditional stereotypes about women. Recent feminist criticism has paid much attention to these portrayals in folktale. As one critic put it, "The pattern of enchantment and disenchantment, the formulaic closing with nuptial rites, and the plot's comic structure seem so conventional that we do not question the implications. Yet, traditional patterns, no less than fantasy characterizations and actions, contribute to the fairy tale's potency as a purveyor of romantic archetypes and, thereby, of cultural precepts for young women."[38] The same critic pointed out that receipt of great wealth and sexual awakening and marriage are often linked in such a way as to indicate that the heroines are being rewarded for adopting "conventional female virtues, that is, patience, sacrifice and dependency," and that " 'Romance' glosses over the heroine's impotence: she is unable to act independently or self-assertively; she relies on external agents for rescue; she binds herself first to the father and then to the prince; she restricts her ambitions to hearth and nursery."[39] Fairy tale is in this sense an ancestor of popular romances for women.[40]

The passivity of many heroines in romantic folktales has been a particular concern of feminist critics. Film versions of fairy tales have attracted special notice. As one critic wittily observed, "if the Grimm heroines are, for the most part, uninspiring, those of Walt Disney seem barely alive. In fact, two of them [among the trio Cinderella, Sleeping Beauty, and Snow White] hardly manage to stay awake."[41] The same critic noted that in folktale "Heroes succeed because they act, not because they are. They are judged not by their appearance or inherent sweet nature but by their ability to overcome obstacles, even if these obstacles are defects in their own characters. Heroines are not allowed any defects, nor are they required to develop, since they are already perfect."[42] In studying folktale from this perspective, feminist critics have found, however, that there are, as one put it, "fairy tales which do present their women as active, intelligent, and courageous human beings."[43]

It has been argued, too, that while fairy tale is clearly the product of a patriarchal culture and society, its origins reach back to matriarchal myths, in which women were the powerful figures and protagonists.[44] As one critic has suggested, "the female's original access to power through her association with nature became perverted and denied, so that more recent versions of fairy tales relegate power held by females to the old, the ugly, and/or the wicked."[45] While this interpretive view is highly speculative, it calls attention to the important question of the effect of changing cultural ideals upon the depiction of sexual roles in folktale. Feminist critics have pointed also to indications that the role of women as tellers of fairy tale romance had a long history:

perhaps Madame d'Aulnoy or her carriage trade ladies differ only in status and style from Basile's townswomen, the French vieilles, or English old wives and middle-class governesses. We may also wish to reconceptualize Madame d'Aulnoy, Mlle l'Héritier, and Madame de Beaumont not as pseudo-masculine appropriators of folkloric tradition, but as reappropriators of a female art of tale-telling that dates back to Philomela and Scheherezade. As such, they foreshadow, indeed perhaps foster, the eighteenth- and nineteenth-century emergence of a passion for romantic fictions, particularly among women writers and readers.[46]

Related questions about social and political implications of the way folktales are invented or shaped have recently been raised, too. The prescription of passive or subservient roles for women is indeed one aspect of this question.[47] This line of inquiry asks, for example, to what extent editors of folktale collections adapted the stories according to the pedagogical aims of particular groups or classes. A leading exponent of this approach concludes, for example, that Perrault, in his *Histoires ou contes du temps passé* of 1697, "directed his energies in writing his fairy tales for the most part to civilize children and to prepare them for roles which he idealistically believed they should play in society."[48] Similarly, in this critic's view, the Grimms in their early nineteenth-century collection "sought to link the beliefs and behavior of the characters in folk tales to the cultivation of bourgeois norms."[49] The point is well taken. It is important for understanding and studying folktales to remember that collectors—and tellers— of folktale have particular audiences and special aims in mind, which may reflect changing structures in society and accompanying shifts in social norms.

While we shall keep in mind these questions raised recently by feminist criticism and related approaches and shall indeed refer to them along the way, the present discussion has a different focus. Accepting the propositions that these stories strongly reflect values and attitudes of a traditional patriarchal society and essentially misogynistic culture and that between the collections of Basile and the Grimms a process of bourgeois "refinement" of folktale occurred, we shall attempt to describe and analyze the handling of sexual desire as a poetic subject within that framework. At the center of our attention will be the fairy tale heroines, the nubile maidens for whom the time to marry has arrived. And our chief question will be how this change or crisis in their lives is depicted.

As an early feminist critic observed, "In effect, these stories [i.e., fairy tales about marriage] focus upon courtship, which is magnified into the most important and exciting part of a girl's life, brief though courtship is, because it is the part of her life in which she most counts as a person herself."[50] While that critic made the observation to object that the implication is that after marriage a woman "ceases to be wooed, her consent is no longer sought, she derives her status from her husband, and her personal identity is thus snuffed out,"[51] we will examine just how, in these stories, this obviously dominant fascination with girls' arrival at marriageable age expresses itself. How is the maiden portrayed as reacting to this change, and how does it affect those around her? Of what concern is it to her brothers, if she has any, and how does it change her relationship with them? How does she relate to her suitors, and how is she affected by the wedding night and attendant loss of sexual innocence? What are the typical changes or crises in the relationship between father and daughter as the prospect of marriage arises? How is the girl's arrival at womanhood greeted by her mother and other older women around her? In those cases where she must act to win the beloved or to keep him, how does she go about it and how does this characterize her? Finally, what differences do we find in stories about marriage where the central figure is the prospective bridegroom, not the maiden, or in which the crisis about love and the wedding night affects the man as much as the woman?

NOTES

1. For early reference to these terms as being the ones current in Perrault's and d'Aulnoy's day and before, see Charles Deulin, *Les Contes de ma mère l'Oye avant Perrault* (Paris: E. Dentu, 1879; reprint, Geneva: Slatkine, 1969), pp. 9–11.

2. Among the several types of folktale, the love stories were perhaps cultivated especially by female storytellers. This opinion was voiced, for example, by Ludwig Felix Weber in his *Märchen und Schwank: Eine stilkritische Studie zur Volksdichtung* (Diss., Kiel, 1904; Kiel: H. Fiencke, 1904), pp. 64–65. A Jungian interpretation of myth and fairy tale as creation of the female psyche or projections of the male anima image was made by Marie-Louise von Franz, *Problems of the Feminine in Fairy Tales* (1972; rev. ed., New York: Spring, 1976).

3. Concerning the vogue of fairy stories from the reign of Louis XIV to the time of the French Revolution, see P. Victor Delaporte, *Du Merveilleux dans la littérature française sous le règne de Louis XIV* (Paris: Retaux-Bray, 1891); Mary Elizabeth Storer, *Un épisode littéraire de la fin du xviiᵉ siècle: La mode des contes des fées*, Bibliothèque de la Revue de la littérature comparée, 48 (Paris: Champion, 1928); and Gonthier-Louis Fink, *Naissance et apogée du conte merveilleux en Allemagne 1740–1800*, Annales littéraires de l'Université de Besançon, 80 (Paris: Belles Lettres, 1966). Perspective on how fairy tales came to be popular in England is provided in Iona Opie and Peter Opie, *The Classic Fairy Tales* (London: Oxford Univ. Press, 1974).

4. Stith Thompson, *The Folktale* (1946; reprint, Berkeley: Univ. of California Press, 1977), p. 8.

5. Ibid., p. 8.

6. Richard Bauman, *Verbal Art as Performance*, with supplementary essays by Barbara A. Babcock, Gary H. Gossen, Roger D. Abrahams, and Joel F. Sherzer (1977; reprint, Prospect Heights, Ill.: Waveland Press, 1984), p. 4.

7. Richard Bauman, *Story, Performance, and Event: Contextual Studies of Oral Narrative*, Cambridge Studies in Oral and Literate Culture, 10 (Cambridge: Cambridge Univ. Press, 1986), p. 3.

8. Ibid., p. 8.

9. Maria Tatar, *The Hard Facts of the Grimms' Fairy Tales* (Princeton: Princeton Univ. Press, 1987), p. 61.

10. See Weber, *Märchen und Schwank*, pp. 38–39, and Walter A. Berendsohn, *Grundformen volkstümlicher Erzählerkunst in den Kinder- und Hausmärchen der Brüder Grimm: Ein stilkritischer Versuch* (Hamburg: W. Gente, 1921; rev. reprint, 1968), p. 35. A still earlier study also focused on the theme of erotic love in folktale, but claimed that love as portrayed in the *Kinder- und Hausmärchen* represented a poetic depiction of a specifically German ideal of the relationship between man and woman; see Marie Luise Becker, *Die Liebe im deutschen Märchen* (Leipzig: Hermann Seemann, 1901). An attempt at a composite characterization of the *Märchen* as romance was made by Marie-Elisabeth Rosenbaum, *Liebe und Ehe im deutschen Volksmärchen* (Diss., Jena, 1929; Klosterlausnitz: n.p., 1932); no clear picture of the *Liebesmärchen* as a folktale genre emerges from her study, however.

11. Thompson, *Folktale*, p. 87.

12. For comment on the veiling of erotic elements in fairy tales, or the argument that the genre prescribes their absence or elimination, see Friedrich Panzer, *Märchen, Sage und Dichtung* (Munich: C. H. Beck, 1905), p. 12; Max Lüthi, *Das europäische Volksmärchen: Form und Wesen*, 2d rev. ed., Dalp Taschenbücher, 351 (1947; Berne: Francke, 1960), pp. 66–67; and Hermann Bausinger, "Anmerkungen zu Schneewittchen," in Helmut Brackert, ed., *Und wenn sie nicht gestorben sind . . .: Perspektiven auf das Märchen*, edition suhrkamp, 973 (Frankfurt am Main: Suhrkamp, 1980), pp. 62–63. The question of hidden erotic meanings has been discussed most recently by Ruth B. Bottigheimer, *Grimms' Bad Girls and Bold Boys: The Moral and Social Vision of the Tales* (New Haven: Yale Univ. Press, 1987), esp. "Eroticism in Tradition, Text, and Image" (pp. 156–66), and Tatar, *Hard Facts of the Grimms' Fairy Tales*, esp. "Sex and Violence" (pp. 3–38). Both Bottigheimer and Tatar, however, are chiefly concerned with indicting the Grimms for softening, hiding, or removing erotic import in the tales, not with investigating the generic tradition of such depiction per se.

13. Generally, literary scholars agree that the European folktale as we know it began to develop during the Middle Ages, and in close connection with the literature of that period; see for example Friedrich von der Leyen, *Das deutsche Märchen*, 3d ed. (1917; Leipzig: Quelle & Meyer, 1930); Albert Wesselski, *Märchen des Mittelalters* (Berlin: Herbert Stubenrauch, 1925), and his *Versuch einer Theorie des Märchens*, Prager deutsche Studien, 45 (Reichenberg: [Bohemia]: Sudetendeutscher

Verlag Franz Kraus, 1931), esp. p. 196; Lutz Röhrich, *Erzählungen des späten Mittelalters und ihr Weiterleben in Literatur und Volksdichtung bis zur Gegenwart: Sagen, Märchen, Exempel und Schwänke mit einem Kommentar,* 2 vols. (Berne: Francke, 1962–67); and Hermann Hubert Wetzel, *Märchen in den französischen Novellensammlungen der Renaissance* (Berlin: Erich Schmidt, 1974).

14. For comment that the manner of a story's telling is inseparable from the conditions under which it is told, see for example Karl Schulte-Kemminghausen, *Die niederdeutschen Märchen der Brüder Grimm,* Veröffentlichungen der volkskundlichen Kommission des Provinzialinstituts für westfälische Landes- und Volkskunde: 3d ser., 1 (Münster in Westfalen: Aschendorff, 1932), pp. 18–19.

15. Linda Dégh, "What Did the Grimm Brothers Give to and Take from the Folk?" in James M. McGlathery, ed., *The Brothers Grimm and Folktale* (Urbana: Univ. of Illinois Press, 1988), pp. 69–70.

16. See Weber, *Märchen und Schwank,* p. 64. Beginning with Hans Naumann's argument that oral transmission of folktales involved "disintegration in the telling" (*Zersprechen*) in his *Grundzüge der deutschen Volkskunde* (Wissenschaft und Bildung, 181 [Leipzig: Quelle & Meyer, 1922], p. 142), there arose a controversy over whether oral or written transmission was chiefly responsible for having maintained the tales relatively intact, and thus whether the oral or literary tradition had a greater claim to authenticity, also with regard to the story's original form and meaning. See Wesselski, *Versuch einer Theorie des Märchens,* esp. p. 178; Walter Anderson, *Zu Albert Wesselski's Angriffen auf die finnische folkloristische Forschungsmethode,* Eesti Rahvaluule Arhiivi Toimetused/Commentationes archivi traditionum popularum estoniae, 4 (Tartu: K. Mattiesen, 1935); Albert Wesselski, *Deutsche Märchen vor Grimm* (Brünn: Rudolf M. Rohrer, 1938); Ernst A. Philippson, "Um Grundsätzliches in der Märchenforschung," *Monatshefte für den deutschen Unterricht,* 37, nos. 4–5 (1945), 135–50; Emma Emily Kiefer, *Albert Wesselski and Recent Folktale Theories,* Indiana Univ. Publications: Folklore Series, 3 (Bloomington: Indiana Univ. Press, 1947); Walter Anderson, *Ein volkskundliches Experiment,* Folklore Fellows' Communications, 141 (Helsinki: Suomalainen Tiedeakatemia/Academia scientificarum fennica, 1951); Paul Delarue, "Les Contes merveilleux de Perrault et la tradition populaire: Introduction," *Bulletin folklorique d'Ile-de-France,* n.s. 12 (1951), 195–201; and Kurt Schier, *Praktische Untersuchungen zur mündlichen Wiedergabe von Volkserzählungen* (Diss., Munich, 1955; Munich: Omnia-Kraus, Weiss und Co., 1955).

The creative and imaginative role played not only by the inventors but also by the oral transmitters of folktales has been emphasized by Sebastiano Lo Nigro, *Tradizione e invenzione nel racconto popolare,* Istituto di Storia delle Tradizioni Popolari dell'Università di Catania: Studi e Testi, 2 (Florence: Leo S. Olschki, 1964); and Felix Karlinger, *Einführung in die romanische Volksliteratur, 1. Teil: Die romanische Volksprosa* (Munich: Hueber, 1969), esp. p. 16. See also Dégh, "What Did the Grimm Brothers Give to and Take from the Folk?"

17. For discussion of the style and content of Basile's stories, as they relate to his life and literary times in early seventeenth-century Italy, see Benedetto Croce, "Giambattista Basile e l'elaborazione artistica delle fiabe popolari," in Giambattista Basile, *Il Pentamerone*, ed. and trans. Benedetto Croce, pp. xiii–xxxv; Ursula Klöne, *Die Aufnahme des Märchens in der italienischen Kunstprosa von Straparola bis Basile* (Diss., Marburg, 1961; Marburg: Erich Mauersberger, 1961); and Giovanni Getto, "Il barocco e la fiaba di Giambattista Basile," in Alessandro S. Crissafulli, ed., *Linguistic and Literary Studies in Honor of Helmut A. Hatzfeld* (Washington, D.C.: Catholic Univ. of America Press, 1964), pp. 185–201.

A readily available introduction to Perrault's life and works has been provided by Jacques Barchilon and Peter Flinders, *Charles Perrault*, Twayne's World Author Series, 639 (Boston: Twayne, 1981). The best-known critical studies of Perrault are those by Marc Soriano, *Les Contes de Perrault: Culture savante et traditions populaires* (Paris: Gallimard, 1968) and *Le Dossier Perrault* (Paris: Hachette, 1972). For a similarly Freudian orientation, see Jacques Marx, "Perrault et le sommeil de la raison," *Cahiers internationaux de Symbolisme*, 40/41 (1980), 83–92. For Perrault's published as opposed to oral sources, see Jeanne Morgan, *Perrault's Moral for Moderns*, American University Studies: Series II: Romance Languages and Literatures, 28 (New York: Peter Lang, 1985). Giovanni Cristini, in *Charles Perrault* (Brescia: "La Scuola," 1954), discusses the extent to which the tales are adult or children's literature. A survey of criticism on Perrault up through the beginning of this century may be found in Theodor Pletscher, *Die Märchen Charles Perraults: Eine literarhistorische und literaturvergleichende Studie* (Berlin: Mayer & Müller, 1906). For a review of the question of Perrault's authorship of the tales, in which it is argued that the stories likely were indeed first written down by his son (he was claimed as the volume's author on the title page), then were reworked, augmented, and readied for publication by Perrault, with assistance from his cousin, Mlle l'Héritier, herself a celebrated author, see Paul Delarue, "Les contes merveilleux de Perrault: Faits et rapprochements nouveaux," *Arts et traditions populaires: Revue trimestrielle de la Société d'Ethnographie Française* (1954), 1–22, 251–75.

Felix Karlinger, in *Einführung in die romanische Volksliteratur*, discusses the literary evidence for the existence of folktale in the Romance countries in the centuries prior to the folklorists' collecting of tales from oral tradition. He goes so far as to conclude that before Basile and Perrault there were no true *Märchen*, or magical folktales, in either Italy or France, respectively.

Regarding the influence of Perrault's stories on German popular tales as represented in the Grimms' collection, see H. V. Velten, "The Influence of Charles Perrault's 'Contes de ma mère l'oie' on German Folklore," *Germanic Review*, 5 (1930), 4–18, and Rolf Hagen, "Der Einfluß der Perraultschen Contes auf das volkstümliche deutsche Erzählgut und besonders auf die Kinder- und Hausmärchen der Brüder Grimm," 2 vols. (Diss., Göttingen, 1954); also Rolf Hagen, "Perraults

Märchen und die Brüder Grimm," *Zeitschrift für Deutsche Philologie,* 74 (1955), 392–410.

18. Alan Dundes, "Fairy Tales from a Folkloristic Perspective," in Ruth B. Bottigheimer, ed., *Fairy Tales in Society: Illusion, Allusion, and Paradigm* (Philadelphia: Univ. of Pennsylvania Press, 1986), p. 266.

19. Rudolf Schenda, "Telling Tales—Spreading Tales: Change in the Communicative Forms of a Popular Genre," in Bottigheimer, ed., *Fairy Tales and Society,* p. 79.

20. Dégh, "What Did the Grimms Give to and Take from the Folk?" p. 68.

21. Concerning the identity and background of the Grimms' informants, see Wilhelm Schoof, "Zur Entstehungsgeschichte der Grimmschen Märchen," *Hessische Blätter für Volkskunde,* 29 (1930), 1–118, and esp. the later, revised version, *Zur Entstehungsgeschichte der Grimmschen Märchen: Bearbeitet unter Benutzung des Nachlasses der Brüder Grimm* (Hamburg: Ernst Hauswedell, 1959); also Heinz Rölleke, "Die 'stockhessischen' Märchen der 'alten Marie': Das Ende eines Mythos um die frühesten KHM-Aufzeichnungen der Brüder Grimm," *Germanisch-Romanische Monatsschrift,* n.s. 25 (1975), 74–86.

22. For discussion of the Grimms' literary shaping of their material, see Hermann Hamann, *Die literarischen Vorlagen der Kinder- und Hausmärchen und ihre Bearbeitung durch die Brüder Grimm,* Palaestra, 47 (Berlin: Mayer & Müller, 1906); Ernest Tonnelat, *Les contes des frères Grimm: Études sur la composition et le style du recueil des 'Kinder- und Hausmärchen'* (Paris: Armand Colin, 1912); Franz Heyden, *Volksmärchen und Volksmärchen-Erzähler: Zur literarischen Gestaltung des deutschen Volksmärchens* (Hamburg: Hanseatische Verlagsanstalt, 1922); Kurt Schmidt, *Die Entwicklung der Grimmschen Kinder- und Hausmärchen seit der Urhandschrift: Nebst einem kritischen Texte der in die Drucke übergegangenen Stücke* (Diss., Halle, n.d.), Hermaea, 30 (Halle: Niemeyer, 1932); Wilhelm Schoof, "Beiträge zur Stilentwicklung der Grimmschen Märchen," *Zeitschrift für Deutsche Philologie,* 74 (1955), 424–33, as well as his "Der Froschkönig oder der eiserne Heinrich: Ein Beitrag zur Stilentwicklung der Grimmschen Märchen," *Wirkendes Wort,* 7 (1956/57), 45–49, and his "Zur Geschichte des Grimmschen Märchenstils," *Der Deutschunterricht,* 15, no. 2 (1963), 90–99; Gunhild Ginschel, "Der Märchenstil Jacob Grimms," *Deutsches Jahrbuch für Volkskunde* (Berlin [East]), 9 (1963), 131–68, and "Aufzeichnung und Bearbeitung der Kinder- und Hausmärchen," in her *Der junge Jacob Grimm: 1805–1819,* Deutsche Akademie der Wissenschaften: Veröffentlichungen der Sprachwissenschaftlichen Kommission, 7 (Berlin [East]: Akademie Verlag, 1967), pp. 212–78; and Alfred David and Mary Elizabeth David, "A Literary Approach to the Brothers Grimm," *Journal of the Folklore Institute* (Indiana Univ.), 1 (1964), 180–96. Jens Tismar includes the Grimms, along with Basile and Perrault, among the authors of artistic fairy tales in his *Kunstmärchen,* Sammlung Metzler, 177 (Stuttgart: Metzler, 1977), because as literary men they told the folktales in their own way.

23. A case for accusing the Grimms of perpetrating literary fraud is made by John M. Ellis, *One Fairy Story Too Many: The Brothers Grimm and Their Tales* (Chicago: Univ. of Chicago Press, 1983).

24. The first dependable scholarly edition of the 1810 manuscript was that by Joseph Lefftz, *Märchen der Brüder Grimm: Urfassung nach der Originalhandschrift der Abtei Ölenberg im Elsaß*, Schriften der Elsaß-Lothringischen Wissenschaftlichen Gesellschaft zu Straßburg: ser. C, 1 (Heidelberg: Winter, 1927). A historical-critical edition, which juxtaposes the texts in the manuscript and those of the first edition on facing pages, has been provided by Heinz Rölleke, *Die älteste Märchensammlung der Brüder Grimm: Synopse der handschriftlichen Urfassung von 1810 und der Erstdrucke von 1812*, Biblioteca Bodmeriana: Texte, 1 (Cologny-Genève: Fondation Martin Bodmer, 1975). For a reissue of the Grimms' original edition of 1812 and 1815, see Friedrich Panzer, ed., *Die Kinder- und Hausmärchen der Brüder Grimm in ihrer Urgestalt*, 2 vols. (Munich: Beck, 1913).

25. Heinz Rölleke, "New Results of Research on Grimms' Fairy Tales," in McGlathery, ed., *Brothers Grimm and Folktale*, pp. 101–2.

26. For two recent studies that use this approach, see Bottigheimer, *Grimms' Bad Girls and Bold Boys*, and Tatar, *Hard Facts of the Grimms' Tales*.

27. Dundes, "Fairy Tales from a Folkloristic Perspective," p. 261.

28. Alan Dundes, "Interpreting Little Red Riding Hood Psychoanalytically," in McGlathery, ed., *Brothers Grimm and Folktale*, p. 18.

29. Dégh, "What Did the Grimm Brothers Give to and Take from the Folk?" p. 68.

30. For a brief but highly illuminating discussion of eroticism in folktale from the historical perspective, see Lutz Röhrich, "Erotik im Volksmärchen: Ein kulturhistorischer Exkurs," *Neue Zürcher Zeitung*, 1–2 Feb. 1986, no. 26, pp. 91–92.

31. The best general introduction in English to the nature and history of folktale studies as a scholarly discipline remains Stith Thompson's *The Folktale*. See also Adolf Thimme, *Das Märchen*, Handbücher zur Volkskunde, 2 (Leipzig: Wilhelm Heims, 1909); Friedrich von der Leyen, *Das Märchen: Ein Versuch*, 4th rev. ed. (1911; Heidelberg: Quelle & Meyer, 1958); Alexander Haggerty Krappe, *The Science of Folk-Lore* (London: Methuen, 1930); Johannes Bolte and Georg Polívka, *Zur Geschichte der Märchen*, vols. 4 and 5 of their *Anmerkungen zu den Kinder- und Hausmärchen der Brüder Grimm*, 5 vols. (Leipzig: Dieterich, 1913–32; reprint, 1963); Giuseppe Cocchiara, *Storia del folklore in Europa*, Collezione di studi religiosi, etnologici e psicologici, 20 (n.p. [Turin]: Einaudi, 1954); Roger Pinon, *Le Conte merveilleux comme sujet d'études* (Liège: Centre d'Education Populaire et de Culture, 1955); and Max Lüthi, *Märchen*, Sammlung Metzler, 16, 2d enl. ed. (1962; Stuttgart: Metzler, 1964).

For an anthology of essays offering a sample of folkloristic (and literary) research on folktale since the turn of the century, see Felix Karlinger, ed., *Wege der Märchenforschung*, Wege der Forschung, 255 (Darmstadt: Wissenschaftliche Buchgesellschaft, 1973) and for a collection of essays reflecting current critical approaches to folktale, see Brackert, ed., *Und wenn sie nicht gestorben sind.* . . .

A good critical bibliography of the post-World War I period was done by Friedrich Ranke, "Märchenforschung: Ein Literaturbericht (1920–1934)," *Deutsche Vierteljahrsschrift für Literaturwissenschaft und Geistesgeschichte,* 14 (1936), 246–304; and for the decade following the end of World War II, see Lutz Röhrich, "Die Märchenforschung seit dem Jahre 1945," *Deutsches Jahrbuch für Volkskunde* (Berlin [East]), 1 (1955), 279–96; 2 (1956), 274–319; 3 (1957), 213–24, 494–514, and his "Neue Wege der Märchenforschung," *Der Deutschunterricht,* 8, no. 6 (1956), 92–116.

32. The geographical-historical approach was introduced and furthered by the so-called Finnish school of folktale studies, the aims and methods of which were first outlined by Antti Aarne, *Leitfaden der vergleichenden Märchenforschung,* Folklore Fellows' Communications, 13 (Helsinki: Suomalainen Tiedeakatemia Kustantama, 1913). In connection with this type of research, two major indices were developed: Antti Aarne, *The Types of the Folktale: A Classification and Bibliography,* ed. and trans. Stith Thompson, Folklore Fellows' Communications, 74 (Helsinki: Suomalainen Tiedeakatemia/Academia scientificarum fennica, 1928; 2d ed. 1961), and Stith Thompson, *Motif-Index of Folk-Literature: A Classification of Narrative Elements in Folktale, Ballads, Myths, Fables, Mediaeval Romances, Exempla, Jest Books and Local Legends,* 6 vols., 2d ed. (1932–36; Bloomington: Indiana Univ. Press; Copenhagen: Rosenkilde and Bagger, 1955–58). See also Maria Leach, ed., *Funk & Wagnalls Standard Dictionary of Folklore,* 2 vols. (New York: Funk & Wagnalls, 1949), and Kurt Ranke, ed., *Enzyklopädie des Märchens: Handwörterbuch zur historischen und vergleichenden Erzählforschung* (Berlin: de Gruyter, 1975-).

An exemplary catalogue of folktales in France and French-speaking countries overseas was begun by Paul Delarue, *Le Conte populaire français: Catalogue raisonné des versions de France et des pays de langue français d'outre-mer* (Paris: Maisonneuve et Larose, 1964; 2d ed. 1976–77). A similar, though less ambitious, survey for Britain was done by Katherine M. Briggs, *A Dictionary of British Folk-Tales in the English Language,* 2 vols. in 4 (Bloomington: Indiana Univ. Press, 1970–71).

33. The notion of "survivals" was popularly introduced into folklore studies by the so-called British anthropological school of the late nineteenth century, centering around Edward Tylor, Andrew Lang, and James Frazer. The view that folktale symbolically depicted primitive ritual was advocated in naive fashion by Pierre Saintyves (pseud. for Émile Nourry), *Les contes de Perrault et les récits parallèles: Leurs origines (coutumes primitives et liturgies populaires)* (Paris: Émile Nourry, 1923). Among more recent, better-founded studies taking related approaches, see Lutz Röhrich, *Märchen und Wirklichkeit: Eine volkskundliche Untersuchung* (Wiesbaden: Franz Steiner, 1956; 3d ed., 1974); Hedwig [Roques-] von Beit, *Das Märchen: Sein Ort in der geistigen Entwicklung* (Berne: Francke, 1965); and August Nitschke,

Soziale Ordnungen im Spiegel der Märchen, 2 vols., problemata, 53–54 (Stuttgart-Bad Cannstadt: frommann-holzboog, 1976–77).

34. Among studies that may be described, in the larger sense, as having an ethnological bent are Gédéon Huet, *Les contes populaires* (Paris: Ernest Flammarion, 1923); Will-Erich Peuckert, *Deutsches Volkstum in Märchen und Sage, Schwank und Rätsel,* Deutsches Volkstum, 2 (Berlin: de Gruyter, 1938); Carl Wilhelm von Sydow, *Selected Papers on Folklore: Published on the Occasion of His 70th Birthday* (Copenhagen: Rosenkilde and Bagger, 1948); and above all Linda Dégh, *Märchen, Erzähler und Erzählgemeinschaft: Dargestellt an der ungarischen Volksüberlieferung* (Berlin [East]: Akademie-Verlag, 1962).

35. A pioneering sociological study was Naumann's *Grundzüge der deutschen Volkskunde.* Among more recent studies, see Linda Dégh, "Grimm's 'Household Tales' and Its Place in the Household: The Social Relevance of a Controversial Classic," *Western Folklore,* 38 (1979), 83–103; Michael Stolleis, "Der Ranzen, das Hütlein und das Hornlein," in Brackert, ed., *Und wenn sie nicht gestorben sind . . .,* pp. 153–64; and, in the same collection of essays, Klaus Lüderssen, "Hans im Glück: Kriminal-psychologische Betrachtungen—mit einem Seitenblick auf die Genese sozialer Normen," pp. 137–52.

36. An anthology reflecting the development of psychological approaches to folktale, since the emergence of psychoanalysis at the turn of the century, was done by Wilhelm Laiblin, ed., *Märchenforschung und Tiefenpsychologie,* Wege der Forschung, 102 (Darmstadt: Wissenschaftliche Buchgesellschaft, 1969).

For two early Freudian approaches, see Franz Ricklin (i.e., Riklin), *Wish-Fulfillment and Symbolism in Fairy Tales,* trans. William A. White, Nervous and Mental Disease Monograph Series, 21 (New York: Nervous and Mental Disease Publ. Co., 1915; orig. German ed., 1908), and esp. Otto Rank, *Psychoanalytische Beiträge zur Mythenforschung: Gesammelte Studien aus den Jahren 1912 bis 1914,* Internationale Psychoanalytische Bibliothek, 4 (Leipzig: Internationaler Psychoanalytischer Verlag, 1919). Broad acquaintance with the Freudian interpretation of folktale, however, has come only since the appearance of Bruno Bettelheim's *The Uses of Enchantment: The Meaning and Importance of Fairy Tales* (New York: Knopf, 1976).

Freud's theories as such have been applied to folktale far less often than those of C. G. Jung. The Jungian approach was prominently employed in Hedwig [Roques-] von Beit, *Symbolik des Märchens: Versuch einer Deutung,* 3 vols. (Berne: Francke, 1952–57; 2d rev. ed., 1960). See also the series of volumes of transcribed lectures by Marie-Louise von Franz, esp. *An Introduction to the Psychology of Fairy Tales,* 2d ed. (1970; New York: Spring Publications, 1973) and her *Shadow and Evil in Fairy Tales* (New York: Spring Publications, 1974). Among other Jungian approaches, see those by Joseph Campbell (*The Hero with a Thousand Faces,* Bollingen Series, 17 [New York: Pantheon, 1949]) and Julius E. Heuscher (*A Psychiatric Study of Myths and Fairy Tales: Their Origin, Meaning and Usefulness,* 2d rev. ed. [1963; Springfield, Ill.: Charles C. Thomas, 1974]).

For studies based on more broadly conceived notions of developmental psychology, or done from a pedagogical standpoint, see esp. Bruno Jöckel, *Der Weg zum Märchen* (Berlin-Steglitz: Dion Verlag Liebmann & Mette, 1939), and his "Das Reifungserlebnis im Märchen," *Psyche*, 1 (1948), 382–95; reprint, in Wilhelm Laiblin, ed., *Märchenforschung und Tiefenpsychologie*, pp. 195–211; Charlotte Bühler and Josephine Bilz, *Das Märchen und die Phantasie des Kindes*, 2d ed. (1958; Munich: Johann Ambrosius Barth, 1961); and Walter Scherf, *Lexikon der Zaubermärchen*, Kröners Taschenausgabe, 472 (Stuttgart: Kröner, 1982). Like the present discussion, the two studies by Jöckel focus specifically on depictions of the process of arriving at sexual maturity.

37. Calls have increasingly been made for collaboration between folklorists and literary scholars, echoing those earlier by, for example, Helmut de Boor, "Märchenforschung," *Zeitschrift für den Deutschen Unterricht*, 42 (1928), 561–81, and Carl Wilhelm von Sydow, "Märchenforschung und Philologie," *Universitas*, 3 (1948), 1047–58; both essays are reprinted in Karlinger, ed., *Wege der Märchenforschung*, pp. 129–54 and 177–93, respectively.

Among early studies of the *Märchen*, or fairy tale, as a discrete narrative genre within folktale, see Weber, *Märchen und Schwank;* Panzer, *Märchen, Sage und Dichtung*, and Berendsohn, *Grundformen volkstümlicher Erzählerkunst.*

Discussion of the structure and characteristics of the *Märchen* as a genre has tended to become more formalistic, abstract, or philosophical following the influential studies by Vladimir Propp, *Morfologija skazki*, Voprosy poetiki, 12 (Leningrad: Academia, 1928; trans. Laurance Scott as *Morphology of the Folktale*, 2d rev. ed. [Austin: Univ. of Texas Press, 1968]) and by André Jolles, *Einfache Formen: Legende, Sage, Mythe, Rätsel, Spruch, Kasus, Memorabile, Märchen, Witz*, 5th ed. (1930; Tübingen: Niemeyer, 1972). Among studies of the *Märchen* genre since Propp and Jolles, see Hans Honti, *Volksmärchen und Heldensage: Beiträge zur Klärung ihrer Zusammenhänge*, Folklore Fellows' Communications, 95 (Helsinki: Suomalainen Tiedeakatemia/Academia scientificarum fennica, 1931); Max Lüthi, *Die Gabe im Märchen und in der Sage: Ein Beitrag zur Wesenserfassung und Wesensscheidung der beiden Formen* (Diss., Berne, 1943; Berne: Büchler, 1943), and his *Das europäische Volksmärchen* and *Das Volksmärchen als Dichtung: Aesthetik und Anthropologie*, Studien zur Volkserzählung, 1 (Düsseldorf: Diederichs, 1975); Jan de Vries, *Betrachtungen zum Märchen: Besonders in seinem Verhältnis zu Heldensage und Mythos*, Folklore Fellows' Communications, 150 (Helsinki: Suomalainen Tiedeakatemia/Academia scientificarum fennica, 1954); Kurt Ranke, "Betrachtungen zum Wesen und zur Funktion des Märchens," *Studium Generale*, 11 (1958); reprint, in Karlinger, ed., *Wege der Märchenforschung*, pp. 320–60; Karl Justus Obenauer, *Das Märchen: Dichtung und Deutung* (Frankfurt am Main: Klostermann, 1959); and Hermann Bausinger, *Formen der Volkspoesie*, Grundlagen der Germanistik, 6; 2d rev. ed. (1968; Berlin: Erich Schmidt, 1980).

38. Karen E. Rowe, "Feminism and Fairy Tales," *Women's Studies: An Interdisciplinary Journal,* 6 (1979), 237–57; p. 248.

39. Ibid., pp. 239–40, 246, 251.

40. Ibid., p. 237.

41. Kay F. Stone, "Things Walt Disney Never Told Us," *Women and Folklore* [special issue of *American Folklore*] 88, (1975), 42–50, see p. 44; that issue also published as Claire R. Farrer, ed., *Women and Folklore* (Austin: Univ. of Texas Press, 1975).

42. Ibid., p. 45.

43. See Rosemary Minard's introduction to Rosemary Minard, ed., *Womenfolk and Fairy Tales* (Boston: Houghton-Mifflin, 1975), p. viii; see also Ethel Johnston Phelps's introductions to Ethel Johnston Phelps, ed., *Tatterhood and Other Tales: Stories of Magic and Adventure* (Old Westbury, N.Y.: Feminist Press, 1978), pp. xv–xxi and to Ethel Johnston Phelps, *The Maid of the North: Feminist Folk Tales from Around the World* (New York: Holt, Rinehart, Winston, 1981), pp. ix–xvi.

44. Heide Göttner-Abendroth, *Die Göttin und ihr Heros: Die matriarchalen Religionen in Mythos, Märchen und Dichtung,* 3d ed. (1980; Munich: Frauenoffensive, 1983), p. 170.

45. Ruth B. Bottigheimer, "The Transformed Queen: A Search for the Origins of Negative Female Archetypes in Grimms' Fairy Tales," *Amsterdamer Beiträge zur Neueren Germanistik,* 10 (1980), 1–12, see p. 12.

46. Karen E. Rowe, "To Spin a Yarn: The Female Voice in Folklore and Fairy Tale," in Bottigheimer, ed., *Fairy Tales and Society,* p. 71.

47. See Jack Zipes, *Fairy Tales and the Art of Subversion: The Classical Genre for Children and the Process of Civilization* (New York: Wildman, 1983), p. 25, and his *Don't Bet on the Prince: Contemporary Feminist Fairy Tales in North America and England* (New York: Methuen, 1986), pp. xi, xii.

48. Zipes, *Fairy Tales and the Art of Subversion,* pp. 13–14.

49. Ibid., p. 47.

50. Marcia R. Liebermann, " 'Some Day My Prince Will Come': Female Acculturation through the Fairy Tale," *College English,* 34 (1972/73), 383–95; p. 394.

51. Ibid.

1

Brothers and Sisters

e shall first consider the question of what happens to a girl's brother when she marries. That is to say, we shall be concerned in this chapter with those fairy tale heroines who have male siblings with whom they share a degree of devotion. In some of the most famous stories, to be sure, this situation does not exist. Snow White and Sleeping Beauty are their parents' only children, and Cinderella has only sisters. And while the heroine in Perrault's "Bluebeard" does have brothers, their role is confined to appearing at the end to rescue her by slaying her wife-murdering husband.

A sufficient number of less-famous tales about heterosexual sibling devotion are found in the collections of Basile and the Grimms, however, to allow us to speak of a brother and sister type of tale (see AT types 450–59). Typically, the sister has reached marriageable age, and the tale ends with her marriage and her brother or brothers joining her and her husband in living happily ever after together.

In early modern times, large families being common, daughters most often did have brothers. The existence of tales about brothers and sisters does not merely attest this fact, however. The focus is on the loyalty and devotion of siblings of opposite sex. Our question is whether any discernible crisis in such relationships is indicated when the sister comes of age. Let us first examine, though, the depictions of love between brothers and sisters who have not yet reached adolescence.

I. INNOCENT DEVOTION

Grimm's Fairy Tales, as the German title *Kinder- und Hausmärchen* suggests, are intended partly for children, and it is therefore no surprise that the stories are sometimes about childhood. The most famous example is unquestionably "Hansel and Gretel" (*KHM* 15). From this tale, we remember, of course, the stereotypically selfish stepmother and her magical counterpart, the evil witch, whose passion for cooking and eating tender infants grotesquely mirrors the mother's greedy unwillingness to share her and her husband's meager rations with her stepchildren. The story's interest, as a portrayal of passion or emotion, centers, however, on the children's devotion to one another; and the simple fact that they are of opposite sex lends to their adventure something of an innocent tale of love. The evil actions of the two older women, the stepmother and the witch, serve to provide the adversity against which the two little siblings—like young lovers in romantic plots—must struggle. These evil doings also result in granting the little brother and sister the opportunity, out of necessity, to demonstrate their devotion by acting as one another's angel of rescue. Hansel bolsters Gretel's courage during their ordeal of being twice exposed in the forest; and Gretel then saves the brother from being boiled and eaten by contriving to push the witch into the hot oven in which she intended to roast Gretel herself for dinner.

Hansel and Gretel's relationship is perfectly innocent. They are far from being of an age to marry or even to experience the first stirrings of desire. Still, their magical adventures, once they find themselves out on their own together, have the quality of a dream, and one involving a type of wish fulfillment not unlike that found in the fairy tales of love. Their discovery of the little house made of sweets not only magically answers their hunger caused by several days alone together in the forest, like an oasis for the thirsting traveler lost in the desert. It also provides them occasion for something akin to a celebration of their now still closer relationship to one another—like the wedding cake for a bride and bridegroom, but on the childhood level of satisfying an appetite for sweets as such, rather than as a symbolic anticipation of gratifying sexual desire.

This "house of sweets" potentially offers Hansel and Gretel not only the means of sustenance in their new independence but also the prospect of cohabitation, of living under one roof together, as in the case of the brides and bridegrooms in the romantic fairy tale. Of course, far from finding shelter in this magical abode, the little "couple" becomes exposed to yet greater mortal danger in the clutches of the old witch. But this new peril serves to cement their relationship still further, and provides them, once they have slain the evil hag, with riches sufficient to set up a household together, were they not still little children but of marriageable age, like the hero and heroine of the romantic fairy tale. And their final magical adventure, their transport across the lake on the back of the friendly duck in answer to Gretel's entreating incantation, suggests a crossing over to a new beginning, not unlike a bride and bridegroom on their honeymoon. The innocence of the children's devotion to one another, however, is demonstrated yet again in the happy ending, for here we are reminded once more that their dream of fulfillment is to return to the life they knew with their widowed father before his marriage to the selfish, unloving stepmother, whose death—as though by way of magical wish fantasy—has seemingly coincided with that of the evil witch.[1]

A portrayal of similarly innocent devotion between two small children of opposite sex is given in "The Juniper Tree" (*KHM* 47). Again, the focus of interest is partly on the punishment of the wicked stepmother, after she has murdered her husband's little son by perfidiously decapitating him with a trunk lid as he accepted her invitation to reach in for an apple. Yet the most touching feature of the story is the daughter Marleenken's suffering in the mistaken belief, encouraged and indeed occasioned by her wicked mother, that she herself was responsible for the half-brother's death. The revenge taken by the slain brother on the stepmother serves to punish the latter's evil deeds, of course (she made the daughter witness, too, the butchering and serving up of the brother to their father for dinner). This revenge also functions, though, to relieve Marleenken of her burden of guilt. The brother's magical restoration to life, and later to human form, and his slaying of the stepmother make possible that same happy life together as brother and sister with the widowed father that represented the innocent wish fulfillment in "Hansel and Gretel."

In "The Juniper Tree" the feeling between the brother and sister is, if anything, more intense than in "Hansel and Gretel." The brother, being the stepchild, has been singled out by the mother for rejection and abuse. As a result, he values the sister's devotion just that much more—perhaps as a substitute for the love of his biological mother, who died in childbirth out of joy over his arrival. At the same time, the mother's mistreatment of the brother has awakened sisterly, and latently maternal, compassion for him in Marleenken. The boy's cruel death, moreover, introduces a further element of the sublime into their relationship—again, not unlike that in the feelings the boy must have for his dead mother, whom he never knew and about whom he can only wonder and dream. Marleenken gathers up the brother's bones in "her best silk scarf" and lays them under the juniper in front of the house—the tree under which his mother lies buried and where she was sitting when, after she had cut herself while peeling an apple, she prayed for "a child as red as blood and white as snow."

As though through the power of the sister's devotion and the dead mother's approval of it, the brother is magically revived in the form of a beautiful bird. The song that the bird sings, as it sets about to gain revenge for the stepmother's evil deed, leaves little doubt as to the brother's thrill over the sister's role as his angel of mercy:

My mother, who butchered me,
My father, who ate me,
My sister, little Marleenken,
Gathered together all my little bones,
Bound them in a silken cloth,
Laid it under the juniper tree
Tweet, tweet, what a pretty bird am I!

Finally, a touch of romantic feeling may be expressed in the bird's choice of a gift for the sister: a pair of pretty red shoes. He tosses the shoes down to her as he sings about how she gathered up his bones and about what a beautiful bird he is; and she then dances and leaps about in the shoes for joy.[2]

If the greater intensity of feeling between the brother and sister in "The Juniper Tree" may be explained partly by their being, unlike Hansel and Gretel, only half-siblings, in the tale "Fundevogel" (*KHM* 51) an even more pronounced erotic element may owe something to the circumstance that the boy and girl are not blood relatives at all, he being a foundling (hence his name, in the title role) who has been raised with the sister since babyhood. The peril confronted by the children is not owing, as in those two stories, to the resentment of an adoptive mother as such, for the villain of the piece is the (evidently widowed) father's old lady cook, who sets about to murder the foundling boy for no apparent reason—other than that she perhaps sees herself as mistress of the house and to that extent as successor to the father's wife. The action takes the form of a chase, with the lady cook first sending her servant men—and then finally going herself— to fetch back the children, who have run away in view of the hag's intent to cook the foundling son in boiling water. The focus of interest, though, is upon the three magical transformations that the children effect upon themselves in order to avoid capture. It is the nature of these metamorphoses which betrays erotic feeling of a somewhat less than innocent sort on the part of the sister, Lenchen (her name's possible association with Helen of Troy is perhaps not coincidental).[3]

The role of saving angel here belongs entirely to the girl. Her motivation, moreover, appears less than spontaneous and not without design, if only unconsciously so. Before Lenchen betrays the cook's murderous plan to Fundevogel she says to him, by way of admonition or warning and rather in the manner of a woman out to secure a man's love (they are lying together in bed), "If you don't forsake me, I won't forsake you either." Also, each of the transformations she proposes for them implicitly casts her in the role of his adornment and him in the role of her protector: first, he as a rose stem and she as the little rose upon it; then he as a church and she as a chandelier in it, and finally he as a pond and she as a duck swimming on it.

This dream of captivating and owning a man which is evident in the girl may shed light on the old lady cook's otherwise uncertain motivation for wanting to murder the boy. The cook, who may harbor secret fantasies regarding the widower father, possibly recognizes—if only unconsciously, like the girl herself—that since the children are not blood relatives they would be free to marry someday, and envies the girl that dream of young bliss. Such envy, perhaps, explains why the cook so vividly paints for her outwitted servant men the picture of how they should have cut off the rose stem to get at the rose and should have destroyed the church to seize the crown, and also why she then is drowned by the duck (i.e., by the girl) as she attempts to drink up the pond (i.e., the foundling boy). Possibly, the hag only wants the girl for herself. It is just as likely, though, that she is out to make Lenchen as miserable as she herself is by destroying the girl's dream of young love. We will return to this type of jealous envy in the chapter on "Hags, Witches, and Fairies."

In "The Little Lamb and the Little Fish" (*KHM* 141), another tale of the Hansel and Gretel type, the stepmother transforms the brother and sister into a fish and a lamb, respectively. A situation thereby is produced that provides opportunity to portray the siblings' intense devotion to one another across a far greater biological divide than that between the sexes— a boundary that perhaps serves as a metaphor for the barrier represented by the incest taboo. The ending of this tale is of particular interest, in that a good witch (*eine weise Frau*) not only restores the brother and sister to human form but also leads them to a small house in a great forest "where they lived alone but contented and happy," almost as though they were the prince and princess of the romantic fairy tale who marry and live happily ever after.

Behind this ending, and the magical separation that leads to it, may lie—if only in the mind of the storyteller—the dream of union with a sibling that is implicit also in the stories discussed above. The lamb (that is, the sister) grieves so over the separation from the brother that she does not eat. (The separation is only partial, since she lives on the meadow next to the pond in which he, as a fish, is constrained to dwell.) And after the cook, on overhearing a tender exchange between the fish and the lamb, spares her from being slaughtered for the stepmother's table, good fortune dictates that the peasant woman to whom the cook brings the lamb turns out to have been the girl's childhood nurse (cf. the nurse's traditional role in literature as a girl's confidante and aide in affairs of the heart). The good witch's action in providing for the siblings' cohabitation is no more clearly motivated than was the evil stepmother's role in separating the brother and sister physically, so that one thus may suspect that both situations hint at the secret role of a subterranean dream of incestuous union.

Cohabitation of the sort found in "The Little Lamb and the Little Fish" is an unusual ending for fairy tales of the brother and sister type. Typically, the children return in the end to live with a parent, usually the widower father, or they are reunited only after they have reached young adulthood and have married or are about to do so, as in "Ninnillo and Nennella," a tale of the brother and sister type in Basile's *Pentamerone* (V, 8). There the stepmother's demand that the father get rid of the children—a demand explicitly motivated by her resentment over having to care for the first wife's offspring—results in the siblings' becoming separated from one another, the brother winding up in the service of a prince and the sister in the belly of a fish. Ninnillo and Nennella find one another again only when they are grown, but with the fortunate result that the prince arranges rich marriages for each of them. In Basile's tale there is little focus on the siblings' devotion to one another, and no erotic element in the portrayal of their adventure. The sister's magical sojourn, though, coincides with her passage from girlhood to womanhood, and ends with her emergence in romantically charming fashion from the fish's mouth, rather like Aphrodite from the scallop shell.

II. THE SISTER AS ANGEL OF RESCUE

Already in "Hansel and Gretel," "The Juniper Tree," and "Fundevogel," we have seen the sister in the romantically appealing role of saving angel. In several other tales of the brother and sister type, however, this role achieves central importance. To be sure, in such a story as "The Three Little Birds" (*KHM* 96) the sister's function as heroine is entirely innocent with regard to romantic devotion. Yet in a number of other stories there are hints of an erotic attraction between the siblings, and especially on the sister's part (as was noted above in the case of Lenchen in "Fundevogel"). This attraction is most pronounced in those tales in which a baby sister yearns for her absent older brothers, who typically have left home for reasons related to the sister's birth.

"The Seven Ravens" (*KHM* 25) is a case in point. Here the seven brothers have vanished as a magical consequence of their father's anger over their tardiness in returning with spring water for the baby daughter's baptism (the father swears, "I would wish that the boys were all turned into ravens!"). When the sister, who has meanwhile grown more beautiful with every day, hears people talking about how she was the cause of the brothers' misfortune, she slips away from home and travels to the end of the earth in an effort to find and rescue them: "She believed she would have to redeem them."

The magical element in the sister's quest—she sets about to consult the sun, moon, and stars as to the brothers' whereabouts—testifies to the intensity of her yearning. And that it is the morning star (often associated with Venus) who finally provides her the means of finding and rescuing the brothers hints at the erotic nature of her yearning. This symbolism is further indicated by the sister's use of one of her small fingers to unlock the door of the glass mountain where the seven ravens dwell. Moreover, the sister's means of identifying herself to the momentarily absent ravens is to place a little ring in the last of the seven goblets, after she has eaten and drunk at each of the brothers' places at the table. That the brothers, in turn, have dreamed of the baby sister as serving one day as their angel of redemption is indicated by their thrill that the sister has now indeed arrived. After the seventh (and youngest?) brother has exclaimed, "God grant that our sister were here, then we would be saved," they and the sister are reunited, the brothers are restored to human form, and the siblings are free to return home together to their parents.

Most striking in "The Seven Ravens," as has been indicated above, are the possible hints of unconscious girlish sexual fantasy in the little sister's adventure. She rescues the brothers with the magic of her desire. The male and female roles appear reversed in that she opens the gate to the magic mountain (cf. the *mons veneris*) with her amputated finger as a substitute for the little chicken bone given her by the morning star (i.e., the planet Venus) which she lost along the way. When she eats from the brothers' plates and drinks from their goblets, she does so evidently not as much from actual hunger or thirst as out of a desire to enter thereby into a degree of intimacy with them, as a token of their now being together under one roof at last. Her use of the ring to signal her presence may also represent an unconscious pledge of fidelity, across the boundary of opposite sex. The brothers' existence as hideous birds of evil color and portent, moreover, may project her feeling of their inaccessibility to her and the potentiality of a forbidden, incestuous love. And her—irrational—sense of guilt as the source of the brothers' misfortune may indicate a (pleasurable) fantasy about herself in the role of *femme fatale*, again as the potential object of incestuous desire.

While the sister in "The Seven Ravens" can hardly be held responsible, objectively speaking, for her brothers' transformation, considering that it happened when she was a newborn baby, the sister in "The Twelve Brothers" (*KHM* 9) commits an act that directly results in the very same metamorphosis. The circumstances surrounding the brothers' transformation here are as suggestive as they are enigmatic. In "The Seven Ravens" the father's angry exclamation produced the fateful change. In the present case, the metamorphosis occurs in connection with the sister's innocent picking of twelve lilies to grace the brothers' places at a feast the siblings have made for themselves. The mystery concerns the question of why this act of innocent sisterly devotion should have such a grievous consequence.

Since she was about ten, the baby sister has been living alone with the brothers in a (magical) hut in the forest. Aided by the youngest brother, Benjamin, she has been serving as cook and housekeeper for the brothers, rather like a substitute mother. By now, though, she must be entering adolescence, raising the possibility that, subconsciously at least, she is beginning to think of herself in the role of spouse, or even to sense that something akin to illicit desire is entering her feelings for the brothers. The brothers' metamorphosis thus may represent a projection of guilt in this regard. Their transformation and resulting disappearance (they are constrained to fly away) effectively remove them as tangible objects of a forbidden love. This possibility would explain, too, why the brothers are restored to human form only after the sister is married, and why the happy ending consists in a resumption of the siblings' blissful cohabitation, this time in circumstances rendered more normal by the presence of the sister's spouse.

The incestuous potential of the cohabitation in the forest is increased by the sister's diminished role as angel of rescue, when compared with that of the sister in "The Seven Ravens." Here the girl is not motivated so much by dreams of a mission to save the brothers (they have not yet been transformed, and the father would not welcome them back), nor by guilt over her birth as having been responsible for their banishment. Rather, she is motivated by a simple, though if anything more intense, yearning to find the brothers and to enjoy the pleasure of their company (and, unconsciously, to have them quite to herself, one may suspect). Her thrill at being united with them can only be increased by their obvious delight at her beauty, a delight so great that they completely put aside, or even lose all memory of, their earlier misogynous oath that "wherever we find a girl, her red blood shall flow." (Does that oath, indeed, express not only boyish aggression toward the opposite sex but unconscious fantasies about deflowering or violating a maiden?) The brothers are so taken with her—she bears a golden star on her forehead as a magical token of her beauty—that they immediately kiss and embrace her.

The conditions that are placed on the brothers' release from the spell also are suggestive with regard to the interpretation made here (the sister learns of these conditions from an old woman who appears next to her, as if by magic, just after the fateful moment; cf. the type of the hag as matchmaker in literature, for example, the *ruffiana* of the *commedia dell'arte*). The girl is told that she must not talk or laugh for seven years, and that if she utters one word her brothers will die. This punishment— or penance, if it can be called that—seemingly would render the sister less appealing to a prospective suitor. She would not, for instance, be able to speak the words "I do" in response to a marriage proposal (or even simply "Yes"; cf. the German expression *ihr Jawort geben*). And evidently to insure that she will not be tempted to laugh or speak—and, in effect, to make it unlikely that she would even meet a suitor—she climbs a tree and occupies herself with spinning, dreaming of the day when she will be reunited with her siblings: "I know for certain that I shall redeem my brothers" (cf. the traditional association of spinning with romantic fantasizing, or "building castles in the air," and current German *sie spinnt*, "she's crazy" or "she's daydreaming").

What happens, though, is that a king, while out hunting, discovers the sister in the tree, is enraptured by her beauty, asks her on the spot to marry him, and is perfectly happy to accept her nod of assent in place of the customary *Jawort*. Indeed, her silence has if anything made her that much more appealing to him. Nature has taken its course with her. The sister's ready assent may be explained further by the fact that her brothers have been the only men she has seen since becoming nubile. With time, however, her enigmatic silence begins to make the king suspect, under the influence of his mother's harping on the subject, that the girl has something to hide—a divination that is true enough, though not exactly in the sense of a bad conscience as the mother imagines, for the wife's silence is motivated by her continued devotion to the brothers. The husband's rage over the beloved's failure to reveal her secret brings him to the point of ordering that she be burned at the stake. The sister's good fortune—or should one say her magical wish fulfillment?—will have it, though, that at the very moment she is about to be consumed by the flames, the seven years have elapsed and the brothers arrive to rescue her, the beloved sister whose devotion has won their return now to human form. At last the sister is free to tell the king her secret; and the husband and wife and the brothers "all lived together in unity up until their deaths."[4]

A similar, though rather less puzzling and therewith more innocent, version of the story told in "The Twelve Brothers" is found in "The Six Swans" (*KHM* 49). Here the girl bears no guilt whatsoever, whether objectively or irrationally, for the brothers' transformation and disappearance. It is the plan of the evil stepmother here (she is the daughter of a witch)[5] to change all of the husband's children by his first wife into swans. Only by chance does she fail to discover the girl. Cohabitation of the brothers with the sister, however, plays no less a role in this story. The siblings first have been hidden from the stepmother by the father in a lonely castle in the woods. Then, after the brothers' transformation, they are briefly re-united in a hut in the forest (where the boys are able to appear in human form, but only for a quarter of an hour each evening). Finally, once the sister's six-year testing period (one year for each brother?) is over, they live together happily ever after at the castle of the king whom she mean-while has married.

The point of the story appears to be that a kind or providential fate, albeit in the ironic form of a malevolent stepmother, has contrived to separate the brothers from the sister during the potentially troublesome period (in terms of the taboo against incest) when the girl is growing into womanhood. The six years of her ordeal evidently span the time from her approaching nubility to her arrival at full maturity—say from the age of twelve to eighteen—since she has in the meantime married and given birth to three children in succession.

The relative innocence of the incestuous attraction here, compared to that in "The Twelve Brothers," may be indicated by the boys' transfor-mation into a type of bird associated with pleasant fantasies (swans instead of ravens). The brothers' fantasies about the sister, assuming they harbor anything of the sort, would appear to run to thoughts of her as an ideal substitute mother, in contrast to the evil witch the father has married. As the brothers tell the sister—and in this tale it is they who divulge the secret—one condition of their redemption is that she must succeed in sew-ing for them six little shirts made from *Sternblumen* (*asteraceae*, a star-shaped flower), much as the stepmother effected their transformation into swans by making little white silk shirts for them into which she had sewn a magic charm (the brothers understandably do not make this connection).

The sister, for her part, may harbor somewhat less innocent, if surely unconscious, feelings toward the brothers. For one thing, a degree of in-hibition is suggested when, after she has discovered the brothers' abode following their transformation, at a time of day when they are constrained to be absent, she refrains from taking her rest in any of their six little beds and sleeps instead upon the hard floor beneath one of the beds. And her subsequent determination to redeem the brothers betrays a note of thrilling exaltation: "The girl, though, conceived the firm determination to save her brothers, and even if she should have to pay with her life." Ironically, it does indeed almost come to that near the end. As in "The Twelve Brothers," the eventual husband finally despairs at her refusal to speak (or to laugh, as the conditions for the brothers' redemption here, too, require) and orders her burned at the stake—for better cause than in the other story, since the mother-in-law here has contrived to make it appear that the wife has slain and eaten his newborn children.

A final hint that avoidance of incestuous passion is the hidden reason for the brothers' transformation may be seen in the circumstance that although the sister, at the fateful moment when the six years are up, has not quite managed to finish sewing the last of the six shirts, the brothers nonetheless are restored to human form and are thereby enabled to save her from a fiery death.[6]

A tale similar to the three stories we have been discussing ("The Seven Ravens," "The Twelve Brothers," and "The Six Swans") is related in Basile's collection, although there the second half of the adventure, the sister's redemption of the brothers, takes the form almost of a philosophical or moral allegory. This tale, "The Seven Doves" (IV, 8), begins with circumstances and adventures that are likewise suggestive of a subterranean romantic attachment between the brothers and their sister. Indeed, the siblings' separation results from the brothers' very wish for a baby sister, a wish so ardent that they leave home and vow never to return unless their pregnant mother bears a daughter this time (the brothers were born successively over a period of seven years). As fate would have it, the midwife, having become confused, gives the wrong sign, so that the brothers mistakenly assume that the child is yet another son. (It perhaps helps explain why the midwife fails to remember the right sign that each signal involves what may be seen as a combination of male and female symbols, the signal for a girl being a spoon and a distaff and that for a boy an ink pot and quill.) Moreover, when the sister, Cianna, later goes off to seek the brothers, her desire to find them is so great that she leaves the mother no peace until the latter consents to her departure. She discovers them at the house of a misogynous wild man of the woods, who kills and eats all the women he can find, as a form of revenge for his wife's having blinded him one day as he lay sleeping.

The figure of the ogre with whom the brothers are living may be something of a projection of incestuous guilt. Their devotion to the sister might awaken a desire in them, too, to "devour" her, so to speak. This is suggested by the circumstance that after they have saved Cianna by slaying the misogynous host, they warn her not to pick any grass from his grave, otherwise they will be transformed into seven doves, effectively putting an end to their blissful cohabitation with her alone in the dead man's forest abode. Is the implication perhaps that by picking grass from the grave she would be "raising" the wild man within the brothers, in the sense of a "misogynous" (i.e., actually incestuous) passion to devour her? When the dreaded event then happens, it results from the sister's overpowering urge to come to the aid of a poor wanderer who has suffered a head wound (she picks some rosemary growing upon the wild man's grave). This role as angel of mercy, in other circumstances, would surely render her all the more appealing in the brothers' eyes, particularly insofar as they might vicariously identify themselves with the victim as the object of her angelic ministrations.

With the brothers' transformation as a result of Cianna's fateful—and romantically appealing—act of mercy, the hints of repressed incestuous attraction between the brothers and the sister appear to end, except that like the sister in the Grimms' "The Seven Ravens," Cianna sets out on an almost cosmic mission to redeem the brothers. Most important, though, is that in the end the sister returns with them to their parents' home, and, as the storyteller reports, "there, through the goodness that Cianna had shown for them, [they] enjoyed a happy life."

A final suggestion of subterranean feelings between the brothers and the sister may be found in the magical moment of the brothers' restoration to human form. The spell is broken as they innocently seat themselves upon the horns of a dead ox, whereupon it is revealed to them "that the horn, as a symbol of plenty, is the pillar of wealth to which Time [in connection with Cianna's cosmic mission of redemption] had referred." But since return to human form and reunion with the sister, not wealth, was the brothers' goal, one may be reminded that the horn's symbolization of Plenty is not unrelated to its representation of potency, or the sexual ardor of the male—that threatening natural force which the brothers may now be seen to have overcome, through its transferral to the level of the sublime or the philosophical. (In this connection it is worth noting that the sister's name may call to mind Italian *ciana* 'loose or bad woman, slut' and perhaps the word root referring to the poisonous substance cyanide as well, e.g., *cianato* 'cyanate').

As a final, and particularly illustrative, example of the type of story in which a sister, out of deep devotion, attempts to prevent or reverse a brother's transformation into subhuman form, one may point to the tale "Little Brother and Little Sister" (*KHM* 11), where the relationship is, moreover, underscored by the title. Here, as in the stories of innocent devotion, we have the more intimate situation in which the sister has only one brother. As in most stories of the brother and sister type, cohabitation plays a role, and here may be said to form a particularly strong focus of interest, especially as regards the extended portrayal of events attendant upon the siblings' arrival at marriageable age.

Since the brother's transformation, the siblings have been living blissfully alone together in a small house in the forest. The problematic nature of this situation, once they have passed puberty, would seem to be suggested by the events leading up to the sister's marriage to a king who—as happens in "The Twelve Brothers" and "The Six Swans"—finds her as he is out hunting. These events are set in motion by the brother's irresistible urge, on hearing the horn sounded by the king's party, to answer the call to the hunt, an urge normal enough in a youth of his age but strikingly unusual in view of his transformation. As a fawn he is joining the chase as the hunted prey, not as the hunter. The explanation for this paradoxical desire may be that despite his transformation the brother has remained at heart very much a young man. Indeed, his urge to join the hunt even if only as the prey may represent a substitute for the surrender to desire, which in his case could only lead to incest.[7] The result of the brother's answering the call to the hunt is, at any rate, the sister's marriage to the king, with the happy prospect it provides the siblings of continuing their cohabitation under a more seemly arrangement, the brother now being a "friend of the family," or in view of his transformed state, a house pet. The sister makes this role for the brother a condition of her acceptance of the king's proposal of marriage, saying "That [the little deer calf] I won't leave behind."[8]

This view of the siblings' relationship as latently incestuous finds further support in the circumstances of the king's discovery of the girl. The sister tells the brother, as he goes off to the hunt, that she will let him back in only on hearing the password, "Dear Sister, let me come in"; otherwise, she says, "I won't open up my little door." On the first two days, everything goes as planned. On the third evening, however, the king, who has found out about the girl and the password, is the one standing on the threshold when she opens the door. The sister's swift acceptance of the king's proposal, made at first sight (he is wearing his crown, evidently the better to impress her), may indicate an instantaneous—and in that sense, magical—passage from girlishness to maidenhood. Still, the condition that the prospective suitor has had to address her as "sister" in order to get her to "open her little door" to him may suggest that her farewell to her childhood and its incestuous attachment is not all that complete.[9]

The situation that produces the brother's transformation in the first place is also suggestive of secretly incestuous feelings between the brother and sister. An evil stepmother functions here, as in "Hansel and Gretel," "The Little Lamb and the Little Fish," and "The Six Swans," to provide the occasion for the siblings' departure from home and their resulting shared adventure. Furthermore, the spell the stepmother has cast on the springs in the forest presents the opportunity for expression of the sister's feelings toward the brother, through her series of warnings to him about the consequences should he give in to his thirst and drink.[10] At the first spring, she warns that he will be turned into a tiger and tear her apart; at the second, that he will be changed into a wolf and eat her, and at the third, that he will be transformed into a deer calf and leave her. In the first two instances, the brother manages to refrain from drinking, indicating perhaps that, for his part, he is able to resist any unconscious urge to ravish the sister—a potentiality that surely plays a role in the sister's unconscious erotic fantasies at least. When he does then surrender to thirst at the third spring and is indeed transformed into a deer calf, he does not leave her, as she feared he would. On the contrary, his transformation has made it possible for the two of them to become in a sense more intimate, because in his new, magical form he is no longer so much a member of the opposite sex as a pet with whom the sister may exchange innocent affection, as for example when she now adopts the custom—albeit after first saying her prayers—of sleeping with her head on the little deer calf's back. The third spring has thus proven to be enchanted rather in the sense of a fountain of love, or of love's sublimations. The storyteller's comment, "if the little brother only had had his human form, it would have been a magnificent life," expresses the girl's conscious feelings about her magical cohabitation with the brother; left unexpressed is the situation's incestuous potential that made the brother's transformation "necessary."[11]

Like the brother's transformation, his eventual return to human form, too, after the sister has married and given birth to a child, is the unintended result of the stepmother's malevolence (she thus functions as a sort of *dea ex machina* in spite of herself). The stepmother contrives to substitute her ugly daughter as the newborn child's mother and to murder the true bride. But the latter's continued devotion to the infant (perhaps significantly, a son), as demonstrated by her magical return from the grave to nourish and care for him, results in her being restored to life "through God's grace." That the sister's attachment to the brother is paramount, though, even after she has become a mother is indicated by her care, before departing after her magical, ghostly visits to the nursery, to stroke the back of the little deer calf as it sleeps in the corner of the room, and by the verses she speaks. Expression of love for the husband is curiously absent. She asks only, "What is my child doing? What is my deer doing?" The stepmother's death, upon the king's discovery of her deceitful and evil deeds, is followed immediately by the brother's sudden restoration to human form, so that "Little Sister and Little Brother . . . lived happily together until their deaths"—which is clearly what both desired from the start.

III. THE BROTHER AS MATCHMAKER

In "Little Brother and Little Sister" the brother serves—unwittingly—to lead the king to the sister as prospective bride, whereby the happy result is provided that an unconsciously incestuous relationship is returned to the bounds of propriety. In several other fairy tales of the Grimms' collection— none of them counted among the better-known stories—the brother's role as matchmaker for the sister is as conscious as it is central. And the secretly desired result generally remains the same: cohabitation with the married sister happily ever after and under decorous circumstances.

A particularly striking case in point is "The Golden Bird" (*KHM* 57), the story of a fox's patient and untiring efforts to insure that the youngest of a king's three sons succeeds in winning and marrying a beautiful princess. Only at the end does one learn that the fox is actually the girl's brother, yet this revelation would seem to hold the key to the fox's persistent devotion to his mission. To be sure, the brother's motivation may be simply the desire to be returned to human form. But since it is indicated that, after the spell cast on him has been broken, the husband, the wife, and her brother live on blissfully together ("And now their happiness lacked for nothing as long as they lived"), one may suspect that the brother's aim all along has been to be reunited with the sister. No explanation whatever is given for the brother's having been transformed into a fox. Precisely because such an explanation is wholly lacking, there is reason to believe that the metamorphosis occurred in connection with a crisis in his feelings about the sister, or simply that it points to the "necessity" of the siblings' separation once the sister has become nubile.

There are several indications that this is secretly a tale of incestuous passion. First, and most tellingly of all, there is the hint of voyeuristic, vicarious fantasy in the fox's instructions to the young prince as to how he must go about abducting the sister (at this point, neither the suitor nor the reader knows yet that the fox is her brother): "at night, when all is quiet, the beautiful princess goes to the bathhouse in order to bathe there. And when she goes inside, leap at her and give her a kiss, then she will follow you and you can lead her away with you—just don't allow her to go take leave of her parents first or it can turn out badly for you." The plan is portrayed so vividly by the brother that one can almost imagine he is speaking from firsthand experience, like one who has made the attempt with her. He certainly displays great excitement about her bathing habits. These habits suggest, too, that the sister is the type to court and even welcome abduction. With such a sister, a brother might well need to be made safe from surrender to temptation by being transformed into something other than a man.

Once the prince has succeeded in abducting the anything but unwilling princess, the fox immediately sets his mind on becoming restored to human form. Since the transformation, however, is dependent on his shooting the fox dead and then cutting off its head and paws, the prince cannot bring himself to grant this odd request, especially considering that the fox has proven himself such a loyal friend. (The prince presumably would not shrink from the deed if he knew it would result in the breaking of a spell,

but the fox's silence regarding that fact evidently is required for his redemption.) That the brother's return to human form does not occur at this
point is perhaps a further hint that his having been changed into a fox was
the consequence of incestuous feelings, for the sister is at this point still
not yet—safely—married to the prince.

The necessary condition for the brother's redemption—that he be shot,
decapitated, and suffer the amputation of his paws—may be a projection
of his incestuous guilt, insofar as it may represent a symbolic punishment:
death for having desired the sister, decapitation for having "lost his head"
over her, and loss of the greedy "paws" with which he yearned to steal a
caress. And that this redemptive punishment should be effected by the
sister's prospective husband is a possible further hint of the brother's need
for expiation of guilt, spiritual purification, or guilty resignation. The restoration of the brother to human form, in the prescribed manner, takes
place only after he, still as the fox, has helped the prince defeat the attempt
of the latter's elder brothers to claim the bride for themselves (yet another
projection of the fox's guilt vis-à-vis *his* sibling?) and after the prince and
the sister have long since been married.

In the light of the present interpretation, the great lengths to which the
fox must go to bring about the sister's marriage, his unfailing loyalty to
the prince, and his persistent determination throughout, appear comic,
especially considering that at every turn the prince, as the type of the
stupid or bungling youngest son (the *Dümmling* of folktales generally), fails
to heed the fox's warnings. That in the end everything nonetheless turns
out as the fox has desired must therefore be attributed to good fortune,
to young love's all-conquering power, or to the intensity of the brother's
wish fulfillment regarding his relationship with the sister. And as to the
brother's role as fox, it is less his shrewdness in laying his plans and in
choosing his agent (the bungling prince) than the slyness in his mode of
dealing with his passion for the sister that marks him as worthy to have
been transformed into a member of that genus. He contrives to marry the
sister to a man whom he has put deeply in his debt, and he thereby
ultimately succeeds in spending the rest of his life in her appealing
presence.

A similar story of a brother's role in providing his sister with a husband
is told in "The Glass Coffin" (*KHM* 163), a tale even more bizarre and
complex than "The Golden Bird." Here the brother's transformation (into
a stag) is explained, to be sure. It is part of an attempt by a magical stranger
to win the sister as his bride. The story behind this adventure, however,
is nonetheless much the same as in the tale just discussed. The magical
stranger enters the picture after the brother and sister have been living
together for some time; and their eventual recovery of that situation is

made possible by the brother's subsequent recruitment of a poor tailor as rescuer and bridegroom for the sister. The magical stranger's role as presumptuous suitor, with the attendant transformation of the brother and magical imprisonment of the sister, is thus perhaps a projection of the siblings' guilt over an unconsciously incestuous attachment; and the tailor's good fortune as bridegroom is a product of the siblings' secret dream of living together happily ever after under more decorous circumstances.

An unusual aspect of this story, when compared with folktales of like type, is that the account of the sister's imprisonment is given by the maiden herself, by way of explaining her predicament to her rescuer and eventual husband, the tailor. While there is certainly no reason to disbelieve her, the simple fact that this part of the story comes from her lips lends an element of the fantastic to the adventure recounted. If her account is not girlish fantasy, one could well imagine it as such.

After she has related how she and her brother, children of a wealthy count, were orphaned "when I was still in my tender youth" and how her parents, in their will, had commended her to the care of her brother, who then raised her, she tells the tailor that a stranger came to the castle, became their houseguest, and then one night, having awakened her with "the sounds of a tender and lovely music," used magical powers to get into her bedroom through two locked doors and proceeded to ask her to marry him. The dreamlike, erotic quality of this nocturnal adventure is enhanced by her report of how she was so tired after she, the brother, and the stranger had stayed up late over dinner that she hurried "to sink my limbs into the soft feathers"; how the charming music awakened her after "I had hardly fallen a bit asleep"; how, unable to understand from where the music was coming, she had waited to call her chambermaid, "but to my astonishment I found that, as though a demon (*Alp*) were weighing upon my chest, my speech had been taken from me"; and how by the light of her nightlamp she saw the stranger enter her room through the locked doors and heard him say "that through the magical powers at his command he had caused the lovely music to sound in order to awaken me and was now himself [as an embodiment of that music?] forcing his way through every lock with the intention of offering me his heart and hand." Interestingly, the sister does not report that she found the stranger himself unappealing. It even sounds as though she might not have been completely disinclined to accept his proposal had he approached her differently: "My revulsion at his magical powers, however, was so great that I did not grant him the privilege of an answer."[12]

There are several indications that the sister's adventure with the stranger may be a symbolic representation of her feelings about her relationship with the brother. As she tells the tailor, she and the brother "loved one another so tenderly and were so alike in our way of thinking and our inclinations that we both formed the determination never to marry but rather to remain together until the end of our lives." Then, after her refusal to respond to the stranger's proposal, the latter made good his vow to punish her haughtiness, by perfidiously transforming the brother into a stag while the two of them were out hunting the following morning. The stranger thus appears to have believed that it was her attachment to the brother that prevented her from accepting him as her suitor. The intensity of the sister's devotion to the brother is demonstrated at this point by her attempt—again, as she relates it—to shoot the stranger with a pistol as he approaches her on horseback leading a beautiful stag on a leash (she has immediately sensed what has been done to the brother) and by her faint when the stranger, from whose chest the bullet has rebounded (instantly slaying the horse she is riding) mumbles "several words that robbed me of my consciousness"—evidently words to the effect that he has taken his revenge on her or that she will now belong to him.

The sister's subsequent awakening to find herself lying naked in a glass coffin (hence the story's title) further suggests that her adventure with the stranger symbolically dramatizes her feelings about her "unnatural" life with her brother. After the magical stranger tries one last time to get her, as she says, to "accommodate myself now to his wishes" by offering to return her, her servants, and her castle to their former state—he says nothing about restoring the brother as well—he disappears. She then fell into a deep sleep, during which she had the "comforting" dream that, among other things, "a young man came and liberated me, and as I open my eyes today I discover you [before me] and see my dream fulfilled," as she sweetly tells the tailor. The girl's curious vagueness (or reticence?) about the other things she saw in her dream may hint that the brother, too, played a role therein. At least, when she proceeds to beg the tailor to help her "bring to pass what happened further in that vision," she is surely thinking partly of the brother's restoration to human form and of reunion with him. As is then reported at the end, "Her joy was increased still more when her brother . . . emerged from the forest in human form." That marriage to the tailor is not uppermost in her mind, and is perhaps even only a means to the end of decorous cohabitation with the brother, may be suggested by the terse wording of the succeeding, final clause: "and that same day the young lady, in accord with her promise, extended her hand to the lucky tailor at the altar."

This interpretation of the story as a portrayal of unconsciously incestuous attachment is further supported by the brother's role in bringing about the sister's liberation from the glass coffin. The events leading to her liberation begin with a fight to the death between a beautiful stag (the brother) and a large black bull (the stranger)—a struggle that, in view of the subsequent revelations in the sister's report of her adventures, suggests a jealous battle for possession of her. This struggle is witnessed by the tailor, who is then carried off, on the stag's antlers, to a stone cliff, where the stag uses his antlers to burst open an iron door and thereupon immediately disappears in a cloud of smoke. The stag's purpose, as is later made clear, is to provide the sister with a liberator and husband, once the unwanted suitor (the stranger in his magical transformation as a bull) has been destroyed.

Since the motivation for the stranger's metamorphosis is not explained, one may perhaps see in this transformation a symbolic representation of his passion for the maiden as being akin to the ardor of such a beast in the mating season. At the same time, insofar as the stranger's role may be related to an emotional crisis in the brother and sister, the stag's defeat of the bull may represent the brother's triumph over the "bestial" incestuous urge within himself. The stag's subsequent abduction of the tailor, to serve as liberator of the sister, amounts to a first step toward restoring the siblings' relationship, which—so we may suspect—guilt over their passion for one another has threatened to destroy. That the urge to incest is not so easily overcome may be reflected in the stag's battering down the iron door with his antlers (cf. the stranger's magical passage through the locked doors to reach the sister's bedroom) and his disappearance in the resulting flame and smoke once he has done so—perhaps lest he be tempted to contest with the tailor the role of rescuer of the sister from her glass coffin (in which, after all, she lies naked, with only her long tresses to cover her). The tailor thus serves the brother, in effect, as a vicarious substitute or stand-in in the role of bridegroom—a role which he himself, as her sibling, cannot properly assume. It is the tailor's chance wandering into the maelstrom of this repressed incestuous passion between the siblings that carries him willy-nilly to the totally unexpected and undeserved good fortune of which the opening lines of the story speak.

Discussion of "The Glass Coffin" has carried us somewhat into the territory of the *conte fantastique* as opposed to folktale (the Grimms adapted the tale from the pages of a novel that had appeared in the early eighteenth century). With the portrayal of a brother's devotion to his sister in "The White Bride and the Black Bride" (*KHM* 135) we are again on familiar ground. Here the brother's devotion to the sister is expressed first through his request to be allowed to paint her portrait, so that he may take it with him to the king's castle where he serves as coachman, and then by his subsequent mission, once the widower king has fallen in love with the sister on seeing the picture, to bring her to live at the castle as the king's bride. Such a union is clearly a delightful prospect for the brother, who would have the pleasure of the sister's charming company again and not have to make do with her portrait. As the brother, Reginer, told her earlier: "Dear Sister, I want to paint you so that I may constantly have you before my eyes, for my love for you is so great that I would like always to gaze upon you." It was Reginer's worship of the portrait then, once he had painted it and hung it in his room at the castle, that caused the king to want to see it for himself, whereupon the latter found that the maiden "resembled his deceased wife in every respect [and] was only still more beautiful, thus he fell mortally in love with the picture."

Reginer's devotion to the sister is then further shown—as he is driving her (and her stepmother and envious stepsister, who have contrived to come along in the carriage) to the castle—by his thrice-repeated refrain: "Cover thyself, my little Sister, / That rain does not soak you, / That wind does not make you dusty, / That you come nice and pretty to the king." The brother's hopes are spoiled, though, by the evil stepmother's treachery in arranging, with the aid of magic, to substitute her ugly daughter for the true bride. The effect of this deceit, happily, is to demonstrate further the devotion of the brother and sister to one another. The girl emerges transformed as a white duck from the water in which the stepmother has hoped she would drown, and laments her misfortune to the kitchen boy at the king's castle, asking each time: "What is my brother Reginer doing?" (and, secondarily, "What's the black witch [i.e., the stepsister] doing in the house?"). The brother and sister are reunited then when the king, on being told by the kitchen boy about the duck's curious visits, cuts off its head and the true bride appears before him in all her beauty, so that the ruse is discovered. Although it is not said that the king, the sister, and the brother live happily ever after, nothing is reported either about Reginer taking a bride, only that the king "rewarded the loyal brother by making him a rich and distinguished man."

"The White Bride and the Black Bride" begins as though it were a pious tale, not a story about love between a brother and sister. This introductory part of the tale explains the sister's beauty as a gift from Heaven in return for the kindness she shows God when He comes to her house disguised as a poor man. God blesses her and asks her to choose three things she would like Him to grant her, and she responds first that she wants to become "as beautiful and pure as the sun"; second, that she desires to be rich ("I would like to have a money bag that would never get empty"), and then, only after a bit of prodding from the Heavenly Father ("Don't forget the best thing") "as the third thing the eternal heavenly kingdom after my death." The favor she has found with God partly explains the passion she awakens in the brother, and then in the king. Moreover, the brother's name "Reginer" may mark him as worshipping her as though she were worthy to be a queen, or were even an earthly counterpart to the Holy Virgin as the *regina caeli,* the Queen of Heaven.

In stories of the brother and sister type, as in fairy tale romance generally, it is not uncommon for the heroine's beauty to be matched by her virtue; and occasionally, as in the story just discussed, her virtue is divinely rewarded. Such was the case, too, in "Little Brother and Little Sister," where the dead sister's maternal devotion resulted in her being restored to life "by God's grace." Indeed, to the extent that a romantic fairy tale involves portrayal of virtue on the heroine's part, it lends itself easily to adaptation as a pious story. "The Girl without Hands" (*KHM* 31) thus is a pious version of the story told in Basile's "Penta the Handless" (III, 2) about the consequences of a brother's madly passionate attraction to his sister. In both tales the heroine lets her hands be cut off in order to avoid evil, which is represented in Basile's tale by the widower brother's demand that the sister marry him and in the Grimms' version by the devil's claim upon the girl's father. In each case, the heroine's virtue is rewarded with a happy marriage and the restoration of the sacrificed extremities. The girl's hands in Basile's version are the source of her appeal for the brother, or so he claims at least when the distraught and outraged sister asks what there is about her that could awaken such great desire in anyone. (The brother's adoration of her hands may involve a guilty substitution for the actual object of his lust; in any case the sister's name "Penta" surely refers to the five fingers of her hand as the focus of the brother's incestuous obsession.) In the Grimms' story, the girl's hands symbolize her purity, not her appeal, for the tears she has shed upon them in lamenting the devil's claim on her have rendered her proof against his power. Similarly, whereas in Basile's version the girl's sacrifice of her hands is required to defeat her brother's shameful purpose—and, in that sense, to defeat the "devil" within the brother—in the Grimms' story the sacrifice is made to prevent the devil from carrying off the girl's father in her stead, after the father unwittingly has promised her to the Evil One in return for escape from poverty and for the prospect of riches.[13]

In Basile's collection, a portrayal of more innocent brotherly passion is found in "The Two Cakes" (IV, 7), where Marziella's brother Ciommo brags about her at the court of the king of Chiunzo, who then asks that the sister be brought to him. As in "The White Bride and the Black Bride," an attempt to drown the sister so that an ugly rival can assume her place provides occasion for demonstrating the sister's equal devotion to the brother. Marziella, whom a siren has saved from drowning, secretly rises from the sea each day to feed the geese which Ciommo now must tend, as punishment for what the king can only view as his deceitful claims about the sister's beauty. The king is pleased by Ciommo's success in fattening the geese; and the brother is then completely restored to favor when the king one day spies the beautiful Marziella rising from the sea, falls madly in love with her, and cuts the magic chain with which the siren had bound her.

Another, more curious example from Basile of a brother's role in providing for a sister's marital bliss—an example that leads us as well to our next topic, "Beauties and Beasts"—is found in the tale "The Three Animal Kings" (IV, 3). Here the brother does not have the role of matchmaker in the usual sense, for the sisters already have married even before he is born. Instead, his devoted search for the sisters, whom he has never met, produces the happy result that their husbands are restored to human form, the brother himself finds a bride, and—this would seem to be the secret dream motivating the whole—the siblings and their spouses live together happily ever after.

The especially peculiar facet of this story is the postponement of the full consummation of the sisters' marriages, in human terms at least, until the brother has been born and has himself reached marriageable age. Moreover, the redemption of the three husbands (who had been transformed into a falcon, a stag, and a dolphin, respectively) occurs as a result of the brother's discovery and rescue of a bride, whom the animal brothers-in-law help him secure for himself. To be sure, the husbands, who are siblings themselves, explain this circumstance as having resulted from their being cursed at birth "because of a vexation which our mother caused to a fairy." But the fact remains that the sisters spend their youth and young adulthood—a minumum of sixteen years from the time of their arrival at marriageable age—in what amounts to celibate isolation with their respective subhuman husbands in their several magical retreats. Married life begins for them really only after the brother has grown and has sought them out, and has enjoyed their "husbands' " aid in rescuing the bride. One thus may suspect that the secret point of the story is the sisters' longing for a brother, even more than for a husband, and that the marriages to the three "animal" suitors serve conveniently, or "magically," as a way of preserving their maidenhood until such time as they and the yearned-for brother can celebrate the consummation of their marriages together. Above all, they then can live on happily and decorously with one another (and their spouses, of course) under the same roof. Indeed, since the brother was born shortly after the sisters' departure with their "husbands," perhaps the girls knew their mother was pregnant and hoped the child would, at last, be a boy.

There are indications, too, that the brother's quest for a bride involves a similar sublimation of incestuous passion. Originally, he did not set out to find a wife but only the sisters, whom he had never met. While he did not think of himself as being on a mission to rescue them and was concerned only to meet them and to satisfy himself as to their well-being, he does prove to be their angel of salvation. Finally, the brother's rescue of his prospective bride from a dragon may hint at a secret, unconscious need to triumph over the menace of incestuous passion within himself vis-à-vis the sisters. In any event, the animal husbands' aid in helping him defeat the dragon and win the bride indicates that the brother's marriage is the veiled condition for their being allowed fully to possess the sisters. That union makes possible a decorous cohabitation of the sisters with the brother, and thereby provides fulfillment of the siblings' secret yearning.

Our survey has shown that when the Grimms' and Basile's fairy tale heroines have brothers, the relationship is almost invariably portrayed as one of devotion. Rivalry between siblings of opposite sex goes undepicted, much in contrast to stories of siblings of the same sex, where as often as not there is no love lost between brothers or between sisters. The moral ideal implicit in both types of depiction—always positive in the case of siblings of opposite sex, often negative when of the same sex—is that siblings ought to be loyal and devoted. Such loyalty and devotion should be free of any element of erotic desire, and in any case certainly not motivated by it. It appears, however, that the tales of brothers and sisters exist precisely because of the perception that devotion between siblings of opposite sex does tend to have erotic overtones.

The devotion between Hansel and Gretel is perfectly innocent and uncomplicated. They are still young children. What will happen, though, when Gretel becomes nubile? Can we imagine that she will marry? If she does, will Hans marry, too? Whether he does or not, will he live happily ever after with Gretel and her husband, assuming that she does marry? Obviously, the Grimms' tale about these still-very-young children does not permit such speculation. Hansel and Gretel go home to their father and live with him happily and forever, as though they will never become adults themselves.

Even in the brother and sister tale as a story of childhood, though, one may speak of "romantic" involvement in that almost invariably the brothers rescue the sisters or the sisters the brothers, or they rescue each other by turn or simultaneously. This element is "romantic" insofar as it represents the situation that typically provides the occasion for falling in love in romances. In the tales of childhood, however, brother and sister return home or otherwise continue to live much as they had before the peril arose that necessitated the rescue.

In tales of adolescence, by contrast, the siblings' rescue of one another is intimately bound up with the sister's finding of a marriage partner. Typically, in these stories, some peril results in the brothers and sisters leaving home. They are thus living together in the forest at the time they are approaching adulthood. They are not allowed, however, to live on happily ever after in this fashion. A magical transformation occurs, usually changing the brothers into animals, birds, or some other subhuman form and thereby effectively creating a biological, physical barrier between them and the sister. This barrier then remains until the sister has married, whereupon it is removed just as wondrously as it was created.

The brothers are transformed and not the sisters because the girl must marry if the siblings are to live decorously together in adulthood. The brothers and sisters are so devoted they cannot bear to part. That is the implication. Having the brothers marry is not the solution. Their wives are not likely to welcome a beautiful, devoted, unwed sister into their households; and in patriarchal society, unwed women typically lived with their parents or in convents or other institutions anyway.

Since the whole point is to get the sister married, it is not surprising that in the most extreme versions of this type of story, the brother plays the role of matchmaker. It does not matter who the suitor is as long as the sister will take him and he can be counted on to let the brother live with them. Since the sister is devoted to the brother, she will not be choosy—quite the opposite of the haughty brides we will meet in our next chapter.

Even the brothers who function as matchmakers for their sisters typically do so while under magical subhuman transformation. Since we can imagine that other barriers to forbidden intimacy between the brothers and sisters might be raised, the metamorphoses hint at an image of the brother as a biological creature. The brother has become for the sister something subhuman, as a projection of her sense that she has been seized by an animal attraction to him, or that this is latently possible. As a member of the opposite sex, he is a potential object of desire, once she has reached adolescence. This biologizing of desire on the part of nubile maidens leads us to our next question: how do the heroines of fairy tale romance react to the wedding night or its prospect?

NOTES

1. For an early reference to this implied identification of the stepmother with the witch in "Hansel und Gretel" see Jöckel, *Der Weg zum Märchen*, p. 127. A special study of the changes in the Hansel and Gretel story between the first edition of 1812 and the Grimms' last version of 1857 was done by Elizabeth Winter, "Ur- und Endfassung des Grimmschen Märchens 'Hansel und Gretel,'" *Pädagogische Rundschau*, 16 (1962), 808–19. Helmut Brackert used the tale as a test case for his discussion of the problem of interpreting fairy tales; see his "Hänsel und Gretel oder

Möglichkeiten und Grenzen literaturwissenschaftlicher Märchen-Interpretation," in Brackert, ed., *Und wenn sie nicht gestorben sind . . .*, pp. 9–38, also pp. 223–39.

2. The likely symbolism of the gift of shoes in the Juniper Tree story as a token of love was noted by Jöckel, *Der Weg zum Märchen*, p. 158. The focus on the devotion between the brother and sister is, if anything, still more evident in a version (entitled "Stepmother") published from the letters of the Brothers Grimm (of the year 1808) by Wilhelm Schoof, "Neue Urfassungen Grimmscher Märchen," *Hessische Blätter für Volkskunde*, 44 (1953), 65–88; see pp. 68–69. In this version, the dead mother plays no role whatever. The stepsister ties the stepbrother's bones together with a red silk thread and casts them under a tall pear tree, whereupon she hears a bird's beautiful singing. Subsequently, whenever she goes to stand under the tree in order to hear the bird sing, something beautiful always falls down from the tree for her. What the bird sings is a song about its sad fate (whereby it is identified as being the girl's dead stepbrother). At the father's suggestion, he and the stepmother go out one day to hear what the bird is singing. When the sister stands under the tree this time, a silk neckerchief drops as a present for her. Wishing a similar present for herself, the stepmother tells the daughter to step aside, so that she may stand there alone, whereupon a millstone falls from the tree and kills her. In this version, that is simply the end of the story; there is no mention of the stepbrother's being restored to human form.

3. The handling of erotic elements in children's fairy tales was commented on by Berendsohn in *Grundformen volkstümlicher Erzählerkunst*, p. 37: "If the *Märchen* is to serve as a children's tale, it must be slightly altered since love, after all, controls and guides everything here. The natural sexual things are not especially emphasized, to be sure, but they also are not avoided."

4. As told in the Grimms' manuscript of 1810, the story of the twelve brothers appears to concern the danger of unwitting incest between brothers and sisters, such as indeed happens between a mother and a son in the tale of Oedipus. In the manuscript, the sister does not seem to know about the brothers' existence at all, and thus cannot recognize that she is the sister of the twelve youths with whom she takes up residence in the forest. Only after she has picked the twelve lilies does she learn from the hag (who addresses her familiarly as "my little daughter") that the boys are her twelve brothers who *now* (i.e., in view of what she has just done) must be transformed into ravens. It is then reported that out of sorrow that she "did it," she cries and asks if there isn't any way to redeem the brothers. The hag thereupon replies, in this version, that she would have to remain silent for *twelve* years, evidently one year for each of the brothers. By the same token, the manuscript offers no hint of attraction or devotion between the girl and the brothers prior to her grief over having picked the lilies. Nothing is mentioned about her age; the youngest brother is not described as being moved by her beauty, nor is anything said even about her being beautiful; and it is not reported at the end that after her rescue the brothers live on happily with her and her husband. The ex-

planation may be that in the manuscript the interest is centered on the girl's unwitting commission of symbolic incest, at which the storyteller may be hinting through the mother-in-law's slanderous claim that the girl has been guilty of "the most shameful things." For the text of this version see Rölleke, *Die älteste Märchensammlung*, pp. 64–69. Pierre Bange alludes to the veiled theme of incest in his "Comment on devient homme: Analyse sémiotique d'un conte de Grimm: 'Les douze frères,' " in Georges Brunet, *Études allemandes: Recueil dédié à Jean-Jacques Anstett* (Lyon: Presses Universitaires de Lyon, 1979), pp. 93–138.

5. Only beginning with the third edition of the Grimms' collection was the wife described as being the daughter of a witch; see Tonnelat, *Les contes des frères Grimm*, p. 139.

6. A Freudian view of the sister's emotional situation in the stories of the twelve brothers, the seven ravens, and the six swans as being one of transfer of attachment from the father to the brothers was offered by Günther Bittner, "Über die Symbolik weiblicher Reifung im Volksmärchen," in Laiblin, ed., *Märchenforschung und Tiefenpsychologie*, pp. 410–17, reprinted from *Praxis der Kinderpsychologie und Kinderpsychiatrie*, 12, no. 6 (1963), 210–13.

7. Jöckel, *Der Weg zum Märchen*, p. 118, makes a similar interpretation of the fawn's eagerness for the hunt in the story of Little Brother and Little Sister, but he views the king's role as a projection of the brother's passion: "In this state of intoxication by the hunt something previously suppressed is elementally liberated: the youth's desirous love breaks through the neutral disguise of the little fawn and finds its appropriate form in the figure of the king."

8. The story's ending was interpreted similarly by Jöckel, *Der Weg zum Märchen*, p. 117: "The ending confirms the supposition: 'Little Brother and Little Sister lived happily together until their end.' These words unambiguously depict the same sibling tie we found in the last scene in the little house in the forest." It should be noted that in the Grimms' manuscript of 1810 and in the first edition of 1812 this ending was not yet made clear; see Bolte and Polívka, *Anmerkungen zu den Kinder- und Hausmärchen*, I, 82–84, and Rölleke, *Die älteste Märchensammlung*, pp. 188–91.

9. Jöckel, *Der Weg zum Märchen*, p. 118, finds in this business, instead, a projection of anxiety about intercourse: "The girl's fear about the brother's awakening manhood sees him in two images: in the wished-for image of the neutral little fawn and in the fearful image of the 'wild man.' That the latter is an expression of the disposition peculiar to her is confirmed through the words 'I will close my little door to the wild hunters.' "

10. In the Grimms' manuscript of 1810, the stepmother's role is lacking. The brother and sister simply go off into the woods of their own volition one day. In this version it is even more evident that the tale concerns arrival at sexual maturity. At each of the three springs there is a sign; and the danger warned about in the first and last signs is dependent on the sex of the person who drinks from the

spring. Whoever drinks from the first one, if it is a man he will become a tiger, and if it is a woman she will become a lamb. Whoever drinks from the second spring will become a wolf, evidently regardless of the person's sex. Whoever drinks from the third, if it is a male he will become a golden stag, but if it is a girl she will become big and beautiful. Moreover, in this version both the sister and the brother drink from the third spring, which suggests that if the sister achieves sexual maturity the brother may not, or had best not, retain his human form. And since in this version the brother is turned into an animal symbolic of male sexual prowess, not into a gentle fawn, it may also be indicated that the sister's transformation as a beautiful woman will, in and of itself, bring on this change in him. In this version, the story behind the story is that of a brother and sister whose devotion and attraction to one another tempt them to drink from the fountain of love as they are enjoying a lonely walk in the forest together. See Rölleke, *Die älteste Märchensammlung,* pp. 188–91.

11. The brother's transformation into a fawn was interpreted by Jöckel, *Der Weg zum Märchen,* p. 117, as projecting the sister's anxiety about the entry of sexuality into their relationship and her desire to suppress the brother's awakening manhood:

> Her words, "Don't drink, otherwise you will become a wild animal and tear me apart," show in frankly drastic form her anxiety about the brother's sexuality that is at this time entering into their previously neutral relationship. . . . In the case before us, it is noteworthy how the awakening sexuality of the brother is deprived of its actual elementariness during the course of the sister's entreaties: it sinks from that of a tiger by way of a wolf to that of a little fawn. As such it not only does not pose a danger to the girl, but is also at the same time the right object for her maternal instinct and female possessiveness. The garter around the animal's neck and the soft rope braided from the rushes speak a clear language; no less so the cohabitation in the little house, where the little sister is the only active partner. That she lays her head on the back of the little fawn at night is to be evaluated as suppression of the little brother's male instincts.

In the version the Grimms published in the first edition (1812), the brother drinks from the first spring they reach; thus, the sister's sexual feelings are less evident there. At the same time, however, the possibility that the brother's transformation into a fawn is a wish fulfillment on the sister's part is strengthened by reference to her—merely—thinking she hears the spring warn her; and the brother drinks because, not having heard the spring speak himself, he pays no heed to the sister's warning. Of similar interest in this version is that the stepmother wanted both of the children turned into fawns, not just the little brother, perhaps because she enviously recognized that, as a young girl, the little sister would make a pet of the brother in his new shape as a cuddly deer. See Bolte and Polívka, *Anmerkungen zu den Kinder- und Hausmärchen,* I, 79–82; cf. Panzer, ed., *Die Kinder- und Hausmärchen der Brüder Grimm in ihrer Urgestalt,* I, 45–49.

12. Ruth B. Bottigheimer, from a feminist perspective, viewed the scene not as a crisis of desire but as a depiction of women's sexual vulnerability: "The evident fact that no amount of security is protection enough for a woman emerges from my reading of 'The Glass Coffin,' where the onset of speechlessness coincides with the revelation of the young woman's vulnerability, that is, her powerlessness against an intrusion that can be read sexually, as well as spatially"; see her *Grimms' Bad Girls and Bold Boys*, p. 77.

13. A monograph on the stories about The Girl without Hands was done by Heinrich Däumling, *Studie über den Typus des 'Mädchens ohne Hände' innerhalb des Konstanze-Zyklus* (Diss., Munich, 1912; Munich: Carl Gerber, 1912). He traces the history of the literary versions back to the Middle Ages, and compares the literary and oral versions of this type of tale. He finds that the incest theme is dominant, and that it most often concerns a father's illicit passion for his daughter. One strand of the tradition avoids this theme by supplanting it with that of an older woman's envy of the young girl's beauty, or of her place in the father's affections.

2
Beauties and Beasts

n the stories focusing upon devotion between brothers and sisters, we encountered a number of examples of the male sibling's transformation into a member of the animal kingdom. In such tales, the sisters are rarely in doubt as to the identity of the transformed sibling, while in the type of story we shall discuss here one finds the opposite case: the girl is often at first unaware that the subhuman creature with whom she is confronted is in reality a man, and indeed a potential suitor (or, in a few cases, merely a would-be seducer). What is the reason for this important difference?

Stories of the Beauty and the Beast type portray crises related to thoughts of marrying or the wedding night.[1] Why is it that whereas in tales of the sibling type the brothers are only occasionally changed into animal forms of the more threatening or "beastly" sort, in the stories now under discussion this type of metamorphosis predominates? Do these tales typically, if secretly, have reference to virginal fantasies about males as predators?

We have seen instances of this view of female psychology in a few of the stories of the brother and sister type. The most striking was in "Little Brother and Little Sister" (*KHM* 11). There the sister imagined that her brother would be turned into a beast of prey before he was actually transformed into an exceedingly tame and affectionate fawn. Similarly, in "The Glass Coffin" (*KHM* 163) this type of fantasy seemed projected in the magical stranger's transformation into a black bull, which the girl's brother, himself in the form of a stag, then destroyed, making possible her marriage to a meek, humble tailor. And in "The Twelve Brothers" (*KHM* 9), the male siblings were turned into ominous birds of prey, likely as a projection of guilt about incestuous desire.

Stories about beauties and beasts invariably have nubile heroines. One of the most famous of all fairy tales, "Little Red Riding Hood," however, is an example of this type as a story about childhood. Red Riding Hood is

still a little girl. The beast she confronts is accordingly not a man transformed into an animal, but purely and simply a wolf, albeit gifted with
speech as both fairy tale convention and a child's imagination allow. The
peril she encounters is not the wedding bed but the bed of her old grandmother, whom the wolf impersonates. The danger is not loss of virginity
but being eaten alive. In the stories about animal suitors, the heroines
discover that the beasts they have wed are in reality only men, and usually
good, kind, devoted husbands at that. Red Riding Hood, by contrast, discovers that "grandmother"—that is, the wolf she takes to be her devoted
grandmother—is in reality a beast of prey. What is the significance of these
parallels between this seemingly innocent tale of childhood and the stories
about beastly bridegrooms? Is Little Red Riding Hood likewise an ironic
objectification of a girl's emotional experience in being the object of erotic
desire?[2]

Perrault, indeed, suggested almost as much in the moral to his version
of the story, "Le Petit Chaperon Rouge," claiming—though perhaps only
half-seriously—that it was a cautionary tale warning innocent young girls
to beware of advances of all manner of "wolves," especially the kindly,
sweet-talking sort.[3] Perrault, accordingly, has Red Riding Hood undress
and get into bed with the wolf, and has her remark then not only on the
size of the animal's ears, eyes, and teeth, but also his limbs, thereby lending
an undertone of paedophilia to the story's ending. In the Grimms' version,
"Little Red Cap" (*KHM* 26), this element is lacking, but the description
of the girl as a "sweet little maid" (*kleine süße Dirne*) to whom the grandmother was so passionately devoted similarly suggests that the granddaughter is potentially the object of illicit passion for men eager to "devour
tender young morsels."

Many interpretations of this famous story have been offered.[4] Some of
these have followed Perrault's lead in seeing it as a tale of seduction, while
many more have not. Recently, a great deal of attention has been focused
on versions of the tale in oral tradition that differ significantly from the
story as given by Perrault and the Grimms. Thus, one critic has observed
that in the oral versions in which the girl escapes the wolf by getting its
permission to go outside to defecate, "the little girl displays a natural,
relaxed attitude toward her body and sex and meets the challenge of the
would-be seducer. In Perrault's literary fairy tale Little Red Riding Hood
is chastised because she is innocently disposed toward nature in the form
of the wolf and woods, and she is *raped* or punished because she is guilty
of not controlling her natural inclinations."[5] Another leading expert on this
tale, meanwhile, has argued that these versions of the story, as told inter-
nationally in oral tradition, are "full of infantile fantasy": "I believe that
the evidence of the infantile nature of LRRH has been available for cen-

turies, but folklorists and literary scholars have chosen not to consider such evidence. The oral cannibalistic eating of the mother's [i.e., Grandmother's] body, the reference to defecating in bed, the toddler's rope (which is a direct allusion to LRRH being a *very* young child), and for that matter the very insistence upon Red Riding Hood's being called *little*." [6] While both of these interpretations are valid if one assumes the prior existence of oral versions that included the motif of the girl's pretension to the wolf about needing to defecate, our concern is rather simply with the meanings that the story appears to have as told by Perrault and the Grimms.

In the Grimms' version, the grandmother's "transformation" into the wolf, in the sense of his impersonation—and incorporation—of her, may hint at an equating of her sort of devotion with that of a man. The girl's nickname, of course, derives from this very devotion on the grandmother's part, which in the Grimms' story is described in terms almost befitting a lover: "There was once a sweet little maid, whom everyone loved who only so much as looked at her, but most of all her grandmother, who absolutely did not know what all she should give to the child. Once she gave her a little cap of red velvet." The granddaughter, in return, has reacted to the gift in the way that a lover might wish his lady to respond: "because it looked so good on her and she no longer wanted to wear anything else, she was never called anything but Little Red Cap."[7]

The possible connection between the doting grandmother and the hungry wolf who impersonates grandmother may be suggested by the wolf's initial queries on encountering Little Red Cap in the woods: "Where are you going out so early, Little Red Cap?' "—"To Grandmother." "What are you carrying under your apron?" Here we see that the wolf, not unlike the grandmother, knows quite well who the child is and what she is called; and his attention is immediately focused upon the goodies she is bringing to grandmother, as well as on the part of the girl's anatomy in front of which she is carrying them (aprons were a sign of gender and an object of erotic fascination for men in those days; cf. German *Schürzenjäger*, literally 'apron chaser', for English 'skirt chaser'). And Little Red Cap's innocent friendliness toward the wolf, including her failure to sense any danger in telling him where her grandmother lives, cannot be attributed simply to typical trusting behavior on the part of little girls in fairy tales; even some of them, like the one in "Little Brother and Little Sister," harbor erotically tinged fantasies about being eaten alive by wolves.

"Little Red Riding Hood" is not a story of the Beauty and the Beast type in the stricter sense, because the wolf is not a prospective suitor, nor even clearly a seducer of maidens as one usually thinks of the matter. His lust for Red Riding Hood's body is portrayed as gluttony, pure and simple. He is truly a wolf, not a man merely appearing in beastly form as a result of the casting of a magic spell. In the stories about animal suitors, grand-mother's bed is replaced by the wedding bed, the wolf by a man in beast's clothing.

I. ANIMAL SUITORS

One of the best-known stories about a girl's involvement with an animal that turns out to be a human suitor transformed by a magical spell is "The Frog King," the tale the Grimms accorded first position in their collection (*KHM* 1). Here the suitor, being a frog (that is, being constrained to appear so until near the end), is an object not so much of the heroine's fear as her revulsion. Thus, if this story is about the crisis of passing from girlhood to womanhood—about arriving at nubility—the princess's magical adventure projects not only initial abhorrence at the thought of marriage and loss of virginity and of losing her position as the pampered youngest daughter of an evidently widower father, but also revulsion at the thought of becoming intimate with a young man.[8]

It is clear enough in "The Frog King" that the princess, who in view of her subsequent marriage to the prince must by now have passed puberty, has remained on the conscious level very much a little girl. Her chief delight is to play with a favorite toy, her golden ball; and she evidently enjoys the role of baby daughter in the household of her royal father, apparently a widower whose elder daughters have already married and gone off with their husbands. Although absolutely nothing is said about the princess's reaction to her arrival at puberty, she cannot help, of course, having noticed the change it has wrought in the shape of her body; and the sisters' prior achievement of nubility and their presumable marriages must long since have caused her, if only unconsciously, to harbor thoughts about marriage and the wedding night. The unadmitted inward crisis of ambivalent feeling to which these perceptions likely have led would appear to be projected in her encounter with the magical frog, after her golden ball has rolled into the well on that fateful day. The toy embodies her wish to remain forever a child; and the circumstance that, in order to have it retrieved for her, she must promise to enter into an intimate relationship with the frog surely hints at her suppressed awareness that the time is approaching when she will have to look to a man other than her father for the fulfillment of her—no longer innocent—desires.

The princess's reluctance to admit to herself the true nature of the crisis confronting her is reflected in her initial treatment of the frog as a funny, silly, and harmless little creature. Her sense of revulsion, horror, and out-rage arises only when the frog pursues her and demands she make good her promise to love him, to let him be her comrade, and to allow him "to sit next to you at your little table, to eat from your little golden plate, to drink from your little goblet, and to sleep in your little bed." The frog's use of diminutives may project the princess's image of herself as still a small girl, and perhaps also her contrary sense of the erotic appeal of her petiteness, for example, vis-à-vis her doting father. The intensity of her emotional crisis is heightened by her father's insistence that she honor her promise to the frog, an insistence that may echo the girl's own feeling that the time has come when she must abandon her filial attachment and cleave to a spouse, "and the twain shall be one flesh," as Jesus ordained (Matt. 19:5).

The princess's revulsion then reaches its peak, of course, when the frog, not content to sleep in a corner of her room, insists that she pick it up and put it into bed with her "or I'll tell your father about it." The girl's resistance to the prospect of entering into that degree of intimacy with the frog (and her guilt about that resistance?) moves her to hurl it against the wall, seemingly in the—perhaps only unconscious—hope that it will thereby perish and she will therewith be rid of it once and for all. Here, of course, the great magical moment in the story has arrived. The girl's evident attempt to slay the frog mysteriously results instead in its being changed into a handsome young prince, or rather, as he then reveals to her, in the prince's being redeemed and restored to human form. The breaking of the spell cast on him by a witch evidently has been conditional upon his success in bringing a beautiful young princess to the point of attempting to destroy him, although no mention of such a condition is made and no explanation is given, either, for the witch's malevolent act in transforming him. The suspicion therefore is justified that the spell functions merely to create a situation in which the nubile princess's ambivalent, unconscious feelings about desire and marriage may be indirectly and roguishly portrayed. This implication is best indicated by the nature of the princess's reaction to the frog's transformation as given in the original edition of the Grimms' collection: "As it hit the wall, however, it fell down into the bed and lay there as a beautiful young prince; whereupon the princess laid herself down beside him."[9] When the moment of sexual consummation arrives, the princess proves to be anything but a prude. The young man's sudden, magical presence in her bed affects her as though it were the fulfillment of a secret dream. The prince's original appearance to her as a frog, though, likely hints at the negative side of her feelings attendant upon the crisis of passing from girlhood to womanhood, or of becoming, as one says in German, *mannbar* ('ready for a man').[10]

A similar portrayal of the passage from girlhood to womanhood as involving confrontation with a suitor in animal form is found in another of the better-known romantic tales in the Grimms' collection, "Snow-White and Rose-Red" (*KHM* 161). Here the element of revulsion, so important in "The Frog King," is entirely lacking; and indeed the emotional situation in this regard is wholly the reverse. In this case the suitor, again as the result of a curse, is constrained to appear as a large but tame and friendly bear. The bear does not force his companionship upon the sisters Snow-White and Rose-Red either. On the contrary, they delight so in frolicking with him in their—widowed—mother's living room that he must beg them to be a bit more gentle in their play. It is precisely at this point in the portrayal, however, that the prospect of marriage is raised, in connection with a broad hint by the bear—amounting indeed almost to a proposal—that he is in reality a young man come a-courting, as he speaks the verses: "Snow-White, Rose-Red, / You're beating your suitor dead." The girls appear not to have noticed the bear's reference to himself as their prospective bridegroom; or perhaps they imagined that he was only jesting in an avuncular way. But when the bear then is constrained to take leave of them the following spring, after a winter of daily visits to their house, yet another hint is given—this time inadvertently—as it appears to Snow-White (who is described as particularly sad that he must depart) that something golden is shining through on the bear where a piece of his hide has gotten caught on the door handle and been torn away.

As in the case of the princess in "The Frog King," the girls at first seem still too young to be harboring thoughts of marriage or to have lost their innocence regarding desire. Snow-White and Rose-Red appear content to continue basking in the warmth of their sisterly devotion to one another and to remain in the bosom of their mother's loving household. The bear's magical entry into this—wholly female—domestic idyll, though, may project a secret dream about involvement with the opposite sex. As far as we learn, the bear is the first male they have encountered. Thus, his sudden appearance may represent an imaginary satisfaction of the girls' curiosity about what it would have been like to have had a father (he evidently died not long after, or possibly even before, they were born), or a devoted uncle or avuncular friend of the family (*Hausfreund*) in his stead. Their delight in romping around the living room with the bear points especially in this direction, as does his good-natured toleration of their sport with him. At the same time, though, this roughhousing with the bear also represents a girlish magical fantasy, of the regressive sort, about teasing, flirtatious intimacy with a lover. The girls' relationship with the bear is possibly even an anticipation of connubial habitation, for he comes every evening to play and to sleep over (albeit only next to the hearth). Between this idyllic winter with the newly found live-in playmate and Snow-White's eventual marriage to the formerly transformed prince sometime later that following year (and, simultaneously, her sister's marriage to the prince's brother) lies the girls' series of encounters with a misogynous dwarf. On each of three successive occasions the two sisters come upon the dwarf in situations of distressful peril such that he is constrained to accept their aid as his angels of rescue. First, he has caught his beard in a tree trunk he was attempting to split with a wedge. Then, his beard having become caught again, this time in his fishing line, he is about to be dragged into the water by the fish he has hooked. Finally, he is about to be carried off by an eagle that has managed to grab him with its claws. Far from being grateful to the girls for having saved him, much less finding them appealing in their—stereotypically romantic—role as his rescuers, the dwarf each time reacts with injured pride over having required their aid and scolds them for having done damage to his person or belongings—in the first two instances to his beard, which they have necessarily had to shorten a bit with their scissors in order to free him, and then to his coat, which, at least so he claims, has suffered a tear in the girls' struggle to separate him from the great bird of prey.

This extended portrayal of the girls' encounters with the dwarf can hardly be just a comic interlude. It very likely has some bearing (no pun intended) on the nature of their relationship to the animal suitor—all the more so since in the end the prince explains that it was the dwarf who changed him into a bear after he "had stolen my treasure." The prince is referring here to his jewels; but in the meantime the two girls, Snow-White and Rose-Red, who have temporarily become occupied with the dwarf, had become the prince's "treasures" in the romantic sense (cf., too, the eighteenth-century French use of *bijou* as referring to the female genitals, as in Diderot's *Bijoux indiscrets*). The dwarf represents another aspect of the male sex in its relationship with the female: the bachelor woman-hater, as opposed to the avuncular bachelor friend. The misogynous dwarf thus may project the girls' image of men as potentially on the run from women, as afraid to succumb to the feelings awakened by female ministrations out of fear of being captured.[11]

In several other tales in the Grimms' collection—and one in Basile's *Pentamerone*—young maidens are confronted with animal suitors whose "transformations" likewise amount to mere disguises (see AT 425). In these stories the moment of crisis comes, as in "The Frog King" (where the transformation into an animal, though, is more complete), when the girl is alone with the suitor in the bedroom. In each of these cases, however, the girl is very much aware that the suitor has entered her chamber as a bridegroom for the purpose of consummating the union. The curious point is that in these stories the girls show themselves to be extremely bold in the face of this unnatural prospect of becoming the bride of an animal suitor, as though they do not shrink from committing sodomy.

In "The Little Donkey" (*KHM* 144), we do not see or hear the princess object when her father betroths her to his pet jackass, or when the time comes to retire to her bedroom to consummate the union with the presumed animal. She merely is quite delighted to discover, once they are in the bedroom, that the creature has only to shed its hide in order to be changed into a handsome young man. Perhaps such a bizarre scene as this is meant to imply that all bridegrooms on the wedding night behave a bit asininely. Why should a girl then be overly shocked at the prospect of taking to bed a bridegroom who seemed a complete ass, especially if he appeared so only outwardly! Likewise, in "The Singing, Jumping Little Lark" (*KHM* 88) the daughter consoles her father in his grief over having inadvertently promised her to a lion. In contrast to the princess in "The Frog King," whose father had to admonish her to fulfill her promise to the frog, the daughter here displays courage, and even confident eagerness, about confronting the adventure that awaits her in the forest with the lion: "Dearest Father, the promises you have made you must also keep; I will go out and calm the lion all right, so that I shall return well and healthy to you." The girl discovers then that the lion is an animal only by day, and a handsome young man at night. And in Basile's "The Serpent" (II, 5) the girl accepts betrothal to a snake without question and enters her bedroom with it. Instead of registering surprise when it thereupon sheds its skin (cf. the bridegroom undressing) and turns out to be a handsome prince, she simply makes love with it—that is, with him. Finally, in "Hans My Hedgehog" (*KHM* 108) one finds an interesting variation on this wedding night scene with the animal bridegroom. In this tale the second king's daughter (there are two kings with daughters here) is betrothed to a creature who was born half-animal: "on top a hedgehog and below a boy." The ostensible problem about consummating the union is therefore in this case purely a matter of the girl's being able to tolerate the pricks of the bridegroom's thorny upper torso. Unlike the daughter in "The Frog King," the princess here displays no revulsion at becoming intimate with the ugly creature: "and he had to go along to the royal table, and she sat down at his side and they ate and drank." The problem is confined to the prospect of going to bed with him: "then she was very much afraid of his spines; but he said she shouldn't be afraid; she wouldn't suffer any harm." And indeed, once they are in bed he has assumed completely human form.

These stories about suitors who can seemingly discard their animal exteriors at will, at least once they have gotten into the bridal chamber on the wedding night, would thus appear to portray various elements in a maiden's feelings as she is about to surrender her virginity. These scenes especially suggest a bride's half-conscious sense that the bridegroom enters the room as a bit of a beast, physically speaking. But then, as desire takes its course, the bridegroom becomes a thing of beauty to her, all the more so once he has shed his clothes—or, as in these tales, his beastly hide. These girls, unlike the princess in "The Frog King," are completely ready for marriage—even to a beast! Only a twinge of physical apprehension, if anything, remains; and the gentle bridegrooms skillfully and swiftly succeed in quieting that.

In several others of the Grimms' tales, the subhuman creature whom the girl encounters is not really beastly, nor even an object of revulsion as is the frog for the princess in "The Frog King," but a small, gentle, friendly, and harmless member of the animal kingdom. The reason may be that these stories reflect more innocent childhood fantasies about romance and less ambivalent feelings about seduction, the wedding night, or sexual desire in general.

In the most enigmatic of these stories, "Little Tales about the Toad" (*KHM* 105)—which actually is a series of three unconnected encounters with toads—it is indeed not clear that the toad is a suitor. In the first of these encounters, a little girl engages in something like a game of mother and child with the toad, scolding it for not eating its bread along with the milk and then tapping it gently on the head with a spoon to enforce her demand. Misunderstanding the girl's action, her mother kills the toad. The girl then, out of grief over the loss of the playmate, proceeds to stop eating, grows thin, and subsequently follows it in death, as a true spouse or beloved might do.

Romantic overtones are, however, evident in the second encounter, where an orphan girl, on seeing a toad come out of the wall (as happened, too, in the first encounter) spreads out a blue silk neckerchief next to herself in order to lure it out again, since such a neckerchief is precisely that "which toads so greatly love and upon which alone they are wont to tread" (cf. the importance of neckerchiefs, or *Halstücher*, as objects of erotic attraction in poetic literature of the late eighteenth and early nineteenth centuries). And, indeed, the toad returns with a little golden crown, places it on the neckerchief, and disappears again into the hole in the wall. The crown would appear to be something of a love token; and the toad's presenting of it to the girl perhaps projects a dream of herself as a bride or princess, or both. Surprisingly, though, after the girl has taken the crown and the toad returns to find it gone, it beats its head against the wall until it dies. The storyteller then suggests that "If the girl had left the crown where it lay, the toad would have brought out more of its treasures from the cave." Perhaps this little scene is thus intended as cautioning against greed. It may also, though, project guilt on the girl's part about accepting the role of bride or beloved too readily, in such a fashion as to lose an admirer or drive him to some manner of irrational despair.

The third encounter similarly portrays feelings of sorrow, yet this time not over the forfeiture of the toad's company or of its gifts but over a sister, Little Red Stocking, who is missing. Here the child who grieves is not identified as a girl and, especially in view of the brother and sister type of story discussed earlier (Chap. 1), may indeed be a boy. This is all the more likely considering the possible erotic overtones of the little sister's name (cf., for example, Little Red Riding Hood, and the red dancing shoes the brother gives to his half-sister in "The Juniper Tree"). In any case, the toad's role here is not that of playmate or suitor, but of potential comforter or source of information about the missing sister's whereabouts.

With another of these stories about encounters with harmless creatures from the animal realm, "The Old Woman in the Woods" (*KHM* 123), we are again on familiar ground with regard to the conventions of the fairy tale romance. In this story, a servant girl who finds herself alone in the forest, after robbers have killed her master and mistress, commends herself to God; and a little white dove thereupon appears and gives her a key with which she finds food, a bed, and royal raiment. One is thus led at first to suspect that the dove represents the Holy Spirit. The bird's role proves, though, to have been rather that of a messenger of love. As a result of the dove's request that the girl do it a favor in return, she finds a handsome prince, marries him, and lives happily ever after.

The situation leading to the girl's discovery of the prince suggests that the adventure amounts to a romantic fantasy about love and marriage. The mission on which the dove sends her is to fetch a simple ring (like those used in the wedding ceremony as a token of eternal fidelity?) from among many jeweled ones which lie on a table in the house of a little old woman. As it turns out, the hag is an evil witch who transformed the prince into a tree. Each day, though, he is allowed to fly about for a couple of hours as a dove. The great magical moment in the story comes when the girl, exhausted by the ordeal of having successfully seized the ring despite the hag's attempt to hide it from her, leans against a nearby tree. The tree embraces her and is therewith transformed into a handsome young man— that is, into the prince, who as a result of the girl's brave deed is now able to regain his human form. As in other stories, like "The Frog King" and "Snow-White and Rose-Red," in which the suitor is constrained to appear to the prospective bride first in animal form, the most intriguing aspect of the tale is the fact that the girl does not recognize—consciously, at least— that her magical adventure has placed her on the road to marriage.

In yet another of the stories involving a girl's encounter with a gentle animal, "The Hare's Bride" (*KHM* 66), we find once more the type of story where the maiden knows full well that her magical adventure is posing the question of marriage. In this case, however, we have a reluctant bride.

Moreover, the portrayal of this aspect of the psychology of desire is rendered particularly interesting by the bride's age. She is—or at least would appear to be—still a little girl. Her adventure thus represents an anticipatory fantasy, from the time before puberty, about marriage and the wedding night. The suitor here, accordingly, is a hare who has been eating (and in that sense, stealing) cabbages in the garden of the girl's mother, who sends the daughter out to chase him away. The result is that the animal—uncharacteristically for a hare, but not for a man—turns his attention from the cabbages to the girl, inviting her to seat herself upon his little tail (under other circumstances, *Hasenschwänzchen* could refer to a hare's penis; cf. also French *mon petit chou* 'my dear', but literally 'my little cabbage')[12] and to go with him to his little hut. The first two times he makes this proposal, the girl refuses; but the third time she accepts his invitation, and does so evidently realizing that the hare means to make her his wife. Before the marriage can be consummated, though—while the hare has gone out proudly to invite the wedding guests and she is left alone in the kitchen to prepare the nuptial feast—she begins to feel sad and lonely and returns home to her mother, putting a straw doll, dressed in her clothes, in her place at the hare's stove. The girl's adventure thus appears to project a fantasy about leaving home and marrying.

Finally, in "The Little Rabbit" (*KHM* 191) we have a story in which a maiden's encounter with an animal suitor of the nonthreatening sort is combined with the motif of the haughty princess. The girl in question is the proud mistress of a castle with twelve magical windows that allow her to see all that is happening, and from each a little better. From the twelfth window she can spy everything "which is above or below the earth." The importance of these magical windows is that they enable the princess to engage in something akin to the infantile game of hide and seek without running the risk of losing. Accordingly, the princess has already had the heads of ninety-seven suitors mounted on posts in front of her castle—no doubt as tokens of the power of her charms and of her invincibility—when three brothers arrive to try their luck. The two elder brothers suffer the same fate as their predecessors, but the youngest brother, with the aid of a magical fox whose life he has spared, succeeds in winning the bet that he will be able to hide himself from her view. Most significant here is the weakness in the princess that the successful suitor manages to exploit: her desire for a cute, harmless little pet. Thus, the suitor turns himself into a miniature rabbit which the fox, transformed as a merchant, sells to the princess, who takes it home with her. When the time comes, then, for the princess to go to her windows to spy the suitor and thereby win her bet for the hundredth time, she is unable to see him, for on the fox's advice the little rabbit has crawled unnoticed under her pigtail.

There are a number of hints that the girl's game of spying out her suitors in their hiding places and her eventual defeat represent a crisis of passage from girlhood to womanhood. The very concept of the game suggests ambivalence about confronting a bridegroom. She wishes the suitor out of her sight (he must hide himself from her view), and yet she wants to find him again (that is her bet). But the moment she sees him again (discovers his hiding place), she has him put to death; and the only suitor she will accept as a husband is the one whom she will not be able to find (whose hiding place she will not be able to discover). She appears to use her magical windows solely for this paradoxical purpose of finding, or spying out, suitors whom she does not want. Most strikingly of all, her eventual defeat by the youngest of the three brothers happens largely as a result of her attraction to him. She accords him alone, of the hundred suitors she has encountered, more than one chance to beat her at her game. Moreover, unlike most haughty fairy tale princesses, she lives alone, not with a doting widower father as is usually the case. Thus, for her the question of finding a man and marrying poses itself that much more compellingly.

The moment of effective surrender occurs when, out of rage at being unable to win the bet, she shatters her magical windows, thereby forfeiting her virginity. Only then is she able to feel the little rabbit under her pigtail (cf. the role of pigtails as symbolizing virginity or its loss, depending on how they are braided). In one final, irrational outburst of maidenly revulsion at the thought of marrying, she hurls the little rabbit to the floor and yells, "Away, out of my sight." Yet when the suitor then returns in his human form as a handsome youth, she is waiting for him as his bride and "submits to her fate." The youngest brother has won because he was able to hide himself on her body. It was this very intimacy with a man which the princess at once dreaded and desired. Her ambivalence had led her to engage in her proud, girlish game with the suitors in the first place, and likewise made her particularly susceptible to the temptation to buy herself a little house pet, as a substitute for a husband.[13] Unlike her counterpart in "The Frog King," the princess here does not discover the secret of the little animal's true identity, for she does not witness his return to human form. Her angry banishment of the pet rabbit is thereby rendered all the more irrational and would appear especially suggestive of a process of unconscious farewell to childhood and maidenhood. Her pet will henceforth have to be a young man.

II. BEASTLY BRIDEGROOMS

The indirect or symbolic portrayal of maidenly ambivalence about marrying is not limited, in fairy tale romance, to encounters with animal suitors. The bridegroom may be portrayed as subhuman or "beastly" in some other way, as for example in the familiar story of Bluebeard, one of the folktales made famous by Perrault's little collection. (Because of the important precedence of "La Barbe bleue" the Grimms dropped their version, "Blaubart," from their collection beginning with the second edition.) In Perrault's telling of the story, the wealthy gentleman's blue beard has "rendered him so ugly and terrifying that there was neither woman nor girl who did not flee at the sight of him." Moreover, the women in his neighborhood have reason to suspect that he may be in the habit of doing away with his wives: "What they further found distasteful was that he had already married a number of women and that no one knew what had become of these ladies." The mysterious gentleman manages to overcome the fears of a neighbor lady and her two daughters, of whom he has asked to be allowed to take one to wife, by showing the three of them a marvelous time on his estates and by proving himself to be a gentle and devoted host. The younger daughter is especially moved by his display of bonhomie, to the point where, we are told, she "began to find that the master of the house did not have so very blue a beard and that he was an extremely nice man"; thus she consents to marry him. After the marriage, and upon learning about the room she is forbidden to enter, curiosity of course gets the better of her; and she discovers the corpses of the previous wives. Somewhat surprisingly, she does not flee upon making this discovery, as she might have done, but instead makes a vain attempt to cover up her act of disobedience. Perhaps she is willing to remain married to Bluebeard even after she has discovered that he is capable of such cruel punishment. It is only when she has been found out and is on the point of being butchered herself that she thinks of rescue and remembers that her brothers have promised to visit her that very day. Thus, in the younger daughter's unconscious, marriage to a man capable of murdering his wife for disobedience may not be an intolerable situation. Perhaps, on the contrary, discovering that her husband is indeed a blue-bearded butcher—as the women of the vicinity have suspected all along—renders the union that much more thrilling. Granted, the first of the two morals offered by Perrault concerns the "regrets" that surrender to curiosity often brings in its wake and, at the same time, the pleasure curiosity causes the fairer sex (this pleasure is itself, perhaps, a form of sublimated erotic desire). Yet the second moral makes the point that one can tell that this story is an old one because husbands are not what they used to be: they are no longer the masters of their houses, much less terrifying and demanding brutes. This is possibly Perrault's roguish way of suggesting it would be hard to find a husband who might prove as "exciting" to a maiden as was Bluebeard for his neighbor lady's younger daughter.

Many other interpretations of Perrault's gruesome tale are possible, of course. Most recently, Bluebeard has been seen as "the victim of sexual jealousy—hence his need to subject each successive wife to a test of absolute obedience. In that test, which becomes as much a test of fidelity as of obedience, Bluebeard's new wife, like all the others before her, fails miserably." The same critic views the heroine, meanwhile, as being possessed not by stereotypically "idle female curiosity and duplicity" but a quite legitimate *cognitive* curiosity (what does her husband have to hide?)[14] Indeed, this is the crucial point. What is clear, certainly, is the heroine's desire to know just what sort of man she has married, and specifically, what murderous crimes he has perhaps committed in view of the rumors she has heard about the disappearences of his former wives.

The Grimms' version of the story differs from Perrault's in certain important respects.[15] Here neither the prospective bride nor anyone else other than Bluebeard himself knows about his previous wives, or anything else about the man, who is a complete stranger (here he is a king, not simply a wealthy landlord, as in Perrault's version). Nor is the effect of his beard on women in particular described; instead it is said only that "he had a very blue beard so that one took a small fright whenever one looked at him" and that "the girl, too, at first was terrified of it and was afraid to marry him." The girl's situation in the family is different here also. She is the only daughter. The parent is her father, evidently a widower. And she and her brothers (there are three, not two as in Perrault's version) are almost as greatly devoted to one another as is the case in the tales of the brother and sister type. Finally, whereas in Perrault's story the girl remarries at the end, in the Grimms' version she simply goes home to the father and—especially—to the brothers, who have fulfilled the role of angels of rescue that she had given them upon riding off to become the stranger's bride. In closing, the storyteller reports, "The brothers took their dearly beloved sister home with them, and all of Bluebeard's riches belonged to her."

The Grimms' Bluebeard tale is thus as much a portrayal of the devotion between a sister and her brothers as of a maiden's involvement with a beastly bridegroom. The terrifying suitor serves to provide a rationalization not only for the girl's escape from marriage but also for her return to the brothers, with whom her relationship has then been rendered all the more tender by their role as her rescuers. In the Grimms' version the girl is an only daughter. There is no older sister to function as companion and as intermediary between the bride and the brothers. Indeed, the girl's first thought upon becoming engaged is to secure a promise of aid from the brothers in the event—which she evidently considers quite likely—that she shall need it: "But because she felt such great anxiety she went first to her three brothers, took them aside, and said, 'Dear Brothers, if you hear me cry out, then wherever you are, drop everything and come to my aid.' The brothers promised her they would do so and kissed her. 'Farewell, dear Sister, when we hear your voice, we'll leap onto our horses and will be with you quickly.' "

In Perrault's version, by contrast, no mention of the brothers whatsoever is made until near the end, and there does not appear to be anything especially passionate in their relationship to either of the two sisters. Moreover, in the Grimms' version the circumstance that the bride herself must summon the brothers to her rescue provides further opportunity for portraying her passionate dependence on them, as she thrice repeats the call, "Brothers, my dear Brothers! Come, help me!"—a summons rendered all the more sublime in view of her pretense to the husband that she has gone upstairs to say her prayers in preparation for death. She sees her help rather in the brothers than in God or Christ. In Perrault's version, although the situation is similar, the girl uses the ruse simply to play for time and to ask the sister repeatedly whether she has yet caught sight of the brothers, who in that version are, by chance, already scheduled to pay a visit that day. Finally, the fact that in the Grimms' version the brothers happen to be drinking wine together in a nearby forest when the call for help is made suggests that they may have been camping all the while within earshot of the king's castle, waiting devotedly for the moment when the sister might summon them, as she has told them she feared she would have to do. One suspects that this "fear" has represented all along her wish for escape from marriage and from the accompanying necessity of foregoing the enjoyment of her brothers' devoted presence.[16]

While the Bluebeard story, in the Grimms' version, represents rather more the brother and sister type, "The Robber Bridegroom" (*KHM* 40) offers an unalloyed case of a maiden's encounter with a homicidal suitor, and with one who is indeed a sex murderer (*Lustmörder*) pure and simple. In this tale nothing in the bridegroom's external appearance renders him particularly terrifying, as does the suitor's blue beard in the other story. Instead, the girl, a miller's daughter, suffers feelings of horror simply whenever she thinks about the fiancé, and without knowing why. The most intriguing aspect of this story, though, is the dreamlike, nightmarish quality of the girl's visit to the robber's house in the woods, including certain indications that this adventure projects the girl's anxiety about the wedding night and the surrender of her body to a bridegroom.

The chief hint that the adventure may objectify a fantasy on the girl's part is that her devoted father, the miller, would hardly have allowed her, prior to the marriage, to venture unescorted into the forest to visit the fiancé at his house, as she does in response to the latter's insistence upon such a visit. This fantastic visit may reflect her feelings about the prospect of following the fiancé to his house as his bride after the wedding. This impression is further reinforced by the nature of the scene she witnesses there from her hiding place: the fiancé and his fellow robbers bring home a young maiden, get her drunk with wine, rip off her clothes, and then, as the storyteller reports, "they laid her on a table, cut her beautiful body to pieces, and sprinkled salt over it. The poor bride behind the barrel trembled and shook, for she saw well what sort of fate the robbers had in mind for her [, too]." The chance landing of the butchered girl's ringed finger in the hidden girl's lap, when the robbers gleefully have chopped it off, also supports this reading of the story. Moreover, the circumstance that it is a friendly hag who warns the girl about the robbers' evil intent, advising her to hide and see for herself, and who then helps her to escape undetected suggests the stereotypical novelistic situation in which an older woman, through vicarious identification with a young maiden as the object of desire, eagerly counsels her about the adventure of the wedding night that awaits her. Finally, the bride's refrain, "My beloved, I only dreamed that," as she tells her adventure to the bridegroom in front of the guests at the ensuing wedding feast at her father's house, is perhaps not merely a tactic in her plan for unmasking him as an ogreish sex murderer. The refrain may also be a hint on the storyteller's part that the visit to the robbers' house is a symbolic representation of the girl's inner resistance to the thought of marriage and the wedding night.[17] The fact that it is the amputated finger with the ring on it that proves the truth of her story further hints that marriage is the object of her preoccupation and revulsion as a prospective bride. The result, in any case, is that the miller's daughter, as far as we learn, retains her virginity and resumes her maidenly existence as mistress of her father's household.

A further example of maidenly confrontation with a homicidal admirer is found in "Fitcher's Bird" (*KHM* 46), a variation on the Bluebeard story. Here there is the interesting difference that the beastly pursuer of young maidens does not approach them at first as a suitor, but disguised as a poor beggar who appeals to their urge to kindness and charity. Like Bluebeard, he seems motivated less by sexual desire than by a misogynistic compulsion to satisfy himself that no woman can be trusted once her curiosity has been aroused—a compulsion, though, that would seem to be a perverse sublimation of desire. In contrast to the Robber Bridegroom, the sorcerer (*Hexenmeister*) here, like Bluebeard, displays no erotically tinged ogreish desire to eat the flesh of beautiful young virgins. The most intriguing variation on the Bluebeard story, meanwhile, is that here it is not the key to the forbidden room that is dropped and receives the ineradicable, telltale bloodstain, but an egg which the sorcerer has enjoined each of the girls, in turn, to protect and which he has advised each therefore to carry in her hand wherever she goes. This otherwise nonsensical requirement is perhaps further evidence of the sorcerer's misogyny, in so far as eggs are associated with the female role in reproduction, and the dropping of this particular egg into the blood in the forbidden room serves as testimony to that sex's inability to withstand the urgings of curiosity.[18]

The elder two sisters in "Fitcher's Bird" succumb to curiosity, are found out, and are duly butchered. The youngest daughter succumbs too, but since she takes care to leave the egg behind before going into the forbidden room, her disobedience is not discovered. Because the sorcerer has failed to prove her guilty of surrendering to curiosity, he is constrained now to do her bidding; and her assumption of that power enables her to restore the sisters to life.[19] The sorcerer's surrender of his magical power to the girl may indicate that his abduction of young maidens involved a yearning to be proven wrong, by finding a girl who could resist curiosity and whom he thus might dare to take as a wife—the fun being here that, unknown to him, the youngest sister was in fact equally unable to resist the temptation.

Taken as a whole, however, "Fitcher's Bird" would seem, like the Bluebeard story, to be a portrayal less of bachelor misogyny than of maidenly resistance to the thought of marrying. The sisters do not go willingly to the sorcerer's house. Rather, they are, one by one, abducted by him, or at least magically seduced, in that when he touches them, after he has appeared as a beggar at their door and they have handed him a piece of bread, they are compelled to leap into the basket on his back and are therewith carried off. Once at the abductor's house, moreover, each of them in turn is confronted, in effect, with the alternative fates of being butchered if she fails the test of resisting her curiosity or of becoming the bride of a murderer if she passes it. To this extent, then, marrying is brought into association with being butchered. Finally, the story's ending concerns the youngest sister's successful avoidance of marriage and the wedding night by using her deceitfully acquired power over the sorcerer to insure that she and her revived sisters manage to return home safely. She tricks him into carrying the sisters home in a sack (he thinks he is carrying gold to her father, evidently as the price for her consent to marriage). Meanwhile, having pretended to him that she was going to make preparations for the wedding, she arranges her own escape by disguising herself as a bird (hence the story's title).

The manner in which the youngest sister effects her disguise may further hint that feelings of revulsion concerning the wedding night are involved. She covers herself first with honey (as a bride might anoint herself with sweet-smelling oils?) and then with feathers torn from her (or the sorcerer's?) bed. And she takes a skull "with grinning teeth," adorns it with a bridal wreath, and sets it in the attic window as a parting taunt and humiliation for the would-be bridegroom. When she, disguised as a bird, then passes him on the road as he is returning from her father's house, she answers his questions in a manner suggesting her abhorrence of the role of dutiful wife: "You *Fitcher*'s bird, whence do you come?" / "I'm coming from Fitze Fitcher's house." / "Then what is my young bride doing?" / "She's swept the house from bottom to top / And is peering out at the attic window." In the end, as in the Bluebeard story, it is the girl's brothers who kill the wicked suitor, in this case by locking the doors to his house, setting it afire, and burning him alive. Far from being the emblematic prisoner of love, the youngest daughter has transformed herself into bird only in order to flee the cage prepared for her and to return to the bosom of her family.

Not all the heroines in the Grimms' romantic tales react with anxiety or revulsion on being confronted with a beastly suitor. In "The Sluggard" (*KHM* 101) the youngest of three daughters gladly and joyfully accepts engagement to a man whose appearance is extremely revolting. In this case we are dealing, however, with a story of a moralistic cast. After the two older sisters have expressed horror at the thought of becoming the bride of such an ugly, unkempt suitor, the youngest agrees to marry him, saying, "Dear Father, he who helped you out of difficulty must be a good man; if you have promised him a bride in return then your word must be kept." In the end, of course, such maidenly virtue is rewarded. The young man is restored to his former, appealingly handsome self; he returns to marry the girl; and her sisters commit suicide out of grief over their lost opportunity. As this story shows once again, fairy tale romance, with its triumph of desire, generally lends itself to adaptation as a moralistic story in which virtue paves the way to bliss, as can be seen especially in the pedagogical versions written for children. In the case of the Beauty and the Beast type, this transformation is rendered all the easier by reference to the saying that beauty is only skin deep.

Basile's *Pentamerone* offers an interesting example of a romantic tale in which virtue, in the form of filial devotion, results in an encounter with an exotic, though not beastly or outright revolting, suitor. The heroine in this story, "The Golden Tree Stump" (V, 4), is rather of the Cinderella type, in that her two older sisters treat her badly. In particular, the sisters refuse to let her graze her pig on the beautiful meadow near their house. Constrained to seek a grazing place in the woods, she finds a golden tree, from which she brings golden leaves to her father that he, a poor gardener, can sell for money. When the leaves are all gone, Parmetella discovers a stairway under the tree's root which leads to an underground palace, where a young Moor tells her he wants to marry her.

As is typical for the heroines in Basile's tales, Parmetella is clearly no prude. Especially entertaining is the roguish description of her loss of virginity, after she has been awakened by the magical stranger's entry into the bed where she is sleeping: "feeling that her wool was being carded without a comb, she was about to die of fright, but seeing then that the thing reduced itself to civil war, she stood firm at the blows." Indeed, it is not until after a second night's lovemaking has ended that she is moved by curiosity to discover her lover's actual physical appearance. A tinge of sexual guilt on her part, though, may be projected in the rebuke that she receives from the youth, after she has discovered that, while he lies with her, he is no longer a black slave but the most shiningly handsome of young men: "Alas, through this fault of yours I shall have to remain another seven years in this cursed penance! Because of you, who with such curiosity has wished to poke your nose into my secrets! Go, run, break your neck, that you may never be able to appear again before me; return to your rags, you who has not known how to recognize your good fortune." Parmetella, by implication, should have been content to enjoy love's pleasures without attempting to find out what her lover looked like, much less who he was exactly. The point, however—in so far as this adventure projects a young maiden's feelings of sexual guilt—is that a girl should not be making love with a stranger at all, and especially not with one whom she must presume is a Moorish slave. And in this connection it is interesting that her lover turns out to be everything that she, in her erotic ecstasy, might wish him to be. Parmetella's reaction to the adventure, now that the magic decrees that he must be taken from her, is to devote herself to regaining his love by outwitting his mother (a witch), who attempts to marry him off to a repulsive bride. In this Parmetella of course succeeds; and she and the youth live happily ever after. His name, Thunder-and-Lightning (*Tuoni-e-lampi*), which she has meanwhile discovered, recalls the suddenness with which he took possession of her.

III. HAUGHTY VIRGINS

Parmetella's complete readiness to abandon her maidenhood before marriage, especially without knowing the identity of the man in bed with her or—most important—without having even assured herself as to his physical appearance, is most unusual in fairy tale romance. Certainly no such example can be found in the Grimms' collection, where the princess's spontaneous lying with the handsome young man in "The Frog King" is as far as any of the heroines go in surrendering promptly and uninhibitedly to desire (indeed, as mentioned earlier, the Grimms told this part of the story somewhat differently in their later editions). In the tales with animal suitors or beastly bridegrooms, in particular, the focus is rather on resistance to the thought of marrying or surrendering to desire, or at least on ambivalent feelings in regard to the matter. The extreme in this type of portrayal is reached in the tales featuring those haughty virgins whose resistance to marrying is not projected—that is, not rationalized—through an encounter with an animal suitor or homicidal bridegroom, but is manifested simply through the maiden's professed inability to find any man whom she could accept as a husband.

We have already seen something of this type of heroine in "The Little Rabbit" (*KHM* 191), where the princess would marry only a man who could succeed in hiding himself from her magically aided, all-perceiving gaze. There the successful suitor had to be changed into a miniature rabbit before he could beat her at her game and win her hand. A similar portrayal, but this time without the need for such transformation, may be found in "The Riddle" (*KHM* 22), where a haughty princess vows to marry only a man who can pose a riddle she cannot solve. That resistance to the thought of marrying lies behind her haughty vow is suggested by her resort to cheating in order to discover the solution of the riddle. In particular, she must stoop to entering the suitor's bedroom in hopes of getting him to talk in his sleep. When her ruse has been found out, she must accept marriage to him as her punishment. Like her counterpart in "The Little Rabbit," the princess here is intent on having each of her suitors beheaded, as testimony to the irresistible power of her charms to move men to risk death in attempting to win her, and perhaps, too, as anticipatory revenge for the defeat and humiliation she unconsciously feels she may have to suffer in surrendering her proud maidenhood on the wedding night.

The tale "The Six Servants" (*KHM* 134) offers yet another example of a proud virgin who would sooner see a suitor dead than marry him. Here a princess, once it appears that she will have no choice but to wed the suitor, declares that, as the storyteller reports, "she would not become his bride until someone would be willing to seat himself in the middle of the wood-pile and endure the fire. She thought none of his servants would burn himself up for him, and out of love for her he would place himself there, and then she would be free." The ostensible motivation for the girl's desperate attempt to rid herself of the suitor is her mother's taunt that it will be a "Disgrace for you, that you will be supposed to obey common folk [i.e., the prince's servants] and are not allowed to choose for yourself a husband to your liking." But the cruel means the princess chooses for trying to dispose of the prince—especially together with her belief that the heat of his passion will move him to attempt to endure the fire in order to win her—may reflect her panic over succumbing to desire's flames. That such panic is involved here is suggested all the more by the curious circumstance that, in the last of the tests set for the suitor, her role has been to remain for a whole night innocently enclosed in his embrace.

"The Six Servants" has in common with several other stories about haughty virgins that the eventual happy ending, or desire's triumph, is only possible after the new bride has been rendered humble through deception practiced upon her by the husband, in this case through the princess's having, for a time, to believe that she has become wedded to a swineherd. The point of such portrayals may appear to be that good marriages are made for love, not for riches or comforts. More likely, though, is an ironic suggestion that haughtiness in virginal maidens is related to a certain revulsion or panic at the thought of surrendering to desire. In such cases, passage to the role of wife requires an experience of humiliation as part of the process of relinquishing protective fantasies or "castles in the air" unconsciously produced in response to the emotional crisis of coming of age to marry.

The classic story of the chastening of a haughty bride, in the Grimms' collection, is "King Thrushbeard" (*KHM* 52). Here the princess finds something to criticize in any suitor who presents himself to her, which suggests that resistance to the thought of marrying is the secret, unconscious reason for her inability to find any prospective husband to her liking. Part of the reason would appear to be that, like her counterpart in "The Frog King," she is the only daughter of an apparent widower, and therefore clings unconsciously to her proud position as maiden mistress of the castle.[20] Moreover, she bears comparison with the heroines who encounter suitors transformed as animals, insofar as her ridicule of the suitors presented to her concerns their physical appearance. In particular, her mockery of the eventually successful suitor consists in her comparison of his somewhat crooked chin to a bird's beak (hence the story's title).

As in other stories of the haughty virgin type, the surprising point is that once the girl no longer has a choice and has married, her pride is swiftly overcome, almost as though by magic; and she proves to be a most obedient and humble wife. In this case, the princess is forced by her father to marry a presumed beggar, a troubadour who sings for his food (but who in reality is the king, "Thrushbeard," whom she has just ridiculed). Angry at her haughty humiliating of the whole group of suitors which he presented to her, the father, for good measure, commands that she leave the castle and go off with the troubadour to live as a beggar's wife.

The princess reacts to this banishment at first with self-pitying remorse. Also, a touch of virginal narcissism is indicated in the phrasing of her lament as she journeys with the presumed troubadour: "Poor tender maiden I, /

Oh, if only I had taken King Thrushbeard!" And when they reach his "tiny, wretched little house" in the forest, the girl, if only unconsciously, is still thinking of herself as a princess when she asks, "Where are the servants?" The turning point comes, evidently, with the physical consummation of the marriage, indicated simply by the laconic report that "they went to bed." After that first night together in the house she makes no further lament about the loss of her earlier status.[21]

Humbly and obediently she attempts to carry out the tasks the husband assigns to her, and proves eventually, because of her extraordinary appeal, to be highly successful at peddling earthen pots in the marketplace. Her beauty is such that many customers simply "gave her the money and left her the pots in the bargain." Her success thus is so great that King Thrushbeard is reduced to disguising himself as a hussar and riding through her pots in order to see that she "fails" at this task as well. The breaking of the pots—as symbolically associated with the loss of virginity—may point to her earlier haughty resistance to marrying that was projected in her ridicule of her suitors. Her last humiliation, too, again involves the breaking of pots, in this case the ones in which she has now been carrying home food from the kitchen of (Drosselbart's own) castle, where she has been working as a scullion. The pots fall from her pockets after she has accepted the invitation of the young king (it is actually Thrushbeard) to dance at his (i.e., their) wedding.

The paradoxical psychic mechanism by which a haughty maiden is "magically" transformed into a humble, devoted, and obedient wife precisely through the loss of the secret source of her disdainful pride—her jealously preserved virginity—is quite openly and roguishly portrayed in Basile's "Pride Punished" (IV, 10). Here the rejected suitor, the King of Belpaese, disguises himself as a gardener and succeeds eventually in being allowed to spend the night in the bedroom of Cinziella, daughter of the King of Solcolungo (i.e., of "long furrow"), by tempting her with beautiful clothes. Obviously, in this girl's case the adornment of her body is more important than the risk of her honor and virginity. At the same time, the progressively more intimate nature of the garments with which the gardener drives his bargains with her—a robe, a petticoat, and a bodice, paralleling his respective demands to sleep in her hall, her antechamber, then her bedroom—suggests that her love of clothes is a form of sublimated desire. To be sure, on the fateful night the princess, before retiring, consigns the gardener to a corner of the bedroom, draws a mark on the floor with charcoal, and threatens him with death if he ventures beyond it. But when the gardener, once she has fallen asleep, "gathers the fruits of love" before she has fully awakened, she not only accepts what has happened but continues at lovemaking with him that night and regularly thereafter. The point, of course, is that the pleasures of the bed, even with a lowly servant, easily supplant the princess's prior love of raiment, which has been nothing more than an unconscious substitute for those then still unknown delights. Moreover, precisely because the princess surrenders to desire without any regard to the question of marrying (which happens only after she has become pregnant and the formerly disguised lover has further humbled her by making her sleep in the stable at his castle), the paradoxical point is made that her rejection of the suitor involved not so much resistance to the thought of becoming subservient to a husband as simply the prospect of losing her virginity.

Another of Basile's tales, "Pinto Smalto" (V, 3), offers an even more striking example of how a maiden's resistance to surrendering her virginity leads paradoxically to that very result. Betta, a merchant's only daughter, refuses to consider marriage, but, under pressure from her father to do so, contrives to have him bring her the necessary ingredients for fashioning, in the privacy of her room, a life-size confectioner's doll which, through ardent prayer to the goddess of love, she manages to bring to life. She then presents the fellow, whom she has dubbed Pinto Smalto ("Painted Enamel"), to her father. Although surprised to see "come out of the room that most handsome youth whom he had not seen enter there," the father agrees to accept this fine specimen as his son-in-law.

We thus have in "Pinto Smalto" the unusual case, for the folktale, of marriage to an unreal, supernatural, or imaginary beloved—to a creature of the heroine's fantasy or wish fulfillment, at any rate—rather than to a mortal (albeit one who has undergone transformation and is then restored to human form). One might suspect that Betta's fashioning of her bridegroom amounts to escape from marriage into an ideal, imaginary love that would be no marriage at all in the usual sense and would thus presumably not involve loss of virginity. Surprisingly, though, she proves to have become pregnant and evidently through intercourse with the doll, although no mention is made of their having slept together and at the wedding the bridegroom is abducted by a queen who has arrived uninvited. The implication is that the impregnation occurred secretly before the wedding, or even that the conception was a magically virginal one, the simple product perhaps of a dream of intercourse with the ideal beloved. In any case, it was made clear from the start—and most humorously so—that the daughter's refusal to marry involved a determination to remain a virgin:

> Once upon a time there was a merchant who had one and only one daughter whom he would greatly have wished to see married; but however much he might strike the chords of this lute he found her a hundred miles distant from his preludes. That airy head, like a monkey among females, hated the coda; like territory set aside and the hunting preserve, it rejected the com-

merce of any man; and it wanted the day off always at its court of justice, vacation always at the schools, court holidays always at the bank; so much so that the father as a result remained the most tormented and desperate in the world.

The fashioning of the doll is thus a magical projection of the girl's revulsion at the thought of intimacy with a man. Her eventual bliss, after she has won back the beloved from the queen, amounts to a fulfillment of the romantic dream of union with an imaginary beloved.

A similar, though less drastic, instance of a haughty maiden's success in magically fashioning a lover to her liking is found in Basile's "Peruonto" (I, 3). Here there is the unusual twist that the virgin becomes pregnant wholly by magic, not through the usual means at all; and the power of transformation belongs to the suitor, not to the girl herself. Princess Vastolla finds herself constrained to marry a penniless, terribly ugly simpleton named Peruonto after he has impregnated her simply by uttering a curse: when she laughed at him, he cried out to her, "Oh, go to, Vastolla, may you get pregnant by me!" The princess turns misfortune to her advantage, however, by making use of the unwanted suitor's gift of magical wish fulfillment to rescue herself, the husband, and her offspring from the sealed cask in which her angry father has set them adrift; to transform the simpleton into an ideal beloved; and to acquire a castle fit for a king. Therefore, in the end her father is quite glad to bless the union and to enjoy playing grandfather to the twin boys who were sired by the simpleton's magical curse on that fateful day.

As a final example of a girl's reluctant passage from maidenhood to womanhood—an example that anticipates our next subject, the relationship between fathers and daughters—one may point to the Grimms' tale "The Iron Stove" (*KHM* 127). Here we have the bizarre situation that the girl, having gotten lost in the forest, finds herself constrained to promise to marry an iron stove—at least, to wed the owner of the voice that has spoken to her from the stove. At first, the princess and her father conspire to prevent her from having to make good her promise, once she has reached home safely thanks to the directions provided by the voice from the stove. But when the two girls they have sent out in her stead prove unable, in turn, to rescue the unknown suitor from the stove in the prescribed manner (by scraping a large hole in it with a knife), the princess herself is forced to make the attempt. That she then succeeds so handily at the impossible task, once she has made enough of a hole to discover that the fellow inside is an extremely handsome prince, is testimony to the heat of her virginal passion (perhaps this is the symbolic significance of the suitor's being imprisoned in an oven, and of the girl's having to open a hole in it sufficiently large to "liberate" or "redeem" him and make him her own).

Once the princess has gotten the prince out of the oven, however, a twinge of ambivalence about marrying appears to come into play. She begs leave to go home first to "say three words" to her father, as she puts it. Because she speaks longer than that with him, when she returns the stove and the prince have vanished. One may suspect therefore that the bridegroom's disappearance and his subsequent taking of another bride—thinking that the princess was dead—project unconscious feelings of guilt on the princess's part about her continued attachment to her father and an unconscious reluctance to surrender her maidenly filial role. In the end, of course, her young love triumphs as she succeeds in winning the prince from the "false" bride.

In the stories of the brother and sister type, the magically depicted crises concerned the heroines' attachment to their male siblings as a potential obstacle to their passage from childhood to adulthood. Typically, the heroines in the tales of beauties and beasts have no brothers. Instead, their attachment, if any, is to their fathers. As one critic, writing from a feminist perspective, remarked, "Many tales implicitly acknowledge the potential attraction between females and the father; but as purveyors of cultural norms, they [i.e., the tales] often mask latent incest as filial love and displace blatant sexual desires onto a substitute, such as a beast in 'The Frog Prince' (AT 440) or 'Snow-White and Rose-Red' (AT 426)."[22] It is the suitor, not the father, who appears as an animal, or who proves to be a "beast." The father is the object of childhood affection, the suitor of animal desire. At the same time, in these stories it is usually very much the father's will and wish that the daughters should marry; and the daughters accept the challenge less out of inclination than filial devotion. Thus, the suitors appear to these beauties in the guise of beasts, not in a form that could awaken romantic passion, albeit one that symbolizes animal desire.

In the tales about animal suitors, the heroines almost always marry, even if they do not leave home. In the stories about bridegrooms who are beastly solely because of their homicidal ways, the opposite holds true. The girls leave home, escape the bloody fate that awaits them at the bridegroom's house, and return home to live as they had before. These brides may be emotionally attached to their fathers or brothers or both; but to judge from the stories' endings, the unadmitted goal is simply to give up being a bride and recover their earlier, maidenly existence, with the nightmarish adventure with the beastly bridegroom providing them the rationalization. The difference between the tales of animal suitors and those about beastly bridegrooms was nicely summarized by a recent critic as follows: "there are two quite different types of beasts in the Grimms' *Nursery and Household*

Tales. First, there are the animal grooms who make life unpleasant for many a female protagonist: these are the frogs, bears, hedgehogs, and other creatures that press themselves on attractive young girls. But these beasts invariably turn out to be handsome young princes in disguise and generally prove to be perfect gentlemen. The real fairy-tale beasts, even if they are beasts only in the figurative rather than the literal sense of the term, turn out to be murderers masquerading as civilized men."[23] The point would seem to be that in the animal suitor stories, the unions are destined to succeed, while the marriages with beastly bridegrooms—with those whom the heroines encounter as men—are doomed to fail.

In contrast to the brides with animal suitors, the haughty virgins staunchly resist their fathers' wish for them to marry, by claiming that they can find no man to their liking. Unlike the girls with beastly bridegrooms, though, they do not return home once they have gone off with the suitor but soon accept the role of bride and seem content with it. Their contentment obviously is not related, as sometimes in the tales of animal suitors, to a desire to please their fathers. Yet, at the same time, they appear to have found in the suitors successors to their fathers as objects of their affections. In this respect, the tales of haughty virgins lead us to our next question: how are father-daughter relationships depicted in romantic fairy tales, as found in the collections of the Grimms, Basile, and Perrault?

NOTES

1. Bettelheim's interpretation of the tales of beauties and beasts is from a didactic or therapeutic perspective: "a radical change in [the heroine's] previously held attitudes about sex is absolutely necessary. What must happen is expressed, as always in fairy tale, through a most impressive image: a beast is turned into a magnificent person"; see *Uses of Enchantment*, p. 282.

Folkloristic studies of this type of story have been done by Ernst Tegethoff, *Studien zum Märchentypus von Amor und Psyche* (Diss., Munich, 1919), Rheinische Beiträge und Hülfsbücher zur germanischen Philologie und Volkskunde, 4 (Bonn: Kurt Schroeder, 1922); Elisabeth Koechlin, *Wesenszüge des deutschen und des französischen Volksmärchens: Eine vergleichende Studie zum Märchentypus von 'Amor und Psyche' und vom 'Tierbräutigam,'* Basler Studien zur deutschen Sprache und Literatur, 4 (Basel: Benno Schwabe, 1945); and esp. Jan-Öjvind Swahn, *The Tale of Cupid and Psyche (Aarne-Thompson 425 & 428)* (Lund: Gleerup, 1955).

As the titles of the studies above indicate, among folklorists this sort of tale is named after the Amor and Psyche story in Apuleius's *The Golden Ass.* For purposes of the present discussion it has seemed better to use a name alluding to the more popularly known tale by Marie Leprince de Beaumont, "La Belle et la Bête," in

Le Magasin des Enfants ou dialogues d'une sage gouvernante avec ses élèves (1756; new ed., 2 vols., Paris: Garnier frères, n.d. [18??]), I, 56–80. For a Freudian interpretation of this story as depicting "Beauty's oedipal attachment to her father," see Bettelheim, *Uses of Enchantment*, p. 307.

2. A folkloristic, or geographical-historical, study of the variants of the Little Red Riding Hood story was done by Marianne Rumpf, "Rotkäppchen: Eine vergleichende Untersuchung" (Diss., Göttingen, 1951). Special attention to oral versions recorded in the nineteenth century, especially in France, is given by Paul Delarue, "Les Contes merveilleux de Perrault et la tradition populaire," *Bulletin Folklorique d'Ile-de-France*, n.s. 12 (1951), 221–28, 251–60, 283–91.

For an interpretation of the story from the perspective of a Freudian clinical analyst, see Lilla Veszy-Wagner, "Little Red Riding Hood on the Couch," *Psychoanalytic Forum*, 1 (1966), 400–408. For a structuralist viewpoint, following the ideas of Claude Lévi-Strauss, see Victor Laruccia, "Little Red Riding Hood's Metacommentary: Paradoxical Injunction: Semiotics and Behavior," *Modern Language Notes*, 90 (1975), 517–34. The interpretation by Carole Hanks and D. T. Hanks, Jr., is pedagogical: in contrast to the Grimms' versions, "Perrault's tale points out that maturing is risky; there *are* dangers in the forest—if the maturing person makes a misstep (not necessarily through any personal fault), then he or she may perish"; see "Perrault's 'Little Red Riding Hood': Victim of the Revisers," *Children's Literature: Annual of the Modern Language Association Seminar on Children's Literature and the Children's Literature Association*, 7 (1978), 68–77.

3. Felix R. Freudmann calls particular attention to the incongruity of Perrault's statements of his tales' morals when those interpretations are compared with the action in the story; see "Realism and Magic in Perrault's Fairy Tales," *L'Esprit Créatur*, 3 (1963), 116–22. For a discussion of humor and irony in Perrault's tales, see Jacques Barchilon, "L'ironie et l'humor dans les 'Contes' de Perrault," *Studi francese*, 11 (1967), 258–70. In his novelistic, almost word-by-word commentary on Perrault's version of Little Red Riding Hood, Georges Londeix views the story as a tale of seduction; see his *Le petit chaperon rouge de Perrault* (Paris: L'Herne, 1970). Lee Burns analyzes the role of eroticism in the tale in his "Red Riding Hood," *Children's Literature*, 1 (1972), 30–36. Marianne Rumpf argues that in the French folktale the wolf had likely been a werewolf, as a particular object of popular belief in sixteenth- and seventeenth-century France; see *Ursprung und Entstehung von Warn- und Schreckmärchen*, Folklore Fellows' Communications, 160 (Helsinki: Suomalainen Tiedeakatemia/Academia scientificarum fennica, 1955), p. 5.

4. For a critical survey of the history of interpretations of Little Red Riding Hood, see Alan Dundes, "Interpreting Little Red Riding Hood Psychoanalytically," in McGlathery, ed., *Brothers Grimm and Folktale*, pp. 16–51, and also Jack Zipes, *The Trials and Tribulations of Little Red Riding Hood: Versions of the Tale in a Sociocultural Context* (South Hadley, Mass.: Bergin and Garvey, 1983), and Hans Ritz,

Die Geschichte vom Rotkäppchen: Ursprünge, Analysen, Parodien eines Märchens (Emstal: Muri, 1981).

5. Zipes, *Fairy Tales and the Art of Subversion,* p. 29.

6. Dundes, "Interpreting Little Red Riding Hood Psychoanalytically," p. 43.

7. Bettelheim's interpretation is similar, in *Uses of Enchantment,* p. 173: "Whether it is Mother or Grandmother—this mother once removed—it is fatal for the young girl if this older woman abdicates her own attractiveness to males and transfers it to the daughter by giving her a too attractive red cloak. . . . Red is the color symbolizing violent emotions, very much including sexual ones. The red velvet cap given by Grandmother to Little Red Cap thus can be viewed as a symbol of a premature transfer of sexual attractiveness." Erich Fromm, agreeing with Freudian critics that the red cap represents menstruation, views the Red Riding Hood story as expressing "a deep aversion toward men and sexuality"; see *Märchen Mythen und Träume: Eine Einführung zum Verständnis von Träumen, Märchen und Mythen,* trans. Ernst Bucher as *The Forgotten Language* (Zurich: Diana, 1957), p. 226.

A political interpretation was made by Hans-Wolf Jäger, who argues that the Grimms, in borrowing certain elements for their version from the fairy tale play *Rotkäppchen* by their German Romantic contemporary Ludwig Tieck, were surely not unaware that in that piece a degree of symbolic association is established between the girl's red cap and the caps worn by the Jacobins, between the wolf and the partisans of the French Revolution, and between the hunter and the servants of monarchical tyranny; see "Trägt Rotkäppchen eine Jakobinermütze?: Über mutmaßliche Konnotate bei Tieck und Grimm," in Joachim Bark, ed., *Literatursoziologie,* vol. 2: *Beiträge zur Praxis* (Stuttgart: Kohlhammer, 1974), pp. 159–80.

In comparing Perrault's literary text with oral versions that have survived and that do not seem influenced by Perrault, Paul Delarue concluded that the red cap or hood, as the particular present the grandmother chooses to give, does not appear necessarily to have belonged to the story as it was being told in Perrault's day; see "Les Contes merveilleux de Perrault," pp. 221–28, 251–60, 283–91; and also Marc Soriano, "Le petit chaperon rouge," *La Nouvelle Revue Franaise,* 16 (1968), 429–43.

8. Bruno Jöckel saw in the princess confronted by the frog "a girl . . . who is about to cross the boundary between childhood and maturing" (p. 205), in "Das Reifungserlebnis im Märchen," reprinted in Laiblin, ed., *Märchenforschung und Tiefenpsychologie,* pp. 195–211, from *Psyche,* 1, no. 3 (1948), 382–95. Bettelheim viewed the girl's revulsion at the thought of intimacy with the frog as a stage in puberty: "The awakening of sex is not free of disgust or anxiety, even anger. Anxiety turns into anger and hatred as the princess hurls the frog against the wall"; see *Uses of Enchantment,* p. 288. For a discussion of the Grimms' suppression of eroticism in this tale, and later erotic transformations of it, especially as done in jokes, cartoons, parodies, and travesties, see Lutz Röhrich, "Der Froschkönig und seine Wandlungen," *Fabula,* 20 (1979), 170–92.

9. Rölleke, *Die älteste Märchensammlung*, p. 146. In that version, the frog's transformation evidently does not take place until the frog hits the mattress, suggesting that the prince can only be restored to human form if he manages to get into the girl's bed (indeed, she has thrown him into the bed, in effect). If a handsome young man can steal his way into a pretty girl's bed everything will then go according to Nature's plan and Desire's magic.

This scene in the manuscript version of 1810 was softened in the first edition (1812), but it remained clear that only when the frog hits the bed is it transformed, and that the princess lies with the prince immediately: "He was now her beloved companion, and she held him in esteem as she had promised, and they fell asleep together contentedly" (n.b. what she actually had promised was to share her bed with the frog, to "esteem" him in that sense); see Rölleke, *Die alteste Märchensammlung*, p. 149. In neither the manuscript nor the first edition is there yet anything about the prince's transformation having been caused by a witch; it is simply a matter of the frog being turned into the girl's lover, and the girl being changed into a—desirous—woman.

10. Jack Zipes finds the 1810 text "explicitly sexual," but as alluding to "a universal initiation and marital ritual (derived from primitive matriarchal societies)," and that "Mutual sexual recognition and acceptance bring about the prince's salvation"; see his *Fairy Tales and the Art of Subversion*, p. 50.

In another version of the Frog Prince that the Grimms give in their notes, the point of the story seems to be somewhat the same, and yet also quite different. On the one hand, the girl's attachment to her father is suggested more clearly, in that the princess (the youngest of three sisters) goes to the spring not to play with her ball but in response to her ailing father's request for a glass of water. She is forced to promise to accept the frog as her lover in return for his rendering the cloudy spring water clear. She does not hesitate to make the bargain because she tells herself that a frog can never be her "treasure" (*Schatz* is the word used here for "lover"). On the other hand, however, the girl rather willingly allows the frog to get into her bed. After he has spent two nights sleeping at her feet, she tells him on the third night that she will not be letting him in again after that. He thereupon leaps under her pillow, and she calmly accepts his presence there. The next morning she awakens to find him standing as a handsome young prince before her bed; and he explains that her promise to be his beloved has transformed him. Thus, the girl here, far from being revolted by the frog, seems to wish, unconsciously, that it might qualify as her lover after all, and even to force it to declare itself, to show itself in its true form, that is, in the form she desires it to take. The prince, for his part, seems to have been romantically attracted to her by her virtue in ministering to her ailing father. See Jacob Grimm and Wilhelm Grimm, *Kinder- und Hausmärchen*, ed. Rölleke, III, 3–5. In the Grimms' telling of this version as "Der Froschprinz," no. 13 in the second volume (1815) of the first edition, the three sisters go out to the spring to get a glass of water for themselves, not for their father. Thus, the focus there is even more clearly on the boldness of the youngest daughter in agreeing to become the frog's "treasure," or lover. She may be the youngest, but she is, by implication, the most eager to marry, perhaps precisely because she is the "baby" sister. See Bolte and Polívka, *Anmerkungen zu den Kinder- und Hausmärchen*, I, 1.

11. In point of fact, though, the story of Snow-White and Rose-Red as the Grimms found it in their source, Caroline Stahl's *Fabeln, Märchen und Erzählungen für Kinder* (Nürnberg, 1818), contained only the dwarf's role. In the end the dwarf is devoured by a bear that is plainly and simply a hungry animal, not an enchanted prince. From the Grimms' summary of Caroline Stahl's story, given in their notes, it appears that the dwarf is merely greedy, not misogynistic; and his bad end serves, in effect, simply to punish his ingratitude toward Snow-White and Rose-Red after they have rescued him on the several earlier occasions. Although Bolte and Polívka suggest that the Grimms possibly took most of the rest of the story from some "French tale of the 18th Century" or other, it is just as likely that the romantic aspect of "Schneeweißchen und Rosenrot" was almost pure invention on the Grimms' part. Wilhelm Grimm admits about as much, for he says in the notes that while he has used Caroline Stahl's story, he has "told it, however, in my own way." He then reports that the verses about Snow-White and Rose-Red beating the suitor to death were found in an undated story by another contemporary author, Friedrich Kind. The indication is that Wilhelm Grimm simply made up the part about the bear from Caroline Stahl's tale being a transformed prince, and accordingly recast the story as a romantic tale. His belief, evidently, was that some such story must have existed in folk song, considering the coincidence of the girls' names in the two sources. See Bolte and Polívka, *Anmerkungen zu den Kinder- und Hausmärchen*, III, 259–60, and Jacob Grimm and Wilhelm Grimm, *Kinder- und Hausmärchen*, ed. Rölleke, III, 243, 334, 504. See also Heinz Rölleke, "Schneeweißchen und Rosenrot: Rätsel um ein Grimmsches Märchen," in his '*Wo das Wünschen noch geholfen hat*': *Gesammelte Aufsätze zu den Kinder- und Hausmärchen der Brüder Grimm*, Wuppertaler Schriftenreihe Literatur, 23 (Bonn: Bouvier, 1985), pp. 191–206; first published in *Wirkendes Wort*, 33 (1983), 152–63.

12. Ruth Bottigheimer recently called attention to the implied equation of an animal's tail with its penis in another Grimm story, "The Wedding of Mrs. Fox" (*KHM* 38); see Bottigheimer, *Grimms' Bad Girls and Bold Boys*, p. 160.

13. The author of a folkloristic study of this type of story concluded that in the original version the "small animal" in question must have been a flea, not a miniature rabbit. As such, the suitor would of course have had a still easier time hiding himself on the haughty princess's body, and many a literary precedent for so doing. See Ingrid Hartmann[-Ströhm], " 'Das Meerhäschen': Eine vergleichende Märchenuntersuchung" (Diss., Göttingen, 1953). Whether the animal is a rabbit or a flea, in either case a degree of erotic symbolism is involved.

14. Tatar, *Hard Facts of the Grimms' Fairy Tales*, pp. 134–35.

15. For the Grimms' Bluebeard story, see Jacob Grimm and Wilhelm Grimm, *Kinder- und Hausmärchen,* ed. Rölleke, II, 465–68; also the relevant note, III, 525–26.

16. Folkloristic studies of the Bluebeard type of story were done by Emil Heckmann, *Blaubart: Ein Beitrag zur vergleichenden Märchenforschung* (Diss., Heidelberg, 1930; n.p.: n.p., 1930), and Josef Herzog, *Die Märchentypen des 'Ritter Blaubart' und 'Fitchervogel'* (Würzburg: Konrad Triltsch, 1938); see also Paul Delarue, "Les Contes Merveilleux de Perrault et la tradition populaire," *Bulletin folklorique d'Ile-de-France,* n.s. 13 (1952), 348–57, and n.s. 14 (1953), 511–17. Heckmann argued that the Bluebeard story originated in mythical tales about Death abducting maidens and testing their obedience, and then was contaminated by elements from ballads about sexual murderers *(Lustmörder).* One critic recently has proposed, rather abstractly, that the lesson the heroine learns is the "unreliability of sight"; see H. H. Mowshowitz, " 'Voir est un acte dangereux': An Analysis of Perrault's 'La Barbe bleue,' " *Proceedings of the Pacific Northwest Conference on Foreign Languages,* 30, nos. 1–2 (1979), 28–30.

17. In the Grimms' manuscript of 1810, the robbers' victim is not a young woman at all, but the heroine's old grandmother. This earlier version, for one thing, lends even more of a nightmarish quality to the heroine's adventure. For another, it suggests an identification, on the girl's part, with her grandmother as a bride and as the "victim" of male lust. In this version the ringed finger that has to be chopped off is the one with the grandmother's wedding band on it. Special attention is attracted to this ring finger in that, while the grandmother has a number of rings on various fingers, the wedding ring is the only one that cannot be removed simply by pulling it off. The Grimms softened the element of horror in their first edition (1812) by omitting the old woman's identity as the heroine's grandmother; but to do that is to miss the heroine's implied identification with the grandmother—like Little Red Riding Hood with hers—as the object of ogreish male lust. For these earlier versions of "Der Räuberbräutigam" see Rölleke, *Die älteste Märchensammlung,* pp. 234–37.

18. Bettelheim's view is much the same: "The egg is a symbol of female sexuality which, so it seems, the girls in 'Fitcher's Bird' are to preserve unspoiled. The key that opens the door to a secret room suggests associations to the male sexual organ, particularly in the first intercourse when the hymen is broken and blood gets on it"; see *Uses of Enchantment,* pp. 300–301.

19. It was not until the Grimms' seventh, and last, edition (1857) that any mystery was introduced regarding the heroine's power over Fitcher. In the earlier editions, she is simply the prospective bride who sets certain conditions on her acceptance of the suitor's proposal of marriage; see Tonnelat, *Les contes des frères Grimm,* pp. 138–39. In any case, the point is that as a prospective bridegroom eager to marry the bride of his dreams—that is, a girl who can withstand the temptations of curiosity—Fitcher is at the heroine's mercy and must do her bidding.

20. For a somewhat different interpretation of the princess's pride in "König Drosselbart" as a compensation for feelings of immaturity and, hence, of inferiority, see Jöckel, *Der Weg zum Märchen*, p. 59.

21. There are some versions of this type of story in which the connection between the girl's haughtiness and her virginity is plainer; see Ernst Alfred Philippson, *Der Märchentypus vom König Drosselbart* (Diss., Cologne, 1922), Folklore Fellows' Communications, 50 (Greifswald: Suomalainen Tiedeakatemia, 1923).

22. Rowe, "Feminism and Fairy Tales," pp. 243–44.

23. Maria M. Tatar, "Beauties vs. Beasts in the Grimms' *Nursery and Household Tales*," in McGlathery, ed., *Brothers Grimm and Folktale*, p. 133.

3

Fathers and Daughters

s the stories discussed thus far show, emotional involvement between parents and children is a frequent object of portrayal in folktales. That this is especially true of the romantic tale should come as no surprise, for in love plots generally the requisite hindrance to the fulfillment of young desire often takes the form of parental objection or intervention. There are surprises to be found here, however. In particular, the romantic folktale offers the possibility of hinting, with seeming innocence, at erotically tinged undercurrents in the relationship between parent and child that do not lend themselves to tasteful direct portrayal.

Fairy tale romance often depicts the child's first experience of leaving home and venturing out on its own, usually in connection with choosing a mate. In the stories of the brother and sister type, resistance to the taking of this step is reflected in a desire to return to the bosom of the family or, failing that, to retain the devoted company of one's siblings. Thus, we have seen how Hansel and Gretel, while prepared to survive together in the forest if need be, are overjoyed at being able to live with their father, and how the sister in "The Seven Ravens" succeeds in restoring her brothers to human form and bringing them home with her. Or when the situation at home precludes returning there—as in "The Twelve Brothers," "The Six Swans," "The Little Lamb and the Little Fish," and "Little Brother and Little Sister"—the siblings set up housekeeping together elsewhere or the sister marries and the brother joins the new household.

The aspect of such stories that occupies us at present, though, is the nature of the parents' feelings toward the children in this crisis, especially those of a father toward a daughter. Although the frequent role of the evil stepmother primarily serves to provide occasion for the brothers and sisters to demonstrate their devotion to one another, the stepmother's intervention may also point to the question of the father's degree of attachment to the children. The answer is almost always that the father's love is unquestioned, but that the changed circumstances in his household render him powerless to take effective action. Thus, the father in "Hansel and Gretel" reluctantly agrees to abandon the children in the forest; his counterpart in "The Six Swans" fails in the attempt to hide the children from the stepmother; in "Fundevogel" the devoted father is simply away from the house when his lady cook—the stepmother-figure there—sets about to do the mischief; and in Basile's "Ninnillo and Nennella" the father's attempt to leave a trail for the children in the forest fails when a donkey eats the clover.

In the stories in which leaving home involves the prospect of marrying, the emotional situation is rendered potentially more complex by the possibility of a degree of erotic attachment between parents and children of the opposite sex. To the extent that the Beauty and the Beast type focused simply on the girl's panic—or surprising lack of it—at the thought of marrying, the issue of her possible attachment to the father was incidental, and was indeed precluded in a number of instances. The girl in "The Hare's Bride," for example, does not appear to have a father and simply runs home to mother. In "Fitcher's Bird," the girls' eagerness to get home likewise has nothing to do with thoughts of their father. And the sisters Snow-White and Rose-Red are the daughters of a widow—although this very lack contributes to their attachment to the bear as houseguest and avuncular playmate. In some of these stories, however, and in a number of others as well, the child's arrival at marriageable age provides the occasion for a display of intensified devotion between a parent and a child of the opposite sex, and occasionally even of jealous or incestuous passion on the part of the parent.

I. PATERNAL DEVOTION

The crisis in the relationship between a father and his daughter may involve nothing more than his parental concern that she make a proper marriage, often in connection with his desire to become a grandfather. Even these decidedly innocent depictions, however, place the father in a position of concerning himself with a matter of most intimate importance to the daughter, the prospect of surrendering her virginity. This degree of intimacy is heightened, moreover, by the almost-universal circumstance that the father is a widower, or that the mother at least plays little or no role or is not mentioned. Thus, as we have seen, the father in "King Thrushbeard" teaches his daughter humility by forcing her to marry a troubadour, while the father in Basile's "Pinto Smalto" finds himself accepting as his son-in-law a magical doll fashioned by the daughter's own hand. The charm of these portrayals lies largely in the wide range of possibilities provided by the ingredient of fairy tale magic.

The father in "The Frog King" (*KHM* 1) does not suggest that the daughter should marry the animal, to be sure, but he does insist that she keep her promises to the creature and is indeed delighted to accept him as son-in-law once he has been restored to princely human form; nor does he object to their having consummated the union prior to the wedding. The father may even unconsciously identify with the young man as having succeeded, under magical circumstances and against great odds, in gaining entry to the daughter's bedroom. By contrast, in "The Iron Stove" (*KHM* 127), where the daughter's promise concerns marriage, the father conspires with her to avoid fulfilling it. His shock is understandable, considering that she made the promise to an iron stove; but there are hints that the attachment between father and daughter is quite strong, especially on her part. She does not tell the father, for example, that the promise was made actually to a young man imprisoned in the oven who claimed to be a prince. One thus may imagine that she fears that the father would then have considered the fellow a suitable match and have insisted that she keep the promise. This impression that the princess is ambivalent about surrendering the role of daughter for that of wife is reinforced by her desire, after she has finally kept her promise to rescue the prince from the oven, to return home to say a few words to her father.

Unlike the daughters in "The Frog King" and "The Iron Stove," the girl in Basile's "Cannetella" (III, 1) avoids marriage, preserves her virginity, and apparently resumes her former role in her father's household. Here we have the case, as in "Pinto Smalto," that the father, wanting progeny, begs the daughter to marry, whereas she is devoted to remaining a virgin, and in this instance has indeed dedicated her virginity to the goddess Diana. The type of the haughty virgin, Cannetella attempts to avoid marriage by setting what she considers to be an impossible condition: the head and teeth of the prospective husband must be of gold. As fate would have it, the condition is satisfied by the king's mortal enemy, the sorcerer Fioravante, to whom the king, not recognizing him, gives the daughter as bride. Fioravante, though, does not appear interested in consummating the union, since he simply locks up Cannetella in a stall, intending to keep her there seven years while he is away. She is rescued by her father's loyal blacksmith; and, fearing that the sorcerer will attempt to abduct her, she has the father put seven iron doors on her room. This measure does not prevent Fioravante from gaining entry, but the spell he has placed on the castle is broken just in time to prevent the abduction. The sorcerer is slain, and the daughter's express desire now to remain forever with the father apparently achieves its fulfillment (though the story ends simply with the would-be abductor's death).

While it is hard to know what to make of Cannetella's adventure, the evident result is that the father is made to forget his desire for progeny and is rendered content to live out his days with the unmarried daughter, whom he clearly adores and who seems equally devoted to him. A possible reading of the story is thus that the sorcerer's role serves to fulfill a secret desire on the father's part for an excuse to retain the status quo in his relationship with the daughter, or a similar wish on the daughter's part, or both. The names of the characters, indeed, may hint at a subterranean eroticism: the father is king of "beautiful little hill" (*bello poggio;* cf. *mons veneris*) and sires the daughter with his wife Renzolla (*renna zolla* 'lump of sand'?), yet only with the magical aid of the goddess Siringa ('lilac' or 'syringe'), after whom he promises to name the daughter, in memory of the goddess's having transformed herself into a *canna* ('pipe', 'tube', etc.; from this imagery it would almost appear that he sired the daughter with the goddess herself, or at least with the goddess in mind). The name of the father's enemy perhaps suggests "flower in front" (*fiore avanti*), referring to the sorcerer's apparent contentment to abduct the girl without then possessing her sexually or, by extension, an unconscious desire on the part of the father himself to retain her virginal presence. Finally, the father's readiness, in the face of the magical threat from outside, to bar the way to the daughter's room with seven iron doors may hint that he is secretly happy to have just cause for joining her in her jealous guardianship of her virginity.

Indications of a particular attachment between father and daughter are provided in a different way in "The Skilled Huntsman" (*KHM* 111). Here the daughter marries in the end, quite happily and very much with her father's blessing. Yet there is the interesting circumstance that the means of identifying the young man who has rescued her from impending abduction by greedy giants include, among other things, two tokens of love and devotion between the king and his daughter that were found by the young huntsman in the tower bedroom where she was in a deep slumber: a pair of slippers under the bed, one with her name on it, the other with that of her father, and a large neckerchief with her father's name on the right side and hers on the left. Moreover, the father seems almost to have set the stage for the daughter's rescue by an eventual bridegroom, which may indicate a degree of anticipatory, vicarious identification with whoever is destined to become the lucky suitor. In an antechamber the young man finds a saber with the king's name on it, which he uses then to slay the giants, and on a table next to the saber a sealed letter in which it is said that "whoever had the saber could slay anything he encountered." Also, there is the curious circumstance that the huntsman finds the slumbering maiden completely sewn into her nightshirt, suggesting that the father envisions her rescue as being such that she will not be violated. And the huntsman fulfills this evidently desired role, for he is content to cut off a small piece of the nightshirt: "Then he went away and allowed her to sleep on undisturbed."[1] That he also takes along all three of the items with the father's name on them—the saber, the slipper for the right foot, and the right-hand half of the neckerchief—indicates that the young man thinks of himself, if only unconsciously, as assuming the father's role as the maiden's fetishistic admirer, since slippers and neckerchiefs—not to forget night-shirts—belong to the more intimate sphere of a maiden's wardrobe.[2] Finally, the father's rage at the daughter's rejection of the—false—rescuer, an un-bearably ugly captain, as bridegroom serves as a final hint, perhaps, that the "rescue" represents the fulfillment of a secret, guilty dream on the father's part.

Often, the father's devotion is a decidedly minor, though still not in-significant, element. In "The Goosegirl at the Spring" (*KHM* 179), the king banishes the youngest of his three daughters for having responded in a seemingly insulting, though actually quite devoted, way to his demand that the daughters express their love for him—a scene reminiscent of that in *King Lear*, of course. In "Rumpelstiltskin" (*KHM* 55) the girl's predic-ament is caused by her miller father's unfounded boast that she could spin straw into gold, a fantastic claim that likely is motivated as much by his excitement over her beauty as by his hope of gaining favor with the king; indeed, it is possible to view Rumpelstiltskin's magical role in getting the daughter out of this mess as related to her father's having gotten her into it, especially since the dwarf's demand to have her child bears resemblance to the concern of widower—and in that sense "bachelor"—fathers in folktale that their daughters produce children. And in "Cinderella" (*KHM* 21), the father's seeming lack of devotion in failing to protect Cinderella from the stepmother's abuse or otherwise to concern himself with his daughter stands in odd contrast to his awareness of her appeal. Twice, with playful teasing, Cinderella escapes the prince's pursuit. First she leaps into the dovecote (cf. the dove as a symbol of Aphrodite), and then into a pear tree (cf. the association of fruit trees with women's seductive wiles, and the resemblance of the pear's shape to that of a woman). Each time, on hearing the prince's report of this, the father asks himself, "Could it have been Cinderella?"

Portrayals of devotion between father and daughter are more pronounced and frequent in Basile's *Pentamerone*. Reference has already been made to the depictions in "Pinto Smalto" and "Cannetella." In Basile's version of the Cinderella story, "The Cat Cinderella" (I, 6), a perfidious governess exploits Zezolla's place in her father's affections to achieve her aim of becoming his wife. Then, Zezolla herself makes use of the father's devotion in getting him to bring home from his travels the magical present that enables her to win her prince, and thereby to escape the oppression of the governess become stepmother.

The circumstances of the magical adventure on which the daughter sends her father are particularly suggestive regarding emotional undercurrents in their relationship. In her misery, Zezolla is confronted by a dove (as symbol of Aphrodite?) who tells her that if she desires anything she should let it be known to "the fairy dove on the island of Sardinia." When, as then happens, the father (a prince) sets out for Sardinia on state business and inquires of Zezolla what present he should bring her, she asks only that he give her greetings to the fairy dove and beg her to send something, but adds the warning that if he neglects to do this for her he will not be able to leave that island. The father does indeed forget and must be reminded of his promise through the good agency of—love's—magic, hinting at a need on his part to suppress all thoughts of the daughter and his paternal duty toward her, perhaps precisely because his devotion to her is secretly still quite intense. The result of his curious mission on the daughter's behalf is that she is provided with the magical means for nurturing and fulfilling her dream of marriage to a prince: through the date twig the father brings her (together with the magical implements for cultivating it), she obtains the magnificent raiment she uses to captivate the beloved.

In the Grimms' Cinderella story (*KHM* 21), the father's mission in bringing such a present to the daughter is likewise of crucial importance. The situation, though, is complicated by the fact that the magical twig's role results from its having been planted on her mother's grave, not from its having been the gift of an exotic fairy. Here the spirit of the dead mother, embodied in the white bird (a dove, evidently) that visits the hazel tree which has grown from the twig, serves as the agent of fulfillment of the girl's dream of marriage (cf. *in die Haseln gehen* = *fensterln* 'paying a nocturnal visit to a girl's room' and *Haselnuß* 'hazel nut' as a symbol of fertility). But the father's—unwitting—contribution to this magical adventure may suggest that he secretly harbors a devotion to the dead wife that has transferred itself to the daughter. In particular, Cinderella's condition that the hazel twig he is to bring her shall be the first one that knocks off his hat as he rides along on his trip points to something like loss of dignity, as though the mother or daughter were magically playing a trick on him or trying to make him "come to his senses." For her part, Cinderella seems initially to have no idea of why she wants such a twig (much less any guarantee that one will indeed happen to knock off the father's hat), and certainly no inkling that planting it on the mother's grave will lead to her winning a prince.[3]

The same sort of magical mission is found also in "The Little Slave Girl," the second tale of the Cinderella type in Basile's collection (II, 8).[4]

In this case, however, the relationship is that between a girl, Lisa, and her uncle, the baron of Selvascura ("Dark Forest"). Moreover, the uncle's feelings toward the niece are complicated by the fact that she is the daughter of his dead young sister, Lilla, to whom he was most devoted, who conceived the child in an unusual and magical fashion during a game with her playmates in which the girls were to jump over a rose without knocking off any of the petals. The pregnancy occurred as a result of Lilla's having cheated at the game, by swallowing the petal she had knocked off without the other girls' having noticed it. The implication is that the pregnancy was a punishment for having committed a shameful, dishonest, or forbidden act—an act, though, that bears some resemblance to the usual way of becoming pregnant, in view of the rose symbolism. This magical circumstance must contribute, one would assume, to a romanticization of Lilla in the brother's eyes, for whom she, as virgin mother, must appear as something like a secular counterpart to the Queen of Heaven. Indeed, since the baby was conceived without being sired, the baron may secretly fancy himself to be the niece's father "in the spirit," so to speak, as a sublimation of forbidden incestuous desire (see the tales of the brother and sister type).

This impression of the uncle as doting on the niece out of an incestuous devotion to his sister is reinforced by subsequent magical events in the story. As a result of a fairy's curse at her christening (the motif especially familiar from the Sleeping Beauty story), Lisa, having reached the age of seven, dies when her mother forgetfully leaves the comb in her hair with which she has been grooming her (cf. the use of this motif in the Snow White story). The girl's corpse is placed inside seven crystal boxes, fitted within one another, and then put in a remote room of the castle. Her mother, Lilla, soon dies out of grief over her loss. That Lilla, on her deathbed, makes her brother promise never to open the room containing the crystal coffins, as she gives him the key to it, implies that she senses he will feel the urge to do just that, out of passionate adoration of the niece, the magically conceived offspring and image of his beloved sister. (The uncle is thereby placed somewhat in the position of the wife or potential bride in the stories of the Bluebeard type.) That it is instead the wife he takes, after a year of grieving over the loss of his sister, who succumbs to the temptation does not lessen the suspicion that the uncle is passionately devoted to the niece. On the contrary, the wife's surrender to curiosity about the forbidden room results in her jealous belief—surely not so very wide of the mark—that the baron has been worshipping the beautiful dead maiden, who has now magically become fully grown (the crystal boxes have grown right along with her).

It is at this point that "The Little Slave Girl"—which, as we have seen, combines elements of the Sleeping Beauty, Bluebeard, and Snow White stories—becomes the Cinderella type. Having inadvertently revived the girl, in her jealous rage, by grabbing her hair and pulling her out of the coffin, the uncle's wife abuses her and turns her into a kitchen maid. On his return from a hunting trip, the uncle does not recognize Lisa, whom the wife presents to him as an African slave girl. When the baron then goes off on another journey, Lisa asks him to bring back three presents for her—a doll, a knife, and a sharpening stone—and warns that should he forget to do her bidding, he will be prevented from completing the trip.

As then becomes clear, Lisa's request reflects her thoughts—perhaps only unconscious—of her uncle as her potential angel of rescue. In the kitchen she repeatedly laments her fate to the doll as though it were a live person, demanding from it a response. When the doll does not answer, she sharpens the knife and threatens to kill it, whereupon the doll gives the— evidently desired—reply that it has heard her better than a deaf person (meaning the uncle?). Finally, the uncle overhears the niece speaking in this manner to the doll and looks through the keyhole into the kitchen. This time, though, Lisa threatens to kill herself if the doll does not answer. The uncle, who has recognized her from the story she has been telling to the doll, kicks open the door, takes the knife, restores the niece to her blossoming beauty, sends the wife back to her relatives, and marries the niece to a young man of her choice. Thus, in the end the uncle has returned to a bachelor life such as he led prior to his sister's death. And most important, his relationship to the beloved niece has been restored. To be sure, he has lost his status as her guardian and custodian, but he has surely gained an even greater place in her affections for having served as her angel of rescue.

Similarly interesting, though rather incidental, depictions of paternal devotion are found in other tales of Basile's collection. In the frame story itself, the tale of Princess Zoza's love for Prince Thaddeus of Roundfield, there is the example of a father who, being a widower, desires nothing more than to see his beautiful daughter laugh. He attempts to cure her melancholy by having a fountain of oil built to amuse her with the sight of people hopping around it to avoid soiling their clothes. The indirect result is that the princess soon turns her thoughts to marrying, a development which suggests that such serious-mindedness in a girl is a sign of latent desire and that the father is bound to lose her someday to a husband. In this sense, then, a father's passionate desire to see his daughter laugh involves something of a secret, forbidden wish to have her relate to him as to a lover. In another story, "Peruonto" (I, 3), the father reacts to his daughter's unexplained pregnancy with a rage colored by irrational thoughts of himself as having been thereby not only dishonored but cuckolded as well. He tells his council, "You all know already that the moon of my honor has gotten horns." Ultimately, the father becomes reconciled to his new role as grandfather, as does the father in "The Raven" (IV, 9), a sorcerer who at the end arrives in a cloud just in time to prevent his daughter from throwing herself from a window and to explain that all of the magical adventures that have beset her, her husband, and his brother were wrought by him as punishment for the brothers' abduction of her and for her susceptibility to the temptation of fine raiment that led to it.

II. JEALOUS PASSION

In the stories discussed above, we have already seen elements or tinges of jealous passion intruding occasionally into otherwise innocent feelings of paternal devotion. There are, however, certain tales in which the father's feelings about the daughter, or his actions in connection with her role as bride, exceed the bounds of propriety. This is perhaps most evident in those stories in which the father one way or another becomes involved in what transpires in the bridal chamber on the wedding night. To be sure, in "Hans My Hedgehog" (*KHM* 108) this involvement occurs at the bridegroom's request: he tells the old king that he should have four men stand guard before the door and make a large fire, in which they are to burn the skin the hedgehog will shed just before he climbs into the marriage bed. Once this has happened and Hans is lying in the bed "completely in human form, but . . . black as coal as though he had been burned," the king calls for his physician, who washes the bridegroom "with good salves and covers him with ointments" so that he is transformed into a handsome young man, very much to the daughter's delight. In "The Two Royal Children" (*KHM* 113), though, a father's jealous love of his daughters, and accompanying envy of the suitor as prospective bridegroom, is indicated by his condition that if the young prince is to have one of the daughters to wife, he must remain awake in her bedroom for nine hours—from nine in the evening to six in the morning—without falling asleep. The—ironic—implication of the father's odd demand may be that he imagines that in this way the young man will be prevented from "sleeping" with the daughter and will thus have to suffer the torments of unfulfilled desire.

As it happens, the eldest daughter and the two younger ones after her trick the father by having the statues of St. Christopher standing in their rooms answer each hour for the young man, who thereby passes the test despite having fallen asleep in the girls' bedrooms (there is no indication that he engages in any intimacy with them, except the laconic reports that he "laid himself on the threshold"). That the father, each of the first two times, goes back on his word by refusing to give the daughter to the prince in marriage and by making him repeat this great accomplishment with the next youngest daughter reinforces the impression that the king harbors a forbidden love for the daughters, as does the circumstance of his hourly visits outside the bedroom doors to insure that the suitor is still awake, and that he subsequently sets three further seemingly impossible tasks once the prince has passed the original test with each of the three girls in succession. Moreover, the presence of a statue of St. Christopher, the guardian saint for children, in the bedroom of each of the girls suggests that the father may think of them as susceptible to the temptations of desire (St. Christopher, if not Daddy, will see what you are doing in your bedrooms), as does the fact that the younger the daughter, the larger her St. Christopher's statue, especially since it is the youngest daughter who proves the most "fetching"—both in the appeal she holds for the prince and in her determination to win him as husband. This impression of the statues' role is strengthened, if anything, by the girls' use of St. Christopher as accomplice in their deceit of the jealous father.

In Basile's *Pentamerone* there are several stories in which the father's attention similarly becomes focused on the daughter's bedroom or on the bridal chamber. The father in "The Beetle, the Mouse, and the Cricket" (III, 5) stipulates that, although Nardiello, the simpleton son of a rich farmer, has met the challenge of making his melancholy daughter laugh, the marriage will be valid only if the youth succeeds in consummating it within the space of three nights. The king, who does not consider Nardiello a suitable mate for a princess, then slips him a sleeping potion each night to prevent the marriage's consummation. In "The Serpent" (II, 5) the king, who has similarly been forced to betroth his daughter to an unwanted suitor (in this case understandably so, since it is a snake), peers in through the keyhole to discover what transpires on the wedding night, and then breaks down the door in order to do away with the snakeskin that the bridegroom has shed in emerging as a handsome prince. And in "Sapia Liccarda" (III, 4) a rich merchant, fearing that his daughters might invite young men into their bedrooms while he is away on a business trip, boards them up in the house—but to no avail, of course.

One of the most intriguing examples of a father's resistance to the thought of his daughter marrying is found in "Old Rinkrank" (*KHM* 196). A king has a glass mountain built and tells his daughter's beloved that whoever can succeed in running over the mountain without falling can have his daughter to wife. Out of a burning desire to be wed to her beloved, the princess eagerly offers to join him in attempting this feat, in order to catch him should he begin to fall. The result is that she falls, the mountain opens up, and she disappears into it, becoming the prisoner of an old man with a long gray beard (the title role) who tells her she must choose between becoming his maidservant and being killed. As the years pass, their relationship develops into something like that of an old married couple, though their cohabitation remains chaste. Eventually, she escapes from the gnomic captor and is reunited with the father and the beloved. The father, daughter, and her beloved succeed in killing Old Rinkrank and, made rich by his gold and silver, live happily on together.

Is there a secret, or ironic, connection between the roles of the father and the gnome, who is perhaps a projection of the father's guilt over a subterranean desire to steal the daughter's youth by keeping her for himself? Rinkrank cohabits—celibately—with the girl until she has grown old; then, the time for jealous love on a father's part having passed, the father, daughter, and bridegroom live happily together under the same roof.

In a number of stories depicting a father's feelings about a daughter, the focus is on the circumstances of her birth. In "The Twelve Brothers" (*KHM* 9) the father, passionately hoping that, contrary to superstition, thirteen will be his lucky number and his wife will finally bear him a daughter, has coffins made for his twelve sons, so that the child may be his sole heir, should it be a girl. The impression is thus created that from the outset he has been yearning to have a daughter and therefore resents the sons, whose successive births have brought him a series of a dozen disappointments.[5] As we have noted, there is a similar, though less drastic, portrayal at the beginning of "The Seven Ravens" (*KHM* 25), where the father, who has yearned for a daughter, is so aggrieved over the prospect that the baby girl might die that he utters the fateful wish that his seven sons be transformed into ravens when they fail to return immediately with water for her emergency baptism. One also finds cases in which the wish for a daughter is fulfilled in an almost fantastic manner, recalling, say, Athene's springing full-grown from the head of Zeus. Thus, in a variant opening of the Snow White story, a count has no sooner expressed the wish, as he is out riding with his wife in their carriage one winter day, that he might have a daughter with skin as white as snow, etc., than such a girl indeed appears, as if by magic, at the side of the roadway.[6] And in Basile's "Viola" (II, 3) an ogre, having emitted a loud fart and then discovered a beautiful young maiden standing behind him, imagines that he has sired her in this manner and dotingly takes her in as his daughter.

There are, to be sure, exceptions to the rule that fathers in romantic folktales are depicted as being devoted to their daughters. In "Rapunzel" (*KHM* 12), the father does not display any remorse over having to surrender the baby daughter to the hag, to whom he has promised his pregnant wife's child in exchange for the rampion required to satisfy the wife's lust for that leafy salad vegetable. And in "The Robber Bridegroom" (*KHM* 40), the miller offers no objection to his daughter's going out alone to visit the fiancé's house in the forest, at the latter's insistence. The points of these stories, though, lie elsewhere.

In the tales of the Sleeping Beauty type, depiction of the father as longing for a daughter becomes related to a crisis involving her eventual arrival at marriageable age. The father's yearning in "Little Briar-Rose" (*KHM* 50) is answered by a frog's announcement to the queen, as she is bathing, that she will give birth to a daughter before the year is out (a travesty, perhaps of the Annunciation to Mary?). The ironic point of this "miraculous" conception is perhaps that with a passion so intense wishing alone might suffice to produce a pregnancy, or even that the king's desire is more to obtain a daughter than to sleep with his wife. The matter of the hag's curse of the baby girl, and the twelfth fairy's amelioration of it, may likewise be viewed as secretly related to the father's doting wish for a daughter since the result is that, befitting a princess, the girl remains ignorant of the onerous distaff chore of spinning. She is thereby also prevented from indulging in the traditionally concomitant pastime of building romantic castles in the air (cf. German *spinnen* in the sense of "fantasizing"). And, most important, she does not take a husband when she reaches marriageable age, but remains in the stage of blossoming maidenhood for fully a hundred years.[7]

The intensity of the father's devotion to the daughter is more evident in two versions of the Sleeping Beauty tale found in Basile's collection. In "Sun, Moon, and Talia" (V, 5), when the girl, in fulfillment of the curse, falls down as though dead, the grieving father locks up her corpse in the sylvan palace where they have been living together and leaves, never to return, in the hope that he might thus forget the great misfortune that has befallen him. At her birth, the father—her mother is not mentioned—gave her the name Talia (i.e., Thalia, Greek *Thaleia* 'the blossoming one'), testifying no doubt to his yearning for a daughter and his anticipation of her arrival at maidenhood. Once Talia has fallen into the deathlike sleep and the father leaves, he plays no further role in the story.

The subsequent events, however, concern a similarly intense passion for the daughter on the part of another older man, a king who is unhappily married. While out hunting one day he discovers the seemingly dead girl and, filled with passionate desire, carries her to a bed in the abandoned palace, "and plucked the fruits of love," as we are told. When he later returns, he finds that she is alive and has given birth (while still in the deathlike sleep) to fraternal twins (a boy and a girl), and he promises to come back for them. The degree to which the girl represents for him an ideal beloved is attested by his subsequent mumbling of her name and those of their children (Sun and Moon) in his sleep, thereby leading to his wife's discovery of his infidelity. The king then, in turn, discovers his wife's plan to do away with the rival and her offspring (she intends to have the children fed to him). He has her thrown on the fire she has prepared for Talia, and lives happily ever after with the beloved and their children.

One suspects that the fulfillment of the king's passion may be in some sense an ironic substitute for similar fulfillment of the part of the aggrieved father, especially since the father's departure from the scene is followed immediately by the king's entry into the story. Had the father acted as this king does upon his discovery of the seemingly dead maiden, he would of course have violated the incest taboo, whereas this king is guilty simply of an act of adultery rendered excusable in view of his wife's evil or jealous nature. At the same time, though, the king's deed amounts to a form of rape and of necrophilia, so that a degree of vice attaches to it after all. His act is thus not so very different from the case in which the father, had he not left the secluded palace immediately after the daughter's apparent death, might have succumbed to the same temptation. The odd circumstance that the father does not bury Talia further suggests that his departure forever from the castle was the product not only of grief but of secret fear that the same passionate devotion that renders him incapable of consigning her remains to the grave might cause him to violate her corpse.[8] This possibility, though, is otherwise not indicated in the text, and thus remains pure conjecture.

In Basile's other tale of this type, "The Face" (III, 3), one does not actually have a *sleeping* beauty. Indeed, only the opening of this story belongs to that type, and as such constitutes rather a travesty of it. Here it is made quite clear that the mysterious danger awaiting the daughter is, first and foremost, simply her arrival at womanhood, with the attendant awakening of desire. And the father responds in a transparently jealous or possessive way, building a tower to house the daughter after it has been prophesied that she is in danger of having "the main sluice of life (*la chiavica maestra della vita*) uncorked by the thighbone of an animal (*per un osso maestro*)."[9] The effect of her incarceration with twelve ladies-in-waiting and a governess and of the king's order that only meat with no bones be brought to her is, if anything, to fan the flames of desire. She flirts shamelessly with the first eligible male she spies from her tower and promises on the spot to run off with him. The magical means of her rescue, not surprisingly, is a bone (a thighbone that a dog brings into her tower); and she immediately rides off with her prince.

The coupling of a father's wish for a daughter with the prospect that she will then leave him is quite plain in another of Basile's stories, "The Three Crowns" (IV, 6), where a king hears a voice ask him whether he prefers to have a daughter who would flee from him or a son who would destroy him. The fact that this voice actually leaves him no choice makes one suspect that he secretly wishes for a daughter. Once the girl is born, he locks her up until he has arranged to marry her off. But the moment she is released from captivity, the prophecy nonetheless comes true, as she is carried off by a stormy gust of wind. This magical event, which prevents her marriage to the bridegroom her father has selected for her, may project her resentment of the father's possessive control of her destiny. In any case, the eventual result of her magical abduction—her marriage to a king whom she, disguised as a boy, has served as a page—suggests that her experience of having been locked away by the father made her yearn all the more to bask in the devotion of an older man. The effect of the mysterious, magical prophecy made to the father is thus to ensure that he will succeed in alienating and thereby losing the daughter, just as in the Sleeping Beauty story the father's doting concern to keep the daughter innocent of anything having to do with spindles ensures that when she first encounters one she will be all the more drawn to it. In this sense, we are dealing in each instance with the proverbial self-fulfilling prophecy.

In yet another of Basile's tales, "The Flea" (I, 5), the devotion that fathers in folktale commonly exhibit toward daughters is transferred to a pet flea. Since the father's fascination with the flea, however, becomes entwined with the question of whom—and whether—the daughter shall marry, it may be suspected that the flea is in some measure a substitute for the daughter. The father's involvement with the flea begins one day when he discovers it biting him on the arm and is about to kill it, but instead suddenly develops an infatuation with the creature. He feeds it daily with blood from his arm until it has grown quite large (here one may be reminded that the daughter represents his own flesh and blood that he has nurtured and raised to maturity). He then—implausibly—has the flea skinned and the hide tanned, and offers to give the daughter in marriage to any man who can guess from what animal the hide has been taken. It is at this point, particularly, that an association of the flea with the daughter, and a hint of repressed jealous passion on the father's part, suggests itself. The father must consider it practically impossible that anyone should be capable of guessing the truth; and he therefore would have a rationalization, of sorts, for not giving the daughter away in marriage. In this sense, the daughter is the pet whom he has nurtured with his life's blood and then "skinned," or cheated, in hopes of retaining possession of her.

As the examples discussed thus far indicate, a father's passionate love for a daughter is a subject that, in view of the incest taboo, calls for delicate handling and veiled depiction. Portrayed openly, the matter is simply too offensive. There is, for example, in a tale of the brother and sister type, "The White Bride and the Black Bride" (*KHM* 135), the case of the widower king who wanted to remarry only if the woman were as beautiful as his dead wife, and then was fortunate enough to find her exact image, yet still more beautiful, in the young sister of his coachman. Thus, one is dealing in that case only with spiritual, as opposed to physical, incest. There is, however, one great exception to this avoidance of portraying a father's openly incestuous desire for his daughter. And the tale in question is represented in all three classic literary collections of folktales: in Basile, Perrault, and the Grimms.

In the Grimms' version of this story, "Allerleirauh" (*KHM* 65), a widower king conceives the mad plan of marrying his daughter.[10] This forbidden, if not entirely unnatural, wish is motivated in part by lingering grief over the death of his beautiful wife, to whom he was passionately devoted. The dying spouse's request that he promise never to take another wife unless he should find a woman at least as beautiful as she is likely an expression of her confidence in the incomparability of her beauty, for the request makes sense only as indirect testimony to a desire on her part that he not remarry (this is her explicit motivation in Perrault's version). The king's promise to the wife is likewise a confession of his eternal devotion, but it subsequently provides as well a justification for his assertion of his right to marry the daughter. In the context of the story, the circumstance of the wife's request and the king's promise offers an explanation of the secret desire that fathers feel toward their daughters. By the time a daughter has reached adolescence, the mother's beauty has begun to fade, or she is in any case no longer the nubile, virginal maiden with whom the father once fell in love (it is of course not necessary, as happens here, that the mother actually has died). The king's failure, during the years that the daughter is growing to adulthood, to find a prospective bride as beautiful as the dead wife may be counted as evidence that his secret desire is for the daughter. That such guilty passion is involved is also indicated by the likely element of repressed awareness in the father's failure to notice, until the daughter has reached marriageable age, that she is equal in beauty to her dead mother. At this point, in any event, the issue is joined. If the father does not marry the daughter, she will leave his household and wed another, as then happens in the ensuing course of the story.

The king's councillors react with horror to his announcement that he intends to wed the girl, admonishing him that "God has forbidden that a father should marry his daughter; nothing good can come of sin, and the kingdom will be dragged along into ruin." The daughter's horror at the prospect is all the greater, of course. Yet the plan she conceives for dissuading the king from his mad folly suggests that she is secretly delighted by the intensity of his passion. The extravagant request she makes as the condition for acceptance of his proposal of marriage amounts to an unconscious invitation to him to demonstrate the degree of his devotion. In stipulating that he must first provide her with three dresses—one as golden as the sun, one as silver as the moon, and one as shining as the stars—and then with a fur coat made from a piece of hide from each and every animal in his kingdom, she is making the sort of demand, only much exaggerated, that one might expect from a spoiled daughter or a haughty bride or vain courtesan. If the girl's secret, unconscious wish is to test how far the father's passion for her will carry him, it certainly is fulfilled; and once he has complied with her demands, she has no choice but to flee. The father's sinful passion is not punished, other than by the loss of the daughter, and with her flight from his castle he disappears from the story. This indicates that the opening episode is, in the last analysis, a roguishly comic depiction of certain aspects of the emotional crisis experienced by many a father and daughter with the latter's arrival at marriageable age.[11]

In Perrault's and Basile's versions of the Allerleirauh story, the focus is so completely on the intensity of the father's passion, and the disgust and revulsion it produces in the daughter, that there is little reason to suspect that she may secretly share his dream. The father in Perrault's "Donkey-Skin" ("Peau d'Ane") displays not the least hesitation in squandering all the riches of his kingdom in the vain hope that the daughter will agree to marry him. In particular, he accedes immediately to her ultimate demand, born of desperation, that he sacrifice the source of his kingdom's wealth, a magical donkey in whose straw each morning golden coins are found (in place of the usual excremental matter). The king's willingness to have the miraculous donkey slaughtered so that the daughter might have its hide (hence Perrault's title) can fairly well be said to offer final proof, as it were, that the father's foolish passion has made an ass of him. Meanwhile, the daughter in this version is removed from suspicion that she unconsciously desires to test the heat of the father's passion, insofar as it is not she herself but the fairy godmother from whom she seeks advice in her adversity who is responsible for suggesting the series of demands to be made in an effort to dissuade him. Since the godmother, though, is possessed of supernatural powers, she may be seen to that extent as a creature of fantasy and a magical mentor. The advice she gives may therefore reflect, after all, a secret desire on the daughter's part to take the measure of her father's devotion.[12]

In Basile's version of the Allerleirauh story, "The She-Bear" (II, 6), the daughter has no opportunity to pose seemingly impossible demands that may satisfy a secret desire to know just how much the father is captivated by her. The father, enraged by her rejection of his proposal, simply orders her to come to his bedroom that evening to consummate the union. The matter of unrestrained and forbidden sexual passion is very much out in the open. As the old woman who serves here as the daughter's adviser puts it, the father, who is behaving like an ass (cf. the symbolism in Perrault's "Peau d'Ane" referred to above), would like this evening "to play the stallion." To punish the father for his outrageous demand and thereby also enable the daughter to escape the fate envisioned for her, the hag gives her a splinter which, when she puts it into her mouth, transforms her into a she-bear. The odd—though certainly most effective—character of this magical remedy likely represents a continuation of the sexual imagery in this episode, especially the hag's words about the father being an ass who would like to play the stallion. The father's unnatural command, in effect, reduces the daughter to the role of a concubine or female animal, since she is offered no choice in the matter. Were the daughter actually to join him in bed, she would feel herself, at best, to be no better than a she-bear.

As in Perrault's and the Grimms' versions of the Allerleirauh story, in Basile's "She-Bear" the new raiment, or in this case the transformed appearance, of the daughter that formed a part of her efforts to defeat the father's plan to marry her subsequently plays an indispensable role in her captivation of her eventual husband. Here the princess's use of her magical appearance as an animal in winning her prince casts retrospective doubt on the complete purity or chasteness of her initial employment of this guise to thwart her father's plan. She appears to enjoy this role of female bear; at least she makes use of it in order to enter into a relationship with a prince as his pet. The prince, "finding himself confronted with this female bear, was about to die of fright; but then, seeing that the animal, all the while crouching and wagging its tail like a little pet female dog, was circling around him, he regained his courage." The implication is that the girl's acquiring of the ability to change herself into a she-bear, which she first used to defeat her father's immoral purpose, is in part a symbolic representation of her nubility. With this new, magical role as she-bear the princess has simultaneously acquired the mating instinct and mastered the art of flirtation. It is as though the father's mad plan to make her his wife served to awaken the woman in her, in this sense.

III. SONS AND MOTHERS

Basile's "She-Bear" is of further interest for its depiction of a mother's involvement in her son's choice of a bride. The portrayal of the mother-son relationship, in this aspect, is much less common in the romantic folktale than the like situation between father and daughter. In Basile's story, the matter is highly comical. The intensity of the mother's devotion is evidenced by her consent, at her lovesick son's request, to allow the pet bear to serve as his nurse. Preziosa is thereby able to demonstrate her own devotion to the prince and her virtue as a prospective wife, thus winning the mother's blessing for their union. Most striking, though, is that Preziosa's resumption of her human form occurs in connection with her granting of the mother's request (at the son's urging) that she kiss the prince in his sick bed to keep him from fainting, out of unfulfilled desire. As the she-bear is kissing him, the splinter falls out of her mouth—"I don't know how," so the narrator roguishly avers. Thus, the mother's role here, like that of the father in a number of stories of the animal suitor type, is that of matchmaker or go-between (the type of the *ruffiana* from the *commedia dell'arte*); and the fun concerns the point that a doting mother would accept even a female animal as a daughter-in-law should this be her beloved son's passionate wish. A variation on this theme of the mother as go-between is found in another of Basile's stories, "Belluccia" (III, 6), where the mother helps the son discover whether the youth who has been sent to keep him company during an illness, and with whom he has fallen in love at first sight, is not in reality a maiden.

Portrayals of mothers bending their efforts to see that their sons are not disappointed in love appear to be lacking in the Grimms' collection. There are, however, depictions of true and tender love between a mother and a son. In "The Little Shroud" (*KHM* 109) a mother grieves so over her seven-year-old son's death that he appears to her in his funeral dress and begs her to desist, because her tears prevent the shroud from drying and he thus can find no peace in the grave. Prior to this scene, the child returned from the grave at night to visit the places where in life he had sat and played, and when the mother wept, he wept too. A similarly touching love between mother and son is depicted, as we have seen (Chap. 1), in "The Juniper Tree" (*KHM* 47). There the mother's wish for "a child as red as blood and as white as snow" is fulfilled with the birth of a son (not a daughter, as in the Snow White story). Her joy at his birth is so great, though, "that she dies" and, according to her wish, is buried beneath the juniper tree under which her cutting of her finger while peeling an apple gave rise to the wish for a child. Moreover, she appears to have identified with that tree during her pregnancy as she watched it, too, blossom and bear fruit. When the son then suffers under the resentment and abuse of his stepmother, his half-sister Marleenken's devotion compensates him for the loss of the mother whom he never knew. The association of the step-sister with the dead mother is suggested, however, only after the stepmother has murdered the boy. Marleenken ties up his bones "in her best silken scarf" and lays them on the grass under the juniper tree: "And when she had laid them there, she felt at once so much better and did not weep any longer. Then the juniper tree began to stir, and the branches spread themselves apart and then came back together again, just as when someone is so very overjoyed and does the same with his hands." A mist came forth out of the tree, and out of the mist a beautiful bird that "sang so magnificently and flew high into the air; and when it was gone the juniper tree became again as it was before; and the scarf with the bones was gone. Marleenken though became quite happy and delighted, just as though the brother were still alive." The half-brother's reincarnation as a bird and his subsequent return to human form, after his revenge on the stepmother, thus result from a collaboration between Marleenken and the dead mother, and as a token of their shared devotion to him. The half-sister therefore appears almost to be the dead mother's agent, as the boy's angel of rescue (cf. *Marleenken* as "Little Mary Ann," i.e., as a little heavenly and virginal mother).

Portrayals of a mother's reunion with her son in connection with his discovery of a bride are found in at least two of Basile's stories. In "The Padlock" (II, 9) there is, indeed, a hint that the mother's feelings for the son, on his arrival at manhood, involve a tinge of incestuous desire, since at the end we learn that the son's absence from home and his amorous involvement with his eventual bride resulted from a witch's curse to the effect that he "should wander about far from his homeland until he might be embraced by his mother and the rooster would not crow any longer." The spell is broken only after the following events have occurred: the girl with whom he has slept finds her way unwittingly to his mother's castle; she gives birth to a beautiful son, whom her former lover comes mightily to adore; a lady-in-waiting overhears him exclaim during these secret visits, "Oh, my most beautiful little son, if my mother knew! She would wash you in a basin of gold; she would wrap you in swaddling clothes of gold. If the song of the roosters were silent, I would never leave you"; and the youth's mother, on hearing about this from the lady-in-waiting, has all the roosters in the city killed, and when the son returns the following night, she embraces him. As the narrator reports, "As soon as he found himself in his mother's arms, the spell was broken and his affliction was ended."

This enigmatic close of the tale suggests that the earlier developments in the story—which concern the youth's appearance to the girl at the well as a handsome Moorish slave boy, her seduction by him, his rejection of her when she contrives to discover his true appearance, and her subsequent wanderings while pregnant with his child—are the result of an emotional crisis regarding his attachment to his mother and his awakening sexual desire. What causes him to show himself again to the girl is the birth of the son, and evidently because the boy's arrival fills him with sweet memories of his relationship with his mother. The words of devotion he addresses to the infant son project his longing to be adored and embraced by his mother; and now that he has become a father, this proves indeed to be possible again. That the mother, though, first takes the precaution of seeing that all roosters in the town have been slaughtered suggests that she feels the danger of incestuous desire is still present. In any case, it would appear that the son had to become a father before the "curse" of an incestuous desire could be broken, laid to rest, or sublimated.

In Basile's other tale of a mother's happy reunion with her son, "The Dragon" (IV, 5), the nature of her relationship to the youth appears far less enigmatic, and seemingly quite innocent. Here the mother, Porziella, is protected from starvation and death, and ultimately released from solitary imprisonment, through the loyal efforts of a magical bird. The bird is actually a fairy whom Porziella, in turn, had saved from being dishonored by a satyr as she lay slumbering in a forest. The fairy's motivation in her efforts on Porziella's behalf is somewhat ambiguous, however. In rescuing her benefactress, the fairy also wins Porziella's son Miuccio as her husband. Moreover, it is odd that the fairy did not manage, or even attempt, to repay Porziella in kind by preventing the latter's violation by the misogynous king of Altamarina. Instead, she only restrained the king's arm when he attempted to slay Porziella with a dagger after he had raped her.

Miuccio is the fruit of the king's violation of Porziella; and the fairy's secret feeding of her during her ensuing imprisonment makes possible the boy's birth and his survival. Therefore, we may suspect that desire for an ideal mate lies behind the fairy's actions. When Miuccio reaches adolescence, he is "adopted" by the king as his page. The queen's envy of this rival for the king's affection is thereby aroused; and this paves the way for the happy ending. The envious queen is destroyed; the king marries Porziella; the fairy asks, as her reward, to have Miuccio as her husband; and the two couples presumably live happily ever after.

The whole of the fairy's involvement in the story may be read, too, as magical wish fulfillment on Porziella's part. Her rescue of the fairy from violation by the satyr may hint at virginal sexual fantasy in anticipation of her own rape by the king. The fairy's restraint of the king when he is about to slay Porziella after having violated her may reflect a fantasy on Porziella's part that her beauty alone would suffice to save her from death (the king, at least, believes that it is Porziella's beauty that held back his arm). Her rescue through the magical powers of the fairy may represent a dream of being saved by her son. And the fairy's marriage to Miuccio may fulfill Porziella's own vicarious wish.

In the stories discussed above, the mother tends to be instrumental in bringing about the son's marriage to his beloved. One also finds, however, the opposite situation in which the mother somehow stands in the way of the son's further involvement with, or marriage to, the maiden of his choice.

This potentiality of the mother-son relationship is usually depicted in connection with the motif of the false bride. Thus, in "The Drummer" (*KHM* 193), a youth who has just rescued a maiden from imprisonment by a witch takes leave of the girl to go home so that he may tell his parents where he has been. The girl warns him not to kiss his parents on the right cheek; but then, in his joy at seeing them again, he fails to think of her admonition. Having greeted his parents with that fateful kiss, he promptly forgets the beloved entirely. The mother meanwhile has selected a bride for him; and as a devoted and obedient son, he agrees to marry the girl of his mother's choosing. This same situation is found in Basile's "The Dove" (II, 7). Here, though, it is specifically a kiss from the youth's mother that causes him to lose all conscious memory of the maiden he has just rescued from the clutches of a jealous witch (in this case, the witch is the girl's mother). Moreover, the girl's mother, because of her own possessiveness regarding the daughter, is responsible for that result, because it is she who places a curse on the youth to the effect that with the first kiss Prince Nardaniello receives—from whomever—he will forget his beloved Filadoro completely.

In another of Basile's tales, "The Golden Tree Stump" (V, 4), the youth's mother—here it is she who is the witch—sets about openly to destroy his desired beloved and attempts to marry him to a repulsive bride who brags about her promiscuity. The youth, Tuoni-e-lampi ("Thunder-and-Lightning"), takes both his beloved and the revolting bride to the wedding chamber, slays the bride with a knife, and sleeps instead with Parmetella. His mother, on discovering this (and that her sorceress sister and her child have perished in an oven) repeatedly rams her head into a wall until she has burst her skull. Finally, in Basile's "The Face" (III, 3) another case of direct intervention by the mother ends tragically. On the wedding night, the son stabs himself after having kissed the false bride and then having recognized, in the page whom he had invited into the bridal chamber, the true bride (she died of a broken heart at witnessing his betrayal of her love). The mother, having already picked out a wife for the son, had summoned him home with a letter claiming she was on the point of death— a letter that arrived when the lovers were, as the storyteller reported, "in the midst of their pleasures."

As we have observed, depiction of fathers' attachments to their daughters is more typical of the romantic stories in Basile's collection than in the Grimms' tales of love. Moreover, such depictions as are found in *Grimm's Fairy Tales* tend to occur in stories that the later German collection has in common with the earlier Neapolitan one, such as Sleeping Beauty, Cinderella, and Thousandfurs (Allerleirauh). The reason is surely that the subject easily offended the sensitivities of a later age and more northern, puritanical climate. In late Renaissance Italy, by contrast, a father's, guardian's, or uncle's foolish love for his pretty daughter, ward, or niece became the dominant subject for comedy. Pantalone, the old fool in love, was the principal figure in the *commedia dell'arte* of Basile's time.

While magic usually plays a role in Basile's tales of the father and daughter type, it is not employed to veil the father's passion nearly to the extent it does in the Grimms' stories. The Neapolitan Renaissance author depicts the older man's devotion or jealous love openly as well as more frequently. In Basile's Sleeping Beauty tale, "Sun, Moon, and Talia," as in the Grimm and Perrault versions, the daughter pricks her finger and falls into a magical, deathlike sleep. Basile, though, has the father and daughter in a more intimate relationship, living together in a secluded sylvan palace, while Perrault and the Grimms have her living with both parents in the father's royal residence. And in Basile's other story about a father's worry over a curse or prophecy about his daughter, "The Face," the father goes so far as to lock her away in a tower. The Cinderella tale, meanwhile, represents a case in which the father's devotion emphasized in Basile's "The Cat Cinderella" has been transferred almost entirely to the dead mother in the Grimms' story, while Perrault completely did without this element in his version. Further, Basile employs the Cinderella story a second time, in "The Little Slave Girl," to depict an older man's devotion to a maiden, in this case an uncle's passion for his adored sister's daughter.

To be sure, both the Grimms' "Allerleirauh" and Perrault's "Donkey-Skin" baldly depict a father's incestuous love of his daughter, as did Basile earlier in "The She-Bear." Here the exception proves the role, though, because this tale renders the father's passion less offensive as resulting from his grief over the death of his beautiful, beloved wife, with whose beauty only the daughter can compare. Moreover, Perrault and the Grimms made the fathers' feelings toward the daughter very tender. Thus, Basile's father does not bother to prove his devotion and try to win his daughter with gifts, as he does in the Grimms' and Perrault's versions, but simply and immediately orders the daughter to come to his bed.

Whereas the existence of a type of story focusing on a father's devotion to, or jealous love of, a daughter is evident, the same cannot be said for the theme of a mother's passion for a son. There are, to be sure, occasional depictions of at least innocent devotion of a mother to her son, as in the second half of Basile's "She-Bear"; and his "The Padlock" and "The Dragon" may hint enigmatically at even deeper, illicit emotional currents. Yet while fathers are expected, by popular tradition, to be sweet on daughters and mothers to dote on sons, and while, in a patriarchal society, a father might be excused or accepted as a fit subject for comedy if his passion for the daughter exceeded the bounds of propriety, depiction of a mother's incestuous feelings toward a son was wholly unacceptable, in the poetic imagination as well as in the prose of everyday life in early modern Europe (and basically remains so even today). Thus, in the *commedia dell'arte* the older woman's role was quite different from that of Pantalone, the older man chasing "sweet young things" who were usually his daughters, nieces, or wards. Instead, the older woman was typically the *ruffiana*, or match-making hag, who participated only vicariously in young love. This role as go-between, or facilitator, is indeed that played by the mother in Basile's "The She-Bear." The older woman's place in fairy tale romance, however, usually was involvement rather in the affairs of young maidens in love; and it is to the description and analysis of this role that we now turn.

NOTES

1. In their notes the Grimms refer to another version in which the young hunts-man impregnates the princess as she sleeps (in this version she is lying naked on the bed). On discovering that the daughter is pregnant, yet claims not to know by whom, the father has her thrown into prison. This version thus appears to lack the symbolic depiction of the father's devotion to the daughter, though it may, at the same time, carry an even stronger suggestion that he is preoccupied with her as an object of desire. See Jacob Grimm and Wilhelm Grimm, *Kinder- und Hausmärchen,* ed. Rölleke, III, 192–93; and cf. Bolte and Polívka, *Anmerkungen zu den Kinder- und Hausmärchen der Brüder Grimm,* II, 503. As Maria Tatar has observed, the eroticism in this version of the tale "must have struck the Grimms as unsatisfactory"; see her *Hard Facts of the Grimms' Fairy Tales,* p. 7.

2. Bruno Jöckel judged that the young huntsman loses his courage as prospective lover because the symbolism of the names on the slippers and neckerchief "leaves no doubt that the daughter is bound to her father by strong ties of love." Jöckel also calls attention to the somewhat contrary implication that the king was seeking a suitor for his daughter: "That the father's name becomes a threat to the huntsman precisely at the point when his passion makes possession of the daughter its object is understandable. Less clear, though, might be the resulting reversal of the position of the huntsman vis-à-vis the king, since through the letter the king made him, on the latter's entry into the castle, the executor of his child's fate, as it were." Jöckel also suggests that the girl's tender age, symbolized by her virginal sleep, may play a role in the huntsman's reticence as a lover: "What does more to prevent him from going further, her sleep—that is, the girl's immaturity—or his fear of her father, is hard to say." See Jöckel, *Der Weg zum Märchen,* pp. 101–2.

3. In Bruno Bettelheim's view, "Cinderella's asking her father for the twig she planned to plant on her mother's grave is a first tentative re-establishment of a positive relationship between the two." Bettelheim, though, interprets the story as

depicting, ultimately, the process of becoming independent of one's parents: "If Cinderella is to become master of her own fate, her parents' authority must be diminished. This diminution and transfer of power could be symbolized by the branch knocking the father's hat off his head, and also the fact that the same branch grows into a tree that has magical powers for Cinderella." See *Uses of Enchantment*, pp. 256–57.

In the Grimms' first edition (1812), the father had no role in procuring the twig. The mother, on her deathbed, tells the daughter to plant a tree, and indeed why she should do so: when she shakes the tree she shall have whatever she wishes, or help in necessity or adversity. In her grief over her mother's death, the girl waters the tree with her tears. Thus, in that version the focus, in this part of the story, is entirely on the devotion between the mother and daughter. See Rölleke, *Die älteste Märchensammlung*, pp. 298–317, esp. p. 299.

4. Folkloristic monographs on all known variants of the Cinderella story were done by Marian Roalfe Cox, *Cinderella: Three Hundred and Forty-Five Variants of Cinderella, Catskin, and Cap o' Rushes, Abstracted and Tabulated, with a Discussion of Mediaeval Analogues, and Notes*, with an introduction by Andrew Lang, Publications of the Folk-Lore Society, 31 (London: Folk-Lore Society, 1892; reprint, Nendeln/ Liechtenstein: Kraus, 1967), and, more recently, by Anna Birgitta Rooth, *The Cinderella Cycle* (Diss., Lund, n.d. [1951]; Lund: Gleerup, n.d. [1951]).

August Nitschke uses the Cinderella story to exemplify his historical-behavioral approach to folktales as a source of information about life in prehistoric times; see his "Aschenputtel aus der Sicht der historischen Verhaltensforschung," in Brackert, ed., *Und wenn sie nicht gestorben sind . . .*, pp. 71–88.

5. The father's passion for the daughter is of course not the chief object of depiction, which is instead the girl's relationship with her brothers, although the father's mad desire for a daughter introduces the underlying theme of incestuous attachment. As Ruth Bottigheimer observed, from a feminist viewpoint, "The basic premise of 'The Twelve Brothers' is that disposing of the brothers will allow for a greater accretion of wealth and power to the sister. Therefore it is surprising that once this statement has set the whole tale moving, no more is heard about the father's (and mother's) kingdom, which the princess is to inherit"; see Bottigheimer, *Grimms' Bad Girls and Bold Boys*, p. 38. The explanation is that the incestuous yearning that seized the father has passed to the children, in the devotion of the brothers to their sister and hers to them.

6. See Jacob and Wilhelm Grimm, *Kinder- und Hausmärchen*, ed. Rölleke, III, 87–88.

7. For a similar interpretation of the father's role in "Dornröschen" as symbolically depicting "his romantic attachment to the daughter," see Jöckel, *Der Weg zum Märchen*, esp. p. 44: "the girl is hindered by her own father in that development which leads, after all, to another man." Bettelheim, meanwhile, takes the view that "the central theme of all versions of 'The Sleeping Beauty' is that, despite all

attempts on the part of parents to prevent their child's sexual awakening, it will take place nonetheless"; see *Uses of Enchantment*, p. 230.

8. Bettelheim's interpretation of Basile's "Sole, Luna e Talia" is similar, but he sees the father's romantic attachment to the daughter, and the other king's attraction to her, as arising in response to seductive behavior on her part: "Might these two kings not be substitutes for each other at different periods in the girl's life, in different roles, in different disguises? We encounter here again the 'innocence' of the oedipal child, who feels no responsibility for what she arouses or wishes to arouse in the parent"; see *Uses of Enchantment*, p. 228.

The view that Basile's tale concerns incestuous and illicit desire is indirectly supported by Ester Zago's argument that Basile, here and in his Allerleirauh tale "L'orsa" (II, 6), deemphasized these themes, compared with his possible sources, out of discretion and a personal reserve regarding sexual matters; see "Giambattista Basile: Il suo pubblico e il suo metodo," *Selecta: Journal of the Pacific Northwest Council on Foreign Languages* (formerly: *Proceedings of the Pacific Northwest Conference on Foreign Languages*), 2 (1981), 78–80.

9. For a psychoanalytic study of puberty rites as reflected in folktale, where girls are made outcasts, secluded, put in towers or in the care of an older woman, protected from imagined dangers, or instructed in the domestic arts, see Alfred Winterstein, "Die Pubertätsriten der Mädchen und ihre Spuren im Märchen," *Imago*, 14 (1928), 199–274.

10. As we know from their notes to another tale, "Das Mädchen ohne Hände" (*KHM* 31), the Grimms were familiar with a version of that story in which the father wants to marry his daughter. When she refuses, he personally cuts off her hands—and her breasts as well—and chases her off into the world. See Jacob Grimm and Wilhelm Grimm, *Kinder- und Hausmärchen*, ed. Rölleke, III, 57–60; and cf. Bolte and Polívka, *Anmerkungen zu den Kinder- und Hausmärchen*, I, 295–96. In the version the Grimms used in their collection, the father does not conceive a passion for the daughter, but instead unwittingly promises her to the devil (trying to get the daughter to commit incest with him, as in the other version, would amount to offering her to Satan, too). As noted earlier (Chap. 1), in Basile's related tale, "La bella dalle mani mozze" (III, 2), the girl has her manservant cut off her hands in order to thwart her brother's mad plan to marry her. The Grimms' "Das Mädchen ohne Hände" is cited by Renate Meyer zur Capellen as an example of how folktales reflect men's feelings about women, and the position of women, in a male-dominated society; see "Das schöne Mädchen: Psychoanalytische Betrachtungen zur 'Formwerdung der Seele' des Mädchens," in Brackert, ed., *Und wenn sie nicht gestorben sind . . .*, pp. 89–119.

11. Jöckel makes a somewhat similar interpretation of the beginning of "Allerleirauh": "In our opinion . . . the father represents for the daughter men in general, the representative of the male principle, toward which the girl must first have adopted a clear, and therefore affirmative, attitude before she goes about choosing

for herself that man with whom she would like to share her life"; see *Der Weg zum Märchen*, p. 62.

12. An analysis of the story using deconstructionist notions of intertextuality was done by René Démoris, "Du littéraire au littéral dans 'Peau d'âne' de Perrault," *Revue des Sciences Humaines*, 166 (1977), 261–79.

4
Hags, Witches, and Fairies

lder women are of course never the heroines in romantic folktales. As we have seen, they most often represent the obstacle or opposition that young love must overcome if it is to be fulfilled. The type of the evil stepmother springs immediately to mind, or the witch—an older woman knowledgeable in occult or magic arts—who has placed one or both of the lovers under an evil spell. Sometimes the older woman's enmity is unrelated to the existence, or potential development, of a bond of love or devotion between young people of opposite sex and thus functions simply to intensify such yearning by providing a hindrance to its fulfillment. In other stories, however, the older woman is rendered an interesting character in her own right through indications that she identifies in some way with young dreams of love and devotion, and that her actions therefore are motivated at least in part by such identification. Growing old has given rise, for example, to feelings of bitterness in the older woman that she has lost her youthful beauty and appeal, if she ever possessed them; and she thus attempts to prevent the fulfillment of young love. This case is indeed the more common. One also finds instances, though, in which an older woman appears motivated to recover something of her lost youth—to dream those dreams of love again—through vicarious participation in the joys of youthful desire. In either case, such portrayals serve to remind us that popular stories, especially those about love, were traditionally referred to as "old wives' tales."[1]

I. HAGS

Not all of the older women are described as being ugly or as practicing magical or occult arts. In some instances merely their mean dispositions and corresponding actions render them fearful and repulsive, and hence deserving to be called hags. The stepmother's urging that Hansel and

Gretel be exposed in the forest is morally as ugly as the witch whom the children then encounter there is physically repulsive. The lady cook who wants to boil Fundevogel in her pot does not have to be described as a hag for us to receive that impression of her. While the selfish stepmother in "Hansel and Gretel" (*KHM* 15) makes no distinction between the two children, in "Fundevogel" (*KHM* 51) the lady cook is intent on doing away only with the boy and seems rather to identify with his little sister, however enviously, as being able to win his loyalty and devotion. In these stories it is just such envy of a maiden's potential for inspiring devotion that renders an older woman exceptionally repulsive. Thus, in "The Two Royal Children" (*KHM* 113) we witness a mother's (not a stepmother's) unseemly involvement in the father's attempt to fetch back their daughter after she has eloped with her beloved young prince—an episode that matches the one in "Fundevogel" in which the lady cook is reduced to going out herself to try to slay the boy and bring the girl back. And in "The White Bride and the Black Bride" (*KHM* 135), the envious stepmother contrives to do away with the beautiful stepdaughter so that her ugly daughter may usurp her position as the king's bride.

The type of the resentful or envious stepmother is a familiar figure in Basile's collection too, of course—for example the second wife in "Ninnillo and Nennella" (V, 8), who dislikes having to care for another woman's children and demands that her husband get rid of them. There are also interesting variations on this type, however, such as the fisherman's wife in "Penta the Handless" (III, 2), who so resents having to care for the beautiful maiden without hands whom her husband has found in a box floating in the sea that she has the girl put back in the box and cast into the water. And in Basile's story of the Sleeping Beauty type, "Sun, Moon, and Talia" (V, 5), the queen, having grown suspicious at hearing her husband mumble "Talia, Sun, Moon" in his sleep, discovers the whereabouts of her husband's beautiful young paramour and their twin children and attempts to have them killed.

Of equal importance, and indeed greater interest, are the older women who identify rather more positively with beautiful young maidens. As we have seen (Chap. 2), the grandmother's doting affection in "Little Red Cap" (*KHM* 26) is described in terms almost befitting a lover. Far more striking, however, is the sudden, seemingly magical appearance of the hag in "The Twelve Brothers" (*KHM* 9), whom the beautiful sister finds standing behind her just after she has fatefully plucked the twelve lilies. While it is likely that the old woman is a witch, and quite possible that she is responsible for the girl's twelve brothers having been changed into ravens, no mention of this is made. On the contrary, the hag's role is rather to advise the sister as to what she must do in order that the brothers may eventually be restored to her. In this sense, the hag serves here in the conventional function of an older woman as adviser to a maiden about affairs of the heart, thus enjoying vicarious participation in the young love now lost to her. At the same time, her reproach of the girl for having plucked the lilies may echo the sister's inner voice of guilt over her continued cohabitation with the brothers in the forest now that she has reached marriageable age.

A rather similar instance of an older woman in the role of aide and counselor to a nubile maiden in a moment of crisis occurs in "The Robber Bridegroom" (*KHM* 40). As in "The Twelve Brothers," an element of the fantastic is associated with the hag's appearance here. As we remember (Chap. 2), the whole of the bride's lonely visit to her fiancé's house in the forest has the character of a nightmare. The hag's function in this fantastic adventure is to warn the girl of the danger that awaits her in the bridegroom's house and, moreover, to enable her to see with her very eyes what an ogre he is. Thus, if the hag in "The Twelve Brothers" is a projection of the sister's unconscious guilt over incipient incestuous urges, the old housekeeper's exposure of the bridegroom here reflects the girl's anxiety about what might await her on the wedding night. In both cases, the depiction is enhanced by the contrast between the innocent virgin and the older woman who is privy to dark and mysterious secrets.

In "The Goosegirl at the Spring" (*KHM* 179), we find a clear case of an old woman's identification with a young maiden as the potential object of desire. After a handsome young count has helped a humorous old woman carry home her burden, she teases him by implying that he might fall in love with her rather old-looking and extremely ugly goose maiden, whom she addresses as her daughter and who calls her "mother." The hag says to the girl, "Get yourself into the house, my little daughter. It's not proper for you to be alone with a young gentleman. One must not pour oil onto the fire. He could fall in love with you." The hag is speaking only partly in jest; for as the count later discovers when he comes upon the girl bathing her face in a spring (hence the title), she is in reality young and beautiful, and a princess to boot. Thus, the hag's role in bringing about the romantic happy ending is motivated by vicarious participation in dreams of young love. This is further suggested by the circumstance that when the girl's parents and the count arrive in search of the maiden, the hag restores her to her princessly beauty, transforms the house into a castle, and disappears.

II. WITCHES

As the hag's transformation of her house and her disappearance at the end of "The Goosegirl at the Spring" remind us, older women in folktale, especially when the subject is love, often possess magical powers or knowledge of occult sciences. The fact that these figures are "wise" women, in that sense, does not mean that their roles in these stories and the motivations for their actions are basically different, of course. Their magical powers chiefly serve to enhance the portrayal of their passions as being especially intense, as for example in the familiar type of the resentful or abusive stepmother. Thus in "Little Brother and Little Sister" (*KHM* 11) the stepmother attempts to continue her evil oppression of the brother and sister, after they have run away from home, by casting a spell on all the springs in the forest. Similarly, in "The Six Swans" (*KHM* 49), when the new bride discovers that the husband has hid the children by his deceased wife in the forest, she is not content that she will not have to trouble herself with them. She deceitfully sews a magical charm into the little white silk shirts she makes for them, so that they will be transformed into swans and fly away. And the stepmother in "The Little Lamb and the Little Fish" (*KHM* 141), we remember (Chap. 1), so resented the little brother's and sister's happiness with their playmates on the meadow that she changed the girl into a lamb and the brother into a fish. Not satisfied, she subsequently ordered that the lamb be slaughtered to feed the guests she had invited to dinner. In such depictions, the chief irony is that the stepmothers' magically aided evil acts set in motion events that lead to a happy ending. Indeed, in at least a couple of stories the heroine even manages to appropriate the stepmother's magic for use in fulfilling her dream of bliss with her beloved. The stepdaughter in "Beloved Roland" (*KHM* 56) steals the wicked stepmother's magic wand and thereby foils her evil attempt to catch and destroy the young lovers. And in "The True Bride" (*KHM* 186) the daughter inherits her evil stepmother's magical castle and thus is enabled to attract the attention of numerous suitors, with one of whom she falls in love.

Most often, of course, the hag endowed with magical powers is not related to the hero or the heroine but is a mysterious stranger whom one of the central figures encounters on some fateful occasion. In "The Frog King" (*KHM* 1), for example, we learn only that the prince "had been cast under a spell by an evil witch, and no one could have rescued him from the spring" save the princess alone, as he explains to her after they have married. Since no motive for the witch's spell is given, we may suspect that her purpose was even the benevolent one of ensuring that the prince might marry the girl of his dreams, especially in view of the outcome. Or perhaps the witch's motivation was that given in another story of the animal suitor type, Basile's "The Serpent" (II, 5), where the prince was transformed for seven years into a snake by an ogress whose unbridled desires he had refused to fulfill. Something like this latter motivation may have been involved, too, in "The Old Woman in the Woods" (*KHM* 123) when the witch changed the prince into a tree, allowing him to fly around as a dove for only a few hours each day—particularly when one considers that the condition for his release from the spell is the theft, by the heroine, of a simple ring (like those used in weddings?) from among many jeweled ones on a table in the hag's house.

The most famous curse in all of romantic folktale is surely that placed on the newborn princess in the Sleeping Beauty story. In the Grimms' version, "Little Briar-Rose" (*KHM* 50), the thirteenth wise woman in the father's kingdom avenges herself for not having been invited to the feast celebrating the daughter's birth by declaring that "The princess, on her fifteenth birthday, shall prick herself on a spindle and fall down dead." The curse is then modified by the twelfth wise woman, who had not yet announced her magical gift to the newborn child when her angry peer burst in to disrupt the festivities. Since the twelfth wise woman cannot remove the curse, only mitigate it, she declares that "It shall not be death, into which the princess falls, but only a deep, hundred-year-long sleep." The angry wise woman's specification that the girl is to perish upon reaching her fifteenth birthday indicates that she is thinking ahead to the time when the princess will have reached marriageable age, and that to her mind having to die without experiencing the joys of courting and marrying is the worst fate that could befall a woman. By the same token, the twelfth wise woman's stipulation that death in this case shall mean a prolonged sleep, extending far beyond the normal life expectancy, suggests that she may be imagining how lovely it would be to remain a blossoming maiden forever, as it were, endlessly indulging in youthful dreams of love and romance. That this magical sleep will begin in connection with spinning points in the same direction, insofar as sitting at the spinning wheel is associated with building castles in the air and a woman's pricking herself with a spindle, needle, or the like usually occurs, in folktales, in association with dreams about becoming pregnant.

Though no hint is given as to the age of the wise women, they are surely beyond maidenhood, and are therefore representative of the type of the older woman whose use of her knowledge of occult arts involves an identification with young maidens as objects of desire. Thus it comes as no surprise that the woman at a spinning wheel whom the princess fatefully discovers on her fifteenth birthday should be a true representative of the familiar type of the hag as stranger. Though the hag is not identified with either the twelfth or the thirteenth wise woman, she must be part of the situation they envisioned the princess as confronting. Under other circumstances, one might have expected the hag, who appears kindly and friendly enough, to initiate the girl into the secrets of love and marriage, instead

of enlightening her about the—in the princess's case forbidden—art of spinning.[2] The result is nevertheless essentially the same. When the princess
awakens from her long sleep, it is no longer a spinning wheel and spindle
she sees before her but the far more appropriate object of curiosity and
desire for a girl her age: a handsome young prince whose passion has moved
him to accept the challenge of making his way through the seemingly
impenetrable thorns (hence the Grimms' title "Dornröschen") so that he
might court the beautiful blossoming rose that lies slumbering within. What
more appealing dream, or "castle in the air," could the hag at her spinning
wheel have conjured up in the imagination of the adolescent princess?

In Perrault's "The Beauty Sleeping in the Forest," from which the name
of the Sleeping Beauty type is taken, the curse is uttered by an old, reclusive
fairy who had not been invited to the feast because she had not come out
of her tower for fifty years and thus was presumed to be dead or to have
fallen under a spell. In this telling, the angry fairy, before making her
declaration, hears the list of magical qualities with which the other fairies,
in the order of their youth, have endowed the baby princess. The youngest
fairy wished that the princess might be "the most beautiful person in the
world," and the wishes of the others then served further to endow her with
all the spiritual and social graces appropriate to enhance that beauty. If
the old fairy already was angry, this list of magical endowments could only
give rise to additional feelings of envy and bitterness, especially since she
appears to possess no such charms and graces herself.

Unlike the wise women in the Grimms' version, Perrault's angry fairy
does not specify the age at which the princess is to die, only that it is to
be by piercing her hand with a spindle. Meanwhile, one of the younger
fairies, anticipating that in her rage the old fairy will make some evil
pronouncement, has hidden herself behind the tapestry. It is left to this
young fairy to envision the fateful event happening, as it then does, when
the princess has reached marriageable age (fifteen or sixteen). She specifies,
namely, that the girl, having fallen into a deep, hundred-year sleep instead
of dying, will be awakened by a young prince. And if there remained any
doubt, in Perrault's version, that the fairies—the younger ones, at least—
identify with the princess as the eventual object of ardent passion, the
narrator makes the implication clear by remarking that, though his source
is silent on the matter, it appears that the good fairy has afforded the
princess, during her long sleep, "The pleasure of pleasant dreams." That
those dreams were about a handsome prince arriving to court her is made
clear by the princess's greeting to him on awakening: "Is it you, my prince?
You've certainly kept me waiting a long time."[3]

In three of Basile's stories one finds similar curses or prophecies regarding a daughter, though in only one of these is there any hint of a witch's

or fairy's identification with the girl. In "The Little Slave Girl" (II, 8), Cilla, having conceived a child by swallowing a rose petal, brings the daughter to the fairies so that they might raise her. One of the fairies stumps her toe in her haste to see for herself just how beautiful the child is, and angrily declares that when the girl reaches her seventh year her mother will forget to remove from the daughter's hair the comb with which she has been grooming her, and that this will cause the child to die. While the fairy's stumping of her toe excuses her ill temper, one suspects that she acts out of envy over the girl's beauty—like the mother in the Snow White story, who herself uses a poisoned comb to groom the daughter.

In Basile's "Sun, Moon, and Talia" (V, 5), the story in his collection that most resembles the Sleeping Beauty tales of Perrault and the Grimms, the prophecy is made not by a fairy or a wise woman but by the wise men and prophets of the kingdom. Here the prophecy is not a curse, nor a declaration motivated by ill will, but on the contrary something like an expression of doting concern that the beautiful little princess might in one way or another be adversely affected by becoming involved with the distaff chore of spinning. Thus, the soothsayers do not specify in their prophecy that the girl shall die or fall into a deathlike sleep (as indeed happens), but vaguely foretell that great danger threatens her from a fiber of flax. Finally, in Basile's third story involving such a prophecy, "The Face" (III, 3), the danger is similarly foretold by male soothsayers. In this case, the peril envisioned quite obviously has erotic overtones, for they warn that the girl (here she is no longer an infant) "runs the risk of having the main sluice of life uncorked by a master bone" (*un osso maestro* 'a thigh bone of an animal'). In the various versions of this part of the Sleeping Beauty story, therefore, the curse or prophecy is made under circumstances which suggest that the soothsayers' underlying or secret concern is with the girl's potential for becoming the object of passionate desire.[4]

In other stories in the collections by the Grimms and by Basile, older women with magical powers place various obstacles in the paths of maidens destined to fulfill young dreams of love. In "Jorinda and Joringel" (*KHM* 69), an old witch transforms all the young virgins who venture too close to her castle into birds, imprisons them in baskets, and places the baskets in a room in the castle. As the storyteller roguishly reports, "She had surely seven thousand such baskets with such rare birds in her castle." To make matters worse for the imprisoned maidens, anyone else who gets within one hundred paces of the castle is frozen in his tracks.[5] In "The Herb Donkey" (*KHM* 122), a hag uses her daughter's appeal to gain possession of a youth's magical gifts, and the girl is forced to do her mother's bidding even though she is in love with the young man. Similarly, in Basile's "Rosella" (III, 9) the girl's mother uses occult powers in her attempt to prevent the daughter's elopement; then, failing that, she uses them to make the girl's beloved forget all about her. And in "The Dove" (II, 7) the mother likewise tries to destroy the daughter's dream of love. First, she assigns seemingly impossible tasks for the lover to fulfill before he can marry the girl. Then, when that does not succeed because the daughter makes use of magical arts learned from the mother to aid the prince in completing the tasks, she issues a magical curse that with the first kiss the prince receives (as it turns out, it is from his mother) he will lose all memory of the daughter.

The most famous of these stories about a magical older woman's efforts to prevent the fulfillment of young desire is certainly "Rapunzel" (*KHM* 12). The hag's demand that the father forfeit the child his pregnant wife is carrying in exchange for the rampions from the hag's garden the wife craves seems motivated by desire for a child. We can imagine that even as a girl the hag was so ugly that no man desired her, or that like the sorceress in "Jorinda and Joringel" perhaps or like the type of the haughty princess, she found the thought of the loss of virginity repugnant. In any case, she obviously perceives the foster daughter's subsequent arrival at puberty as a threat to the continuance of their relationship; for when Rapunzel reaches the age of twelve, the hag closes her up in a tower in the forest.

Though the hag is described as a sorceress, she actually works no magic. The only wondrous element in the story is that, as the tower has neither door nor stairway, the hag is able to use Rapunzel's incredibly long tresses to pull herself up to the small window that is the sole entrance. The young prince who discovers the girl's presence in the tower is similarly able to avail himself of this means of entry. This property of Rapunzel's hair is a magical endowment, if it can be called that, which was given to her at birth or with the arrival at puberty, as an added token of her beauty and desirability.

Even if the sorceress is responsible for this remarkable "gift," once it has been given she no longer controls the use to which it may be put. Indeed, we may suspect that the hag has allowed the girl's hair to grow because issuing the command "Rapunzel, Rapunzel, let down your hair for me"—much as a bridegroom might say to a bride on the wedding night—provides her a form of sexual gratification, as recompense for the erotic fulfillment she likely has never known. Precisely this need on the hag's part leads to the defeat of her dream, because it serves to teach Rapunzel an art familiar to girls not so jealously hidden away as she, namely, how to help hoist a lover into one's bedroom (in those days, usually by means of a rope and a basket, hence perhaps the German expression *jemandem einen Korb geben* 'to reject an offer of marriage'—literally 'to give someone a basket', as when the girl dropped the rope, leaving the would-be lover with the basket). That the hag's feelings toward Rapunzel are essentially those of a jealous lover is suggested, too, by the wording of her curse of the prince once his liaison with Rapunzel has been discovered: " 'Aha,' she sneeringly cried, 'you want to fetch the dearest lady, but the beautiful bird is no longer sitting in the nest and sings no more; the cat [referring to herself?] has fetched it and will scratch out your eyes for good measure. Rapunzel is lost to you; you will never behold her again.' "[6]

This type of the envious older woman who holds a beautiful young maiden captive is encountered in other stories as well. In Basile's version of the Rapunzel story, "Petrosinella" (II, 1), the element of possessiveness, as opposed to jealous love, is emphasized. When the hag learns from a neighboring gossip about the prince's nocturnal visits to the girl, she is not seized by passionate rage but calmly contents herself with the belief that a magical spell she has cast on the girl will prevent her escape.[7] In two of the Grimms' stories the older woman seeks to prevent the girl's marriage by assigning seemingly impossible tasks to her suitors ("The Drummer" [*KHM* 193] and "The Six Servants" [*KHM* 134]; in the latter story, the older woman is not a witch but the girl's mother, a queen who has ordered that all of the young men who fail to fulfill the tasks be decapitated). Yet in Basile's "The Three Crowns" (IV, 6), by contrast, the devotion of a witch, to whose house the girl has been transported, is indicated by her providing the maiden with magical means for venturing safely into the world, where she finds and wins a lover.

The most passionate reaction of a sorceress to a girl's budding charms is found in the famous tale of Snow White ("Little Snow White" [*KHM* 53]). This is a story not of possessive love or mere envy but of jealous vanity. The stepmother (in some versions it is the girl's own mother) cannot abide the thought that the daughter's beauty surpasses her own.[8] Her reaction to this perception is the naked urge to kill. Once the queen has discovered that her order to her huntsman to slay the girl has failed to produce the desired result, she is reduced to having to make the attempt herself.

The means the queen chooses for killing Snow White reflects her intense preoccupation with the matter of female sexual appeal and casts her in the unflattering, comic role of the ugly hag who compensates herself for her lack of captivating charms by vicariously identifying with a blossoming maiden. Thus in her guise as an old peddler woman she offers to enhance the girl's appearance with a new bodice lace, then to groom her with a comb, and finally to render her, in effect, a full daughter of Eve or Aphrodite by handing her an apple. The stepmother thereby betrays her own sense of what it means to be a woman, or what means most to a woman.[9] And the fact that these tempting gifts are offered out of an intent to kill testifies

further to the queen's recognition that the girl's youthful charms are su-
perior to her own fading allure. Insofar as her jealous vanity was premature
or anticipatory, arising when the girl was still only seven, it is rendered
that much more amusing. And if the jealous queen and the mother who
wished for a beautiful baby daughter are, as in some versions, one and the
same, the mother's subsequent rage once she perceives the daughter as a
potential rival is sublimely incongruous—quite in accord with mankind's
paradoxical nature. The queen's mirror, of course, is magical only in the
sense that it answers her from the depths of her own jealous vanity.[10]
Moreover, if one thinks of the queen as the girl's own mother instead of
a stepmother, the mirror speaks with the voice of a narcissism that cannot
conceive of any serious threat in the matter of beauty except that which
might issue from one's own flesh and blood.[11]

III. FAIRIES

As critics long since have remarked, fairies as such do not play a role in
the Grimms' collection. One does find, however, the type of the older
woman as magical helper of a maiden in distress. Though these figures
tend to be described, like their counterparts in Basile, as wise women,
sorceresses, or even witches, they have the same function as the good fairies
in Perrault, in Madame D'Aulnoy, and in stories by other authors in that
French tradition which is responsible for our term "fairy tale." Like the
fairies in Perrault's Cinderella and Sleeping Beauty tales, their entry into
the stories tends to occur as rather a magical wish fulfillment in response
to the emotional situation of the young heroine. The role of such kindly,
magical older women thus has something of the character of a dream experience; and these figures tend to be not so much persons in their own
right as reflexes of the psychic state of the maidens who receive their aid.
    In some tales involving this type of character, the magical older woman
serves as a substitute mother. In "The Holy Virgin's Child" (*KHM* 3) this
foster parent is none other than St. Mary, the veritable heavenly mother.[12]
Here the girl is adopted, as it were, by the Holy Mother when she is three
years old, because her parents are too poor to be able to feed her. The
story focuses, though, on the girl's passage from childhood to maidenhood.
When the daughter has turned fourteen, the Virgin goes off on a journey
and entrusts to her the keys to the thirteen rooms of the heavenly kingdom—suggesting a possible association of paradise with the girl's thirteen
years of childhood. She tells the daughter not to open the thirteenth door,
saying that that room is forbidden to her (aside from the number's association with bad luck or evil, it may allude here to the girl's arrival at
nubility and the concomitant awakening desire or curiosity and beginning

loss of sexual innocence). Although what the girl discovers behind the forbidden door is the Holy Trinity sitting "in fire and splendor," not the corpses of Bluebeard's wives or some other scene destructive of childhood innocence in any usual sense, the effect on the girl is similar to Eve's eating of the apple: she has acquired the knowledge of good and evil in the process of committing a forbidden act and then of lying about it; and the result is that, as the Virgin tells her, she is "no longer worthy to be in heaven." The telltale gold that rubbed off on the girl's finger when she succumbed to the urge to touch the Trinity is a symbol of her coming of age, recalling God's words to Adam and Eve that once they have eaten from the tree of knowledge they must leave the garden, for if they were now allowed to eat from its tree of life they would be his equals (*rührte an dem Glanze* has the metaphorical meaning "to tarnish the image," in the sense of diminishing, or appropriating, something of God's glory).

The Holy Virgin's putting the girl to the test, and punishing her for having failed it, would appear antithetical to the role of the good fairy, except that as a result of her expulsion from heaven the girl is subsequently discovered by a king who is out hunting and who takes her home with him and marries her. Thus, the girl's "punishment" leads to the fulfillment of the maidenly dream of marrying and becoming a queen; and the magical foster mother's testing of the girl has indeed made possible—or, psychologically speaking, simply marked—this passage from childhood to womanhood. From the pious viewpoint of this tale, however, the girl is a "false" bride insofar as she has not accepted the obligation of confessing and repenting the trespass that led to the fulfillment of her maidenly desire. The Virgin punishes her stubborn refusal to confess and repent by taking away her newborn children. As a result, the young queen is suspected of having eaten her children and is condemned as an ogress. Once the heroine, faced with death, meets the pious obligation to confess and repent, the children are restored to her; and with heaven's blessing she is permitted to enjoy the full measure of earthly bliss as a wife and mother.

This connection between a magical older woman's testing of a young girl's virtue and a maiden's dream of beauty, wealth, or marriage is not uncommon. In "Frau Holle" (*KHM* 24), the girl's sojourn with a substitute mother in a magical subterranean realm does not result in marriage, only in the compensatory fulfillment of a desire to be praised, loved, and rewarded for goodness and virtue; for this is not a tale about the passage to womanhood but one about the yearnings of an abused and persecuted stepdaughter whose despair is so intense as to engender an urge to suicide. The girl's dreaming while spinning at the well may be about a Prince Charming, but it is more likely about a mother's love; and her obedience to the stepmother's demand that she fetch the spool she has absentmindedly let fall into the water may involve a feeling that the stepmother wishes she were dead (cf. such expressions as *meine Pläne sind in den Brunnen gefallen* 'my plans have come to naught' or literally 'have fallen into the well' and *den Brunnen zudecken, wenn das Kind hineingefallen ist* 'to shut the door after the horse has bolted' or literally 'to cover the well after the child has fallen in'). In Basile's story of the Frau Holle type, however, the unwanted stepdaughter's testing by three fairies and the rewarding of her virtue are followed by her marriage to an aristocratic youth who fell passionately in love with her at first sight despite the rags that the abusive stepmother constrained her to wear ("The Three Fairies" [III, 10]). The connection between a fairy's reward and romantic appeal, moreover, is quite direct in another of Basile's stories, "The Two Cakes" (IV, 7). The hag's blessing causes pearls and garnets to fall from the girl's hair when she combs it, roses and jasmines to issue forth from her mouth when she speaks, and lilies and violets to spring up wherever she steps. It thereby becomes inevitable that a king will fall madly in love with the girl and marry her in the end.

In the Grimms' Cinderella story (*KHM* 21), the girl's good fairy is the ghost or spirit of her deceased mother (in Perrault's version it is her godmother, who happens to be a fairy). Here the persecuted stepdaughter's secret, or unconscious, dream is to marry a handsome prince, and the magical mother's intervention surely concerns her maternal determination, from the grave, that this maidenly wish shall not go unfulfilled. Two doves (as symbolically associated with Aphrodite?) serve as the dead mother's agents: they help the girl with the seemingly impossible chores that the stepmother has assigned to her to keep her from going to the ball; their aid suggests to the girl that she will find dazzling raiment at the tree under which the mother is buried; they alert the prince to the impostures on the part of the two stepsisters; and they confirm the identity of the true bride by perching on her shoulders (indicating her dead mother's pride in her daughter's beauty, as that of a still-virginal Aphrodite?).

In Basile's version, "The Cat Cinderella" (I, 6), doves play a similar role, yet in this case are associated not with the stepdaughter's deceased mother but with the fairy realm. A dove tells Lucrezia that if she is ever in need of anything she should direct her request to "the dove of the fairies" on the island of Sardinia. And whereas in the Grimms' story the father brings the daughter a hazel twig that she then plants on her mother's grave, here he brings her a date twig he has received from a wondrously beautiful young woman at the fairy grotto in Sardinia. Lucrezia plants the twig in a beautiful flower pot and cultivates it with a hoe, a little golden pail, and a silk towel that the fairy sent along for that purpose. Within the space of four days the twig grows as large as a woman, and a fairy emerges from it to ask Lucrezia what she desires. In response to her wish, the fairy provides her with the raiment and equipage of a queen so that she, like her stepsisters, may go to the festive balls. Thus, in Basile's story the function of the tree as projecting the stepdaughter's secret, half-conscious romantic wishes is rendered quite obvious, as is the connection between doves, as agents of fairy magic, and the cult of the goddess of love. Moreover, in this story the girl, who murdered her first stepmother by slamming a trunk lid on her head, is far less a paragon of virtue than is the Cinderella figure in other versions. It is her romantic desire alone that secures for her the magical aid of the Sardinian dove of the fairies.

In Perrault's "Cendrillon, or the Little Glass Slipper," one finds a still clearer depiction of the fairy's role as a magical substitute for a mother who might aid and counsel the daughter in the matter of winning the man of her dreams. The godmother appears in response to Cendrillon's sufferings at the hands of her envious stepmother, particularly the latter's determination to prevent her from going to the ball. She sets about immediately to use her fairy magic to provide Cendrillon with the clothes and carriage she needs to capture the attention of the princely suitor. The godmother's magical identity as a fairy, so it is implied, helps her divine the cause of the girl's distress: "Her godmother, who saw her all in tears, asked her what was the matter. 'I would very much like . . . . I would very much like . . .' She was crying so hard that she could not finish. Her godmother, who was a fairy, said to her, 'You would like very much to go to the ball, isn't that it?' 'Yes, alas,' Cendrillon said with a sigh."

The role of magical "mother" is also in evidence in the Grimms' "The Juniper Tree" (*KHM* 47). Here there is the interesting difference that the magical helper aids in undoing the evil wrought by the girl's own mother, not by a stepmother. Also, since this is a story about childhood, as opposed to adolescence, the secret wish that is magically fulfilled does not involve desire for a suitor but love for a brother. Marleenken's horror and grief over her mother's murder of her half-brother moves her to place the boy's remains under the juniper tree where his dead mother was buried; and she does so doubtless out of a sense that his mother was the sort of loving parent she wishes she had. The boy's magical return to life in the form of a bird, which happens evidently in response to the wishes of his dead mother's spirit, represents a fulfillment, on the childhood level, of a dream of love: through the efforts of the magical bird Marleenken's evil mother is destroyed, so that she, the half-brother, and their father may live on in peace and happiness together. In this sense, the spirit of the boy's dead mother has the role here of fairy godmother to the girl.

A fairy's role need not, of course, be that of a substitute mother. The fairy's underlying function is to make possible the fulfillment of a dream of love. Only to the extent that this is thought of as a mother's typical concern is the fairy's role portrayed as maternal. The fairy is sometimes a stranger who enters the story briefly to pave the way for love's triumph. Thus, in Basile's frame story about Taddeo and Zoza ("Introduction" and "Ending" [V, 10]), three fairies give the princess the three presents that she ultimately uses to gain entry to the beloved's castle and to unmask the false bride as an impostor. Similarly, in "The Flayed Hag" (I, 10) seven fairies come to the aid of an old woman whose intended, the king of Roccaforte, upon discovering the secret of her ugliness, has thrown her from the window of his bedchamber. In return for their good laugh over the sight of the hag hanging by her hair from a tree, they reward her by turning her into a beautiful maiden with the face of a fifteen-year-old, so that the king, when he sees her the next morning, marries her on the spot. And in "Peruonto" (I, 3), a fairy proves indirectly responsible for a poor, lazy youth's marriage to a princess after her granting of three wishes to him has led to his inadvertently impregnating the girl by cursing her with an offhand wish that that might happen. Thus, fairies prove most often to be, as it were, agents of Venus in their role as magical helpers. Indeed, these magical ladies occasionally become themselves the object of a man's passion, as in Basile's "The Myrtle" (I, 2), where a prince falls oddly in love with a twig that proves to be a most beautiful fairy.

Fairies do, nonetheless, tend to play a maternal role, and almost always in the capacity of helping a maiden secure marital bliss. In Basile's "The Seven Skins of Lard" (IV, 4), a mother is responsible for getting her daughter in a tight situation by pretending to a rich merchant who happens by that she has been beating the girl for having worked too hard at spinning, when just the opposite is the case. The merchant, impressed by this report of the girl's supposed compulsive virtue, takes her to wife and promises her the full measure of his passion if, on his return from a business trip, she has succeeded in spinning twenty bundles of flax. During his absence, several fairies who happen to catch sight of the lazy, gluttonous girl gorging herself when she should be spinning reward her for the amusement thus afforded them by magically transforming the flax into cloth for her. The fairies thereby undo the mother's mischief and secure for the daughter the husband's devotion. In the Grimms' version of this story, "The Three Spinning Ladies" (*KHM* 14), the maternal aspect of the magical helpers' role is more pronounced. A queen promises to marry the girl to her eldest son if she succeeds in spinning three rooms of flax into yarn. Since the lazy girl does not want to do the spinning, and is incapable of the task in any case, she enlists the aid of three ugly hags who happen by. The familiar element of vicarious identification with the prospective bride is provided by the hags' setting of the condition that the girl must invite them to her wedding, pass them off as her relatives, and arrange for them to sit at the table with her. Moreover, whereas the girl's mother had been beating her for her failure to spin when the queen passed by, the hags inadvertently free the girl from any further obligation to spin; for when the bridegroom discovers, at the wedding feast, that spinning caused the deformities that render the hags so ugly, he decrees that his bride shall never be permitted to do any spinning again. Since the specific natures of the respective deformities serve to associate the hags with the three Fates of myth, the impression is created that the girl, by virtue of her laziness and revulsion against spinning, was destined or "fated" to be relieved of this onerous chore and that the hags, therefore, have the role of fairies in providing for the girl's complete marital bliss, as she might have hoped that an ideal mother would have done.

A further story of how magical aid in the performance of distaff chores provides for a girl's romantic bliss may serve as a final example of fairy godmothers in the role of Venus's agents.[13] In the Grimms' "Spindle, Shuttle, and Needle" (*KHM* 188), a girl's godmother, on her deathbed, bequeaths her distaff implements to the adoptive daughter so that she, like the godmother before her, may make a modest living from them, now that she will be left all alone in the house. The girl subsequently employs these emblems of female domestic virtue in attracting, fetching, and winning a handsome young prince who passes by her window one day on his horse. The magic that the girl finds residing in the spindle, shuttle, and needle likely reflects unfulfilled desire on the part of the godmother (evidently a spinster), and perhaps also the godmother's wish that the girl may find the marital bliss that she has lacked (the adoptive daughter is fifteen when the godmother dies). Thus the girl, out of her yearning to win the prince after he has ridden off, repeats the words she often heard the godmother utter when the latter sat at spinning: "Spindle, spindle, go thou out, / Bring the suitor to my house." Apparently by her own invention, but using the godmother's sorrowful—or perhaps only playful—incantation as a model, the girl additionally enlists the aid of the other distaff objects as well: "Shuttle, shuttle, weave very nice, / Lead the suitor to me here"; and "Needle, needle, sharp and fine, / Make the house for the suitor clean." The girl's incantations produce magical results where the godmother's did not, because she is young, beautiful, and full of chaste passion and hope—and surely not least because the fulfillment of the girl's dream of love is undoubtedly the devoted, self-identifying wish of the godmother's spirit from beyond the grave.

In our examples of hags, witches, and fairies as characters in the tales about romance and marriage, we have found that the older woman typically acts either to aid or to hinder the fulfillment of young love. Thus, she has the role either of the older woman as matchmaker, the *ruffiana* of the *commedia dell'arte* and traditional comedy, or of its reverse, the villainess who seeks to prevent the dream's realization.

The figure of the older woman understandably has attracted attention from feminist critics. They have viewed these depictions differently, or at least considered them in other contexts. There has been comment on the element of sexual envy, however, as in the observation by one critic that "For the aging stepmother, the young girl's maturation signals her own waning sexual attractiveness and control. In retaliation they jealously torment the more beautiful virginal adolescent who captures the father's affections and threatens the declining queens."[14]

Because feminist criticism is largely concerned with questions of what is called "sexual politics," the issues of control and of power are typically emphasized. Thus, another critic, while noting that "it is at puberty that Rapunzel is locked in a tower, Snow White is sent out to be murdered, and Sleeping Beauty is put to sleep," finds only part of the answer in the recognition that "In the specific tales mentioned, this restriction reflects anxiety about competition with other women that increased sexuality offers." The restriction of women at puberty is seen in reference to a broader aspect of patriarchal society as well, for it "can also be interpreted as a reaction of men to the threat of female sexuality"[15]—an aspect visible in our earlier investigation of stories depicting fathers' feelings toward daughters.

Feminist criticism has also raised the possibility that the role of older women in folktale may involve survivals from an earlier matriarchal culture in which the priests were women; and one critic has taken this approach in reflecting on the prevalence of the role of the older woman in tales about love and marriage: "Although her characteristics have been considerably downgraded, the old woman in Grimm's tales has partially retained her role as guardian of rites and tradition. . . . If such is her function, one can at last understand the paradox of the tale which, at all times intended for children, gives preferential treatment to the subject least appropriate to children's literature: the erotic quest for the beloved through a thousand painful trials."[16]

The present investigation, too, has found that older women typically play an important role in tales of love. The role belongs to the realm of comedy, by older definitions, because these fairy tale romances invariably end happily, not "tragically." Sexual politics, or at least the traditions of a patriarchal society, may be seen as responsible for this typical role, insofar as romantic love was considered a specially appropriate preoccupation of women, young and old alike. In this cultural tradition, men were supposed to have other things to think about. The older woman's role was comic, not romantic, because it was the young heroine, not she, who was to become the object of erotic desire and to marry. The older woman was left to participate vicariously, whether as matchmaker or envious villainness.

Seen in a larger and longer cultural context, however, this "comic" depiction of older women was ultimately part of a general celebration of desire, as in the cult and worship of love goddesses like Venus. Thus, as we saw in the previous chapter, Venus's power made old fools in love of the fathers of daughters, too, as it did in the contemporary *commedia dell'arte* and its descendants on the early modern European stage. But Venus's power being what it was poetically made out to be, did the heroines of folktale ultimately depend on the help of matchmaking older women? We turn now to the question of how well these young women understood how to attract men quite on their own.

NOTES

1. Jungian interpretations of the role of older women in folktale as maternal figures have been made by Wilhelm Laiblin, "Das Urbild der Mutter," in Laiblin, ed., *Märchenforschung und Tiefenpsychologie*, pp. 100–150, reprinted from *Zentralblatt für Psychotherapie und ihre Grenzgebiete*, 9, nos. 2–3 (1936), and by Sibylle Birkhäuser-Oeri, *Die Mutter im Märchen: Deutung der Problematik des Mütterlichen und des Mutterkomplexes am Beispiel bekannter Märchen*, ed. Marie-Louise von Franz, psychologisch gesehen, 28–29, 7th ed. (1976; Stuttgart: Adolf Bonz, 1983).

2. Bruno Bettelheim views this scene as a symbolic analogue of sexual initiation: "Seeing the old woman spinning, the girl asks: 'What kind of thing is this that jumps about so funnily?' It does not take much imagination to see the possible sexual connotations in the distaff"; see *Uses of Enchantment*, p. 233. Bettelheim was not the first to interpret the story as a tale about sexual awakening. Steff Bornstein saw the princess's pricking herself with the spindle as associated symbolically with menstruation and defloration, and the thorn hedge as projecting an inimical anxiety about men on her part; see "Das Märchen von Dornröschen in psychoanalytischer Darstellung," *Imago*, 19 (1933), 505–17. And Bruno Jöckel considered the spindle to be "a decidedly male symbol that points directly to sexual intercourse" and saw a connection between the sort of giddiness produced by climbing a winding staircase, as the princess does in this scene, and the sensation experienced by a "young person at the onset of physical maturity"; see *Der Weg zum Märchen*, p. 46.

Others have found the symbolism to lie in a spiritual direction. Max Lüthi's view was that "The tale of Little Briar-Rose is more than a fancifully stylized love story that portrays a young maiden's retreat into herself and the breaking of the spell by a youth in love; one involuntarily takes the princess to be simultaneously an image of the human soul: the tale depicts the endowing, threatening, paralyzing,

and redeeming of not only some girl or other but of mankind in general"; see
"Dornröschen: Vom Sinn und Gewand des Märchens," in his *Es war einmal . . .:
Vom Wesen des Volksmärchens*, Kleine Vandenhoeckreihe, 136/137 (Göttingen: Van-
denhoeck & Ruprecht, 1962), p. 8. Similarly, with specific reference to the Grimms'
version of the story, William F. Woods characterized fairy tale per se as "a story
of self-meeting, and its eternal promise is that of self-realization, the blossoming
thorn, the curse turned to joy"; see "Sleeping Beauty and the Art of Reading Fairy
Tales," *CEA Critic: An Official Journal of the College English Association*, 40, no. 2
(1978), 18–22, esp. p. 22.

3. For a study of the influence of Perrault's Sleeping Beauty tale on the Grimms'
version as it was modified through successive editions, see Alfred Romain, "Zur
Gestalt des Grimmschen Dornröschenmärchens," *Zeitschrift für Volkskunde*, 42
(1933), 84–116. Barbara J. Bucknall considers various interpretive possibilities for
Perrault's tale in " 'La belle au bois dormant' par Perrault," *Humanities Association
Review*, 26 (1975), 96–105. A comparison of the versions of the Sleeping Beauty
story in Perrault, Basile, and the Grimms was done by Jan de Vries, "Dornröschen,"
Fabula, 2 (1958), 110–21.

4. Representative of earlier interpretations of the Sleeping Beauty story as having
originated in a myth of the seasons—the princess as symbolizing springtime (cf.
Basile's "Talia," meaning "budding woman")—is that by Friedrich Vogt, "Dorn-
röschen-Thalia," in *Beiträge zur Volkskunde: Festschrift für Karl Weinhold*, Germa-
nistische Abhandlungen, 12 (Breslau: Wilhelm Koebner, 1896), pp. 195–237.

5. In their notes, the Grimms refer to a version of the Jorinda and Joringel story
in which the sorceress transforms a little boy, who then has to be rescued by his
sister. The tale has thereby become a children's tale of the brother and sister type.
See Jacob Grimm and Wilhelm Grimm, *Kinder- und Hausmärchen*, ed. Rölleke, III,
119; and cf. Bolte and Polívka, *Anmerkungen zu den Kinder- und Hausmärchen*, II,
69.

6. Max Lüthi showed that the Grimms' immediate source for "Rapunzel" was
a German translation of Mlle de la Force's "Persinette"; see "Die Herkunft des
Grimmschen Rapunzelmärchens (AaTh 310)," *Fabula*, 3 (1959), 95–118, reprinted
as "Rapunzel" in Max Lüthi, *Volksmärchen und Volkssage: Zwei Grundformen erzäh-
lender Dichtung* (Berne: Francke, 1961), pp. 62–96 (Lüthi provides a juxtaposition
of the full texts of Mlle de la Force's tale and the German translation used by the
Grimms). Lüthi noted in passing (p. 79) that the German translator's change of
the girl's name results in the loss of a certain erotic symbolism: "Rapunzel sounds
better in the German tale than Persinette, it has a more forceful sound than *Pe-
tersilchen* [i.e., the name of Mlle de la Force's heroine as meaning "little parsley"]. . . . To be sure, in folk beliefs the plants called 'Rapunzel' do not play any
important role, quite in contrast to those . . . such as parsley and fennel, apples
and pears, to which are attributed eroticizing and talismanic powers."

7. Ernest Tonnelat observed that in the Grimms' first edition, Rapunzel is depicted as noticing a physical change in the wake of her liaison with the prince, since she remarks to the hag, "Why tell me, dear Godmother, why my little clothes are getting so tight on me and don't want to fit me anymore." This reference to pregnancy was suppressed beginning with the second edition (1819), and was replaced with Rapunzel's supposedly naive question about why it is harder to pull up the godmother to her window than the prince. As Tonnelat noted, this change is not satisfactory, because, although Rapunzel may not know what the consequences of sexual relations can be, she clearly has been indulging in such activity with the prince by this point, considering that she subsequently gives birth to twins; see *Les contes des frères Grimm*, pp. 98–99.

8. In the Grimms' manuscript of 1810 and in their first edition of 1812, the jealous older woman is Snow White's own mother. Moreover, in the manuscript the mother herself takes the girl into the forest to get rid of her. She tells the girl to pick her some of the beautiful red roses growing there, and then abandons the daughter by driving off in her carriage. See Rölleke, *Die älteste Märchensammlung*, pp. 244–65. An interesting interpretation of the introduction of the stepmother's role has been made from a feminist perspective. According to this view, the queen's jealousy is the product of a patriarchal society:

> there is clearly one way in which the King *is* present. His, surely, is the voice of the looking glass, the patriarchal voice of judgment that rules the Queen's— and every woman's—self-evaluation. He it is who decides first, that his consort is "the fairest of all," and then, as she becomes maddened, rebellious, witch-like, that she must be replaced by his angelic, innocent and dutiful daughter, a girl who is therefore defined as "more beautiful still" than the Queen. To the extent, then, that the King, and only the King, constituted the Queen's prospects, he need no longer appear in the story because, having assimilated the meaning of her own sexuality (and having thus become the second Queen) the Queen has internalized the King's rules: his voice now resides in her own mirror, her own mind.

See Sandra M. Gilbert and Susan Gubar, *The Madwoman in the Attic: The Woman Writer and the Nineteenth-Century Literary Imagination* (1979; New Haven: Yale Univ. Press, 1984), pp. 37–38.

9. An orthodox Freudian interpretation was made by J. F. Grant Duff, "Schneewittchen: Versuch einer psychoanalytischen Deutung," *Imago*, 20 (1934), 95–103; reprinted in Laiblin, ed., *Märchenforschung und Tiefenpsychologie*, pp. 88–99. Bettelheim justifiably interprets Snow White's susceptibility to the hag's temptations as a matter of sexual awakening: "As Snow White becomes an adolescent, she begins to experience sexual desires which were repressed and dormant during latency. With this the stepmother, who represents the consciously desired elements in Snow White's inner conflict, reappears on the scene, and shatters Snow White's inner peace"; see *Uses of Enchantment*, p. 211. For an interpretation of the tale as

symbolically relating to rites of initiation for females, but in a social and religious rather than a strictly psychological or psychoanalytic sense, see N. J. Girardot, "Initiation and Meaning in the Tale of Snow White and the Seven Dwarfs," *Journal of American Folklore*, 90 (1977), 274–300. A critical discussion of interpretive positions on this tale, as exemplifying the problem of interpreting fairy tales generally, has been offered by Bausinger, "Anmerkungen zu Schneewittchen," in Brackert, ed., *Und wenn sie nicht gestorben sind . . .,*" pp. 39–70.

10. In their notes, the Grimms refer to a version in which the queen does not address the question about who is the most beautiful to her mirror but rather to Snow White's faithful dog Spiegel (meaning "mirror"); see Jacob Grimm and Wilhelm Grimm, *Kinder- und Hausmärchen*, ed. Rölleke, III, 87–90; and cf. Bolte and Polívka, *Anmerkungen zu den Kinder- und Hausmärchen*, I, 450–52.

11. In the Grimms' manuscript of 1810, the father's relationship to the daughter is important. The king's going off to war provides the opportunity for the queen to abandon Snow White in the forest; and at the end, it is the king, returning from battle, who discovers Snow White's corpse at the dwarfs' house. He orders his physicians to revive the beloved daughter, which they accomplish with a radical method that, in its description, sounds like the first half of the torture known as drawing and quartering. See Rölleke, *Die älteste Märchensammlung*, pp. 244–65. In the manuscript, and then again in their published notes, the Grimms refer, moreover, to another version, in which it is the husband, not the wife, who yearns for a beautiful daughter. This wish has hardly been uttered before it is granted, for soon they come upon just such a beautiful girl standing beside the roadway. The count immediately invites the girl into the carriage; and just as quickly, the countess begins to calculate how to get rid of her. This she achieves by dropping her handkerchief and having the girl step out of the carriage to fetch it, whereupon she orders the coachman to drive on. See Jacob Grimm and Wilhelm Grimm, *Kinder- und Hausmärchen*, ed. Rölleke, III, 87–90; and cf. Bolte and Polívka, *Anmerkungen zu den Kinder- und Hausmärchen*, I, 450–52.

In the first edition (1812), the Grimms made a young prince, not the father, the rescuer of the princess. Yet in this version there remains, as in the manuscript, an element of comedy in the scene depicting the maiden's recovery from her deathlike state; and there is also a hint of necrophilic inclination on the prince's part. After receiving the coffin from the dwarfs, the prince has it placed in his parlor, where he sits by it the whole day. If he must go out, the servants have to carry the coffin along. One of the servants tires of this duty, lifts the lifeless maiden out of the coffin, and vents his anger by poking her in the back. This causes the piece of poisoned apple to fall from her mouth, and she revives. The first edition refers also to another version in which the prince has the presumed corpse taken from the coffin and has it dressed up and placed on his bed. See Rölleke, *Die älteste Märchensammlung*, pp. 244–65.

A folkloristic study of all variants of the Snow White story known at the time was done by Ernst Böklen, *Schneewittchenstudien*, 2 vols. (Leipzig: J. C. Hinrichs, 1910–15).

12. The story is told in a secular version in the Grimms' manuscript of 1810. The adoptive mother is not the Holy Virgin, but an aristocratic spinster (*Jungfrau*) dressed in black who drives up in the forest just as the distressed man is about to hang himself. In exchange for wealth the man promises to the virgin in black that which is hidden in his house. Unknown to him, the virgin in black has in mind the child, a girl, with which his wife is pregnant. The strange woman evidently is interested chiefly in having the girl live with her when she reaches puberty, because she allows herself to be put off in collecting on the bargain every three years until the girl has reached the age of twelve.

What the girl then discovers in the forbidden room are four virgins in black, like the strange woman, who seem to be engrossed in reading books. As her necessary forfeit, by way of punishing her disobedience, the girl elects to relinquish the gift of speech, which she then loses when the virgin in black hits her across the mouth hard enough to make blood flow. The symbolic import of this business may be that the "terrible secret" of the forbidden room is that the virgin in black, and the three others like her in the castle, are condemned to a lonely life of reading books since their virginity has remained intact. This fate likewise awaits the girl, as the virgin in black's adopted daughter, unless she perceives the danger. Making blood flow from the girl's mouth and thereby causing her to fall silent amounts to a rite of passage from childhood innocence to maidenly modesty and ripeness for intercourse (cf. "pudenda" as referring to the genitals).

In the end, when the heroine is about to be burned at the stake as an ogress, the virgin in black arrives in her carriage to put out the flames. The four virgins, now dressed in festive attire, explain that they had been put under a spell, but are happy once again; then they take their leave. The point of this ending may be that the four virgins, through the heroine, have vicariously savored the joys of marriage and motherhood. The first virgin in black became the heroine's surrogate mother; and the other three subsequently became, in turn, foster mothers to the heroine's three children, after she had married and her wicked mother-in-law attempted to drown the children and denounced the daughter-in-law as an ogress.

This story of the four virgins in black, then, is an instance of older women's positive identification with blossoming maidenhood. At the same time, although this is a secular, not a pious, version of the story, there is something nunnish in the four virgins' life together in the castle, and in their actions on behalf of the heroine. Finally, it may be that the books the four virgins are reading in the secret room are tales of romance—of magical exploits, love, and marriage—and that their adoption of the girl reflected their secret desire to play a role, vicariously, in such romantic adventure. For the texts of this version, which the Grimms relegated to their notes, see Rölleke, *Die älteste Märchensammlung*, pp. 278–83; and cf. Jacob

Grimm and Wilhelm Grimm, *Kinder- und Hausmärchen*, ed. Rölleke, III, 7–9, and Bolte and Polívka, *Anmerkungen zu den Kinder- und Hausmärchen*, I, 16–17.

For a Jungian interpretation of an Austrian version of the story in which there is only one lady in black, see Marie-Louise von Franz, "Bei der schwarzen Frau: Deutungsversuch eines Märchens," in *Studien zur analytischen Psychologie C. G. Jungs*, vol. 2: *Beiträge zur Kulturgeschichte* (Zurich: Rascher, 1955), pp. 1–41; reprinted in Laiblin, ed., *Märchenforschung und Tiefenpsychologie*, pp. 299–344. A folkloristic study of this type of story was done by Edeltraud Seifert[-Korschinek], "Untersuchungen zu Grimms Märchen 'Das Marienkind' " (Diss., Munich, 1952). Seifert judges that the original version was like the Grimms' variant with the virgins in black, which was thus only in time made over into a pious tale (*Legende*).

13. Ruth Bottigheimer has studied this theme from a feminist perspective and concluded that "throughout the [Grimms'] tales the act of spinning emerges as highly undesirable despite the surface message that it will lead to riches. . . . Despite the good face that Wilhelm Grimm tried to put on spinning as a pursuit, incontrovertible internal evidence appears to tell us just the opposite"; see her "Tale Spinners: Submerged Voices in Grimms' Fairy Tales," *New German Critique*, 27 (1982), 150, and also the chapter "Spinning and Discontent" in her *Grimms' Bad Girls and Bold Boys*, pp. 112–22, esp. p. 122.

14. Rowe, "Feminism and Fairy Tales," p. 241.

15. Stone, "Things Walt Disney Never Told Us," pp. 46–47.

16. Marthe Robert, "The Grimm Brothers," in Peter Brooks, ed., *The Child's Part*, Yale French Studies, 13 (New Haven: Yale French Studies, 1969), pp. 49–50.

5

Fetching Maidens and True Brides

s the story "Spindle, Shuttle, and Needle" (*KHM* 188) suggested, the heroines of folktale are perhaps not as passive about romance as they often are thought to be. Sleeping Beauty and Snow White, to be sure, make no move to captivate their charming princes. Yet these and other similar exceptions would only prove the rule, since these heroines are prevented, by deathlike sleep or the equivalent, from acting to attract a lover. We shall now ask whether there are young maidens in folktale who do display a capacity for actively winning a young man's devotion. Is there an exact countertype to the haughty princess who exhibits disinterest in love and marriage? Do we find cases in which the girl's interest in men shows itself through an urge to service or rescue? Do some indeed prove their abilities as flirts or teases? Do others resort even to physical pursuit of the beloved? Although the romantic folktale heroine's beauty and appeal are virtually sufficient in themselves to win any man's heart, is opportunity often provided for some of them to exhibit an instinct for attracting the opposite sex?[1]

I. FETCHING MAIDENS

In tales of the brother and sister type, we noted examples of a girl's urge to seek out and join the male siblings whom she has never met ("The Twelve Brothers" [*KHM* 9]; "The Seven Ravens" [*KHM* 25]; "The Seven Doves" [Basile IV, 8]). These sisters, of course, do not engage in flirtation to gain the brothers' devotion. Yet each belongs to the type of the fetching maiden insofar as her yearning to be united with the brothers causes her to set out on her own to find them; and her beauty and charm then secure her the brothers' adoring love, not least because the brothers recognize that the sister's devotion has led her to risk all manner of danger to join them. Among these tales, indeed, we find in "The Glass Coffin" (*KHM*

163) a sister who procures herself a husband by casting the young man in the role of suitor as she tells him the story of how she came to be imprisoned naked in the coffin from which he has just released her at her request.

In certain other types of story, the girl's active role in winning or securing a lover is almost as evident as in the case just cited. Rapunzel (*KHM* 12), though imprisoned in a tower and thus unable to set out in search of a man, cooperates in fetching up her suitor to her window by responding to his request that she let down her hair for him so that he may join her. In the Grimms' version of the story, the girl is portrayed as being innocent about love and desire. But in Basile's Rapunzel tale, "Petrosinella" (II, I), there is a more usual flirtation from the window and an agreement that the two of them shall spend the night together once the girl has given the hag a sleeping potion. The heroine in Basile's "The Face" (III, 3), being separated from her admirer by a window with bars, shows herself even more actively determined to answer the call of desire. After having teasingly flirted with the admirer from the window, she uses a large femoral bone that a guard dog has carried to her room to remove a stone from the tower wall and to lower herself to the ground by means of sheets she has tied together to make a rope. As these examples from Basile suggest, his heroines of the fetching maiden type tend to participate actively in their seduction or abduction. Thus, in another of his stories, "Green Meadow" (II, 2), at her admirer's suggestion, each time that she desires him Nella sends up a smoke signal with the powder he has given her so that he may run naked from his castle to her bedroom through the eight-mile-long underground crystal passageway he has fashioned for that purpose.

Heroines of the fetching type are of course portrayed in other ways than as being adept at getting lovers into their bedrooms, or, failing that, at escaping imprisonment so that they may make love elsewhere. There are instances in which the girls assume the role of angels of rescue or help the lovers accomplish seemingly impossible tasks that have been imposed to prevent their union. In Basile's "Green Meadow" Nella slays an ogre and his wife to secure the fat from their bodies that is required to staunch the flow of blood from the mortal wounds her lover received as he ran through the crystal tunnel after her envious sisters had smashed it. Similarly, Princess Grannonia in Basile's "The Serpent" (II, 5) uses her maidenly capacity for sweet talk to outsmart a fox and thereby obtain the magical means of healing her bridegroom's wounds suffered when, in the form of a dove, he attempted to escape through a window in the bridal chamber. (He took flight out of displeasure over her father's having burst through the door to destroy the snakeskin the bridegroom had just shed as he prepared to join her in the wedding bed).

Examples of the fetching maiden as her suitor's magical helper occur also in the Grimms' collection. In "The Two Royal Children" (*KHM* 113), a princess helps her suitor carry out three tasks that her father has placed in the way of their union. When she brings out the suitor's lunch to him at noon on each of the fateful days, she first puts him to sleep by picking lice from his head and then summons friendly gnomes from under the earth to accomplish the tasks as he slumbers with his head in her lap. And when she and the prince elope, after her father has imposed the new condition that her two elder sisters must marry first, she contrives to frustrate her parents' pursuit by changing her suitor and herself, respectively, into a thornbush with a rose on it, then a church with a pastor inside, and finally a pond with a fish in it. Very much the same role is played by the princess in "The Drummer" (*KHM* 193). At her request, the young man, a drummer, lays his head in her lap and falls asleep after he has eaten the lunch she has brought him. While he sleeps, on each of the three consecutive days, she uses her magical wishing ring to complete the impossible tasks set for him by the witch who holds her prisoner: to empty a pond with a thimble, to cut down a whole forest, and to build a fire with all the wood from the forest. Then, she warns the youth not to fear when the witch— as the princess knows she will—assigns him some further tasks; and she adds, "but if you are afraid, then the fire will take hold of you and consume you." Having been thus forewarned, or one might almost say threatened, the youth does not hesitate to venture into the flames to pull out the one log that is not burning, as the witch demands. As soon as he lays the log on the ground, it is transformed into the maiden herself, who now stands before him as the beautiful princess of his dreams. He then casts the hag into the flames, as the princess has told him to do, and the princess is liberated.

In Basile's "The Dove" (II, 7), the maiden likewise magically assists her suitor in performing seemingly impossible tasks and thereby escaping from a witch, who in this case is the girl's mother. Here it is quite evident that making love is the girl's goal. For example, she roguishly remarks to the youth in promising to plow a large field for him in the space of a day, as her mother has demanded of him on pain of death, "think not, dearest, that you shall have to work any other territory than the garden of love."

It is more usual for maidens to be rather less forward, or somewhat more coy, in winning their man. This is reflected in examples of the type of the tease or flirt. One does not usually think of Cinderella in this way; but she is portrayed in the Grimms' version (*KHM* 21) as not at all lacking in such skills, however instinctively or unconsciously she may employ them. In particular, there is no reason why she rushes away from the ball each evening and hides from the prince when he tries to pursue her, other than that she wants to assure herself as to the degree of his devotion and, especially, to fan the flames of that passion to a fever pitch by appearing mysterious and unattainable. She renders herself all the more fetching to the prince, and thereby ultimately "fetches" him, by making him chase her.[2] Basile, in "The Cat Cinderella" (I, 6), portrays her in much the same way, although there the prince does not follow after her himself but sends his servant instead. In Perrault's "Cendrillon," to be sure, her hasty departures from the ball are motivated by the godmother's warning that at the stroke of midnight the magical spell placed on her beautiful raiment and magnificent equipage will be broken. But since the fairy's role is a magical wish fulfillment on Cendrillon's part, the implication regarding her instinctive sense of how to inflame a man's passion remains very much the same.[3]

As has often been remarked, the princess in "Allerleirauh" (*KHM* 65) is essentially the same type as Cinderella. This is especially so in the way she goes about winning her prince, once her father's mad plan to take her to wife has helped make her aware of her irresistible beauty and appeal.[4] Using the three magnificent dresses, each more dazzling than the other, that she had demanded of her father in hopes of bringing him to his senses, she thrice begs leave from her work as kitchen maid in the prince's castle in order to appear briefly at the balls being held upstairs. Her intent to attract the prince's attention is indicated by her pretense to the cook that she is only going up to peek in at the ballroom door, and of course by her care to put on the beautiful dresses and quickly groom herself for the occasion. Her tearing herself away from the prince each time, as she is dancing with him, is motivated by her need to return to the kitchen, lest the cook should discover the ruse. But surely she senses, as well, that her hasty departures serve to increase the prince's curiosity and desire.

Allerleirauh shows herself instinctively skilled at winning her man not only through displaying social grace at dancing, but—in contrast to Cinderella—also through proving to him her domestic capabilities. The way to a man's heart—not least of all a prince's—is through his stomach. In her role as kitchen maid she gives sufficient loving touch to the soup she prepares for him to cause him to exclaim, without knowing who has prepared it, that it is the best he has ever tasted and to demand to see the person who cooked it. This opportunity is of course what Allerleirauh secretly desires, and she knows how to make the most of this very different chance to confront the prince. Now she may appear to him disguised as a scullery maid, clad in her curious coat of many furs—that is to say, as rather more of an elemental creature or in her erotically stimulating aspect as something like a female animal. To render herself even more of a puzzle and to turn the prince's thoughts toward love and marriage, she places three precious golden trinkets, in turn, at the bottom of his bowls of soup: first a ring, then a spinning wheel, and finally a reel. While the lovingly prepared soup has cast the prince in the role, so to speak, of a husband complimenting a bride on her cooking, the three little presents suggest her willingness to become his wife and to carry out domestic tasks. Though the presents are tokens of her love, she claims to know nothing about them, and thereby shows that she is not averse to telling outright lies to achieve her purpose of further intensifying the prince's desire to learn her identity.

Basile's Allerleirauh figure, Preziosa in "The She-Bear" (II, 6), similarly wins her prince by showing herself to him from two aspects: in her resplendent natural beauty and in degraded, beastly form. In this version, however, the maiden approaches the prospective lover first in the beastly form, which in this case is not merely a guise but the magical transformation into a she-bear that she used to thwart her father's incestuous passion. Preziosa oddly chooses to win the prince's devotion first as his pet, confronting him in the forest as a tame animal, circling him on all fours and wagging her tail. She continues this teasing mystification after the prince has seen her from his window in her true beauty; before he can rush down into the garden, she turns herself back into her ursine form. When the prince then falls mortally ill out of lovesick despair, she retains that form while serving, at his request, as his nurse. Only after the prince's mother, in response to his entreaties, has begged the supposed she-bear to kiss him, does Preziosa restore herself permanently to human form (as Basile's narrator coyly puts it, at this moment the magical splinter fell out of her mouth, one knows not how). The effectiveness of her teasing game is then attested by the prince's declaration to her that she is "caught at last."

The Allerleirauh figure's mode of fetching herself a prince differs yet again in Perrault's "Donkey-Skin." The flirtation here is far closer to that of the Grimms' heroine than to that of Basile's roguishly elemental maiden. Indeed, Perrault's princess is the most reserved of the three, but is still clearly characterized as the fetching type. That she has an instinct for these matters is indicated by her awareness (in the narrator's opinion) that the prince has spied her, in all her radiant beauty and magnificent attire, through the keyhole of the door to her tiny room in the dairy and has fallen madly in love with her at first sight. And when his royal parents, at his request, order that the girl (who is serving as a lowly kitchen maid on their estate) make a cake for him, she not only takes care to use the finest and freshest ingredients, but (accidentally on purpose, the narrator suggests) bakes an emerald ring into it, as a token, surely, of her regal eligibility and her willingness to become his bride. Moreover, she must secretly foresee that the—lovesick—prince will seek to fit the ring to the hand whence it came, and will surely recognize that her ring finger (like Cinderella's foot) is uncommonly small. Then, after she has finally been summoned for the test and passed it, she takes care to shed her donkey-hide coat before she is presented to her intended, so that she may show herself to him once again in her dazzling raiment—those magnificent dresses that her father, in his mad passion, had had made for her.

As in these last two versions of the Allerleirauh story, a youth's love-sickness likewise provides the opportunity for a maiden to reveal her true identity in Basile's "Belluccia" (III, 6). In this case, though, the girl's ruse concerns her sex. When a wealthy man, the best friend of Belluccia's father, asks him to have one of his children keep his son Narduccio company during an illness, he is so embarrassed to admit that he has sired nothing but daughters (seven of them) that he sends Belluccia, the youngest, to the friend's house dressed as a youth. Narduccio's illness gives way to lovesickness as he almost immediately senses that the youth is actually a girl, who has come "to waylay my heart." Although he is mistaken about Belluccia's conscious intentions, since she has acted only as a dutiful daughter—saying she would turn herself into an animal to please her father—she appears perfectly happy to marry the young man once the ruse has been discovered. And while her uncommon devotion to her father may explain her uncanny display of mastery at the masculine arts of riding and shooting, the effect of these feats is to fan the flames of Narduccio's passion all the more.

In another of Basile's stories, "Sapia Liccarda" (III, 4), a virtuous and obedient daughter shows a similar instinct for winning and testing a youth's devotion. Sapia's father, a rich merchant with three eligible daughters, boards them up in the house when he leaves on a business trip. The two elder daughters promptly unboard the house and invite over three young princes from the castle across the way to spend a night of lovemaking with them. Sapia, however, locks herself in her room. The two sisters get pregnant and, out of envy of Sapia's having avoided their plight, conspire with the "cheated" youngest prince, Tore, to get Sapia into his clutches; but she evades him yet a second time and preserves her virtue. When the two elder sisters later place their baby sons in the beds of the elder brothers at the castle, thereby getting the two princes to marry them, Sapia teasingly lays a rock in Tore's bed. Then, on the wedding night she puts a confectioner's doll in the bed in place of herself. Her teasing has the desired result of proving that Tore is not indifferent toward her, for after he has stabbed the doll, meaning to kill Sapia, he tastes the "blood" on the dagger and is filled with remorse over having slain such a sweet beloved in his fit of lover's rage. Sapia's manner of winning a husband is a reminder once again that appearing unattainable is a chief strategem of the fetching maiden.

A still more striking example of such teasing protection of one's virtue as part of winning a husband is provided again by a youngest daughter, Viola, the title role in another of Basile's stories (II, 3). She is the object of mad passion on the part of a young prince, Ciullone, who sets about to seduce her. Every time he tries to speak to her, she tells him to his face that she is smarter than he. She agrees to marry him only after he has acknowledged the truth of her assertion. This game of love reaches its culmination in Ciullone's prank of contriving to enter Viola's bedroom, not in order to seduce her but to have occasion to tease her about it on the morrow. She then returns the favor by managing to steal into his bedroom the next night. Viola thereby reveals herself to be not the type of the haughty maiden Ciullone may at first have thought her to be, but a saucy lass who knows quite well how to transform a would-be seducer into a devoted lover.

While Basile's fetching maidens display an unerring instinct for getting their man, they do not always so jealously guard their virtue. In "The Padlock" (II, 9), yet another youngest daughter, Luciella, having agreed to go to the well for her impoverished mother after the two elder girls had refused, readily accepts the invitation of a handsome Moorish slave to go with him to his grotto, on his promise that there he will give her "so many beautiful little things" (she asks only that she be allowed first to deliver the well water to her mother). Among the rich gifts that Luciella receives is a magnificent bed in the youth's underground palace. As she sleeps in the bed each night, rendered oblivious by sleeping potions that the youth has secretly given her, he engages in intercourse with her. That Luciella is of the fetching type is revealed when, on discovering what has been happening in the bed, she does not react with any trace of shock or horror whatsoever. And on finding that her secret lover in reality has the fairest and rosiest complexion, she utters to herself an oath that he shall never ever "escape from my hands."

As we have seen, the fetching maidens of folktale are nothing if not patient. In the Grimms' "The Poor Miller's Boy and the Cat" (*KHM* 106), the princess is prepared from the outset to wait seven years before revealing her identity and making it to the altar. The reason in this case, though, may be that the youth on whom she has set her cap is not yet fully grown, since at the end of the seven years the clothes he was wearing when he arrived at the castle no longer fit him. The situation is rendered all the more intriguing by the youth's unawareness that, instead of entering the service of a cat, he actually has moved in with an enchanted princess and her similarly bewitched chambermaids. Moreover, while he is trading seven years of service for a horse, in order thereby to gain his master's mill as an inheritance, the enchanted princess is secretly out to see that he gets her as his bride in the bargain. Her hidden identity as fetching maiden is hinted at quite early through her abortive attempt to get the youth to dance with her after dinner on their first night together at her castle and, that having failed, by her command to her feline chambermaids to accompany him to his room, undress him, and put him to bed in a manner befitting a prince. Her patience is then demonstrated by her willingness to refrain from further romantic advances, while still accustoming the lad to life as a prince. Thus, she provides him with tools of silver for use in doing the chores that constitute his part of the bargain with her. And once she has revealed herself to him, his two fellows, and his master and has completed her part of the bargain, she simply takes the youth off with her in her carriage and has herself married to him at her castle, without any word of her having asked his consent in the matter.

Similar patience is shown by the fetching maiden in "The Raven" (*KHM* 93). When she was still a young girl, an oath uttered by her mother in anger over the child's misbehavior unintentionally resulted in the little princess's transformation into a raven. After years of living alone in the forest in this condition, the girl accosts a man who happens by, identifies herself to him as a princess who has been cast under a spell, and invites him to serve as her redeemer. The man initially fails the test, succumbing three times to hunger and thirst, and thence to sleep, when he is supposed to remain awake and wait for the raven-princess to ride by. The enchanted maiden then invites him to try again at another location, the golden castle of Stromberg, where she is sure he will be able to succeed. The castle, however, proves to be atop a glass mountain; and a year passes before the man, with the use of a magical horse stolen from robbers, finally manages to get up to the castle. The princess meanwhile, no doubt to insure that he does not forget about his task or lose interest in her, rides around the castle each day during the course of that year. Once the man has redeemed her, he takes her in his arms, indicating that he fully understood that her plea that he redeem her was at the same time an invitation to possess her physically. The princess's reaction to his embrace shows that, indeed, redemption was closely associated in her mind with love and marriage: "she, though, kissed him and said, 'Now you have redeemed me, and tomorrow we shall want to celebrate our wedding.' "

The Grimms' "Spindle, Shuttle, and Needle" (*KHM* 188), too, is essentially a portrayal of the fetching maiden. Alone in the house that she has inherited from her godmother, the girl is sitting at her spinning wheel, undoubtedly building romantic castles in the air, when in answer to such dreams a handsome prince who is riding by looks in at her window. The situation is sufficiently classic that the narrator need not intrude, but does so anyway: "and when she noticed that the prince was looking in, she turned red all over, lowered her gaze, and went on spinning; whether the thread this time came out quite even, I do not know, but she kept spinning until the prince had ridden away again. Then she stepped to the window, opened it, and said, 'It is so hot in this room,' but she followed him with her gaze as long as she could still make out the white feathers on his hat."[5] What the narrator is at pains to show is that the girl's modesty prevents her from admitting to herself that her blushing has made the room seem hot to her and that, moreover, it is above all her dream of marrying that has brought her to the window. This struggle within her between her chaste modesty and her passionate yearning is then further depicted through her physical return to spinning but continued spiritual pursuit of the prince. Such pursuit is revealed in her incantations and projected in the magical activity of the spindle dancing out after the prince with its thread to summon him back; of the shuttle weaving him a beautiful welcoming carpet fit for a prince; and of the needle scurrying about making coverings for the furniture and windows to render the modest living room more presentable for receiving him.

II. TRUE BRIDES

Winning a man is one thing, keeping him quite another. Yet the heroines in fairy tale romance prove equally adept at displaying their fetching instincts after they have achieved the position of beloved. Romantic inconstancy—might one say fickleness?—on the part of men is sometimes depicted in folktale as a curious matter of specific temporary amnesia, in which for some magical or other wondrous reason a young man forgets all about his intended.

A particularly entertaining example is Basile's "Rosella" (III, 9). A young prince, Paoluccio, as a result of a curse put on him by the mother of his beloved Rosella, loses all memory of her once he sets foot again on his native European soil. Like Basile's fetching maidens, the forgotten beloved here shows herself to be a saucy tease when the situation and her romantic goals demand it. Rosella goes to the capital of the prince's native realm and, finding herself the object of passionate desire on the part of the male courtiers, agrees, in exchange for gifts of fine clothes, to spend a night of love with each of three of them. Her purpose is to get the would-be lovers to denounce her at court for having magically prevented them from collecting their part of the bargain, and thereby to appear before the prince, explain her actions, and thus break the evil spell that has caused him to forget her.

In this story, the succession of magically prevented actions Rosella requires the prospective lovers to undertake suggests that she is looking forward to her wedding night with the intended. She tells the first admirer to lock the door before joining her in bed. The door reopens by itself every time he closes it, so that, as the narrator roguishly puts it, the poor cavalier spends the whole night "with a cursed door without being able to make use of the key." The would-be lover then has to suffer her taunt the next morning that he was unable "to lock a door yet had had pretensions to open the coffer of Love's pleasures." The next evening she tells the second admirer to blow out the light before coming to bed, so that, engaged in this attempt the whole night, "he consumed himself like a candle." Then, she tells the third admirer she cannot go to bed without combing her hair. Once he has predictably offered to do it for her, he is magically constrained to waste the entire time at the task. Again the narrator indicates that in this activity both Rosella and her admirer have the pleasures of the bed in mind, each in a different way: "the more he strained himself to unknot that ruffled head, the more entangled the region became, so that he spent the whole night without getting anything straight, and, in trying to put a head in order, he put his own in disorder." Locking the door, blowing out the candle, and grooming the beloved for the night of love are such things as Rosella must hope her intended will do when she has won him back. And on that occasion she will use the magic of her charms to insure that he performs as desired.

The Grimms' true brides, in such stories where the intended forgets his beloved, display more modesty and decorum. In the tale that alludes to the type in its title, "The True Bride" (*KHM* 186), there are no such bedroom scenes. The prince, on going home to ask his father's permission to marry, suffers the typical loss of memory. The girl sets out after him, taking care to bring along three wondrously magnificent dresses with which to adorn herself. On three successive nights she attends wedding balls in honor of the prince's imminent marriage to a princess. As he dances with the former beloved each time, the fond memory of her begins ever so slowly to return, until on the third night he asks her who she is and whether he does not know her. She thereupon asks in reply whether he does not remember what she did when he took leave of her and kisses him on the left cheek, just as she had done when he departed to seek his father's permission to marry her. Her instinct proves correct that, though his mind may have forgotten her—out of sight, out of mind, as one says—his cheek well remembers that one sweet kiss. In this depiction of tender, true love, the maiden's devotion is demonstrated, during her time as a shepherdess near the beloved's castle, by her lament to one of her lambs, as though to a lover, in which she begs it not to forget her as the prince has done (one day when the prince overheard the shepherdess's lament he paused, "as though trying to remember something," but then rode on).

The heroine in "Beloved Roland" (*KHM* 56) is at once more reticent, even resigned, and still more devoted yet. This characterization is especially touching here, because in this case her beloved's lapse of memory is explained. When Roland reached home to make preparations for the wedding "he fell into the snares of another girl, who brought things to the point that he forgot the maiden." The forsaken girl, who as a token of her true love and as a measure of security turned herself into a red fieldstone by the roadside to await Roland's return, transforms herself now into a flower, thinking someone will surely step on her and thus end her misery. Her true love is demonstrated anew by her subsequent polite and gracious refusal of a friendly offer of marriage from a shepherd, whom she has covertly served as magical housekeeper out of gratitude for his having found her to be so beautiful, in her guise as sorrowing flower, that he plucked her and carried her home with him. In a final demonstration of the modest humility that characterizes her in her tender, sorrowful passion for the prince, she agrees to attend his wedding only when the other maidens insist that not only is every girl in the land invited but each is required to sing. Roland then recognizes her voice as she sings, remembers her, and promptly declares that he can marry only her and none other. In this case, then, it is the sweetness of the devoted maiden's voice that has proven unforgettable.

The prince's lapse of memory is explained, or motivated, too in "The Twelve Huntsmen" (*KHM* 67), though quite differently. He is summoned home to the bedside of his dying father, who obtains from him a promise to marry a princess whom the father has selected for him. Thus, in this case the prince's forgetting of his intended has nothing to do with his having become attracted to another woman. It is simply a function of his filial duty toward his father. Meanwhile, the forgotten bride here proves herself to be no shrinking violet. She takes advantage of her aristocratic familiarity with the chase to offer her services to the prince disguised as a hunter, so that she may in this way be allowed to be near him and that he might thus, despite her disguise, find himself attracted to her anew. The fact that she brings along eleven girls from her father's kingdom who closely resemble her (and are likewise disguised as huntsmen) suggests that she wants to be all the more certain that the memory of her will be rekindled. The intensity of her devotion, and of her dream of winning him back, is indicated by the fact that she faints at the word that the bride chosen for him by his deceased father is arriving. It is her faint that leads then to the prince's recognition of her identity and his rediscovery of his passionate love of her.

Since the forgotten beloved in this story shows herself to be more of a fetching maiden than a sorrowing bride, the depiction is largely humorous. The comic situation is provided by her disguising of herself as a man and by her concern to avoid detection before the prince has rediscovered his passion for her. As she surely knows he must, the prince senses that she and the other eleven look-alike huntsmen are secretly women. This suppressed awareness, though, is projected in the clairvoyance of the prince's pet lion, which insists to his master that the twelve hunters are female. The girls, having been forewarned by the prince's servants, manage to avoid the snares set for them by the prince at the lion's suggestion. They adopt a masculine gait in walking over the peas that have been strewn over the floor; and they pretend not to notice the twelve spinning wheels that have been set up to appeal to their distaff concerns. When the prince then does discover his favorite's secret identity, the action leading to the revelation is motivated by passionate concern for "his dear hunter's" well-being. After she has fainted, he rushes to help her, removes her glove, and spies the ring that he gave to "his first bride." The removing of the glove, since it bears no relation to offering aid, suggests that he is more concerned to offer comfort, or even that he actually is moved by an unconscious memory of the beloved and the ring he gave her. At any rate, as the forgotten beloved betrayed her passion by fainting at word of her rival's approach, the prince now displays his manhood by shedding the boyish role of dutiful son and asserting himself as true lover, for he sends a messenger to the second bride to request that she return to her father's kingdom.

As the story of "The Twelve Huntsmen" shows once again, the bridegroom's lapse of memory in these stories may function largely to provide occasion for the maiden to display her qualities as a fetching beauty. In some tales, indeed, the lover has not forgotten the beloved, but simply has been prevented from marrying her by a less-astounding circumstance. Thus, in "The Iron Stove" (*KHM* 127), the prince prepares to marry another girl because he mistakenly believes that the beloved is dead. She, meanwhile, takes a position at his castle as kitchen maid and uses three wondrously beautiful dresses to tempt the vanity of his bride and thereby gain entry to his bedroom on three successive nights. On the first two nights, the bride manages to protect her interests by giving the prince a sleeping potion before he goes to bed. On the third night, however, he does not drink the potion and thus finally hears the beloved's lament about how, though she had earlier rescued him from his imprisonment in an iron oven and then managed to find him once again, he has failed to respond to her confessions of love in his bedroom. The two lovers then flee together, taking care to steal the bride's clothes so that she will be unable to get out of bed and pursue them; and they live together happily ever after in an enchanted castle.

In the stories in which the bridegroom does not forget the bride, the hindrance to their union is most often an imposture.[6] The prominence of this true and false bride type is indicated by Basile's use of it in the frame story of his collection. The telling of the stories in the Pentamerone occurs in connection with Princess Zoza's plan for exposing a Moorish slave girl's imposture as Prince Taddeo's rightful bride. The perfidious slave girl, Lucia, usurped Zoza's position by shedding the few remaining tears necessary to fill a jug that Zoza had cried almost full before the seemingly impossible task so exhausted her that she fell asleep. Taddeo thereupon married Lucia and sired a child with her, since the curse that had been laid upon him destined him to marry the girl who would reverse his transformation into a marble statue by crying the jug full of tears. Zoza, in turn, having herself been placed under a curse that she will never marry unless it be to Prince Taddeo, has no choice but to expose the imposture if she wants to become a bride. Thus, she is cast in the familiar role of the true bride as fetching maiden and sends three beguiling magical gifts to her rival, the third of which is a gold-spinning doll that fills the pregnant false bride with an irresistible desire to hear stories. Zoza is thereby afforded the eventual opportunity of telling a tale that leads to the revelation of the slave girl's imposture and that provides occasion for an indirect portrayal of herself in the role of true and devoted bride.

Zoza's story, "The Three Citrons" (V, 9), is thus likewise a tale of the true and the false bride. After a young prince has fallen passionately in love at first sight with a beautiful fairy whom he has released from her imprisonment in a citron, he has her hide in a tree at a spring until he can return with proper attire and appropriate retinue for introducing her at court as his bride. His absence provides a Moorish slave girl with the opportunity to attempt to murder the intended, while supposedly combing her hair, and to usurp her place. The girl then contrives to render her imposture plausible by telling the prince that while he was gone she was thus transformed. Being a fairy, the true bride avoided being killed by changing herself into a dove, whereupon she flew to the castle. The false bride has the bird killed by the cook and made into stew; but the dove's feathers, which fell into a flower pot, cause a citron tree to grow. The tree reminds the prince of how he discovered the fairy; he therefore takes three citrons from it with him to his bedroom, where he is reunited with the true bride. In this, the fairy's characterization as a fetching maiden or true beloved is enhanced by the nature of her two transformations, first into a dove, as the bird associated with the cult of Aphrodite, then into a citron, as the form in which she had originally appeared to the prince and from which she emerged with a languishing thirst that he was required to slake if he wished to possess her.

In other stories of the true and false bride type, the slain maiden likewise magically reappears in the form of a bird, whereby the false bride's imposture is similarly discovered. In the Grimms' "The Three Little Men in the Forest" (KHM 13), the true bride returns as a duck. Her stepmother and stepsister had seized her in her bed and hurled her from a castle window into the stream flowing by below. Then, the stepmother's ugly daughter usurped her place in the bed, where she had just given birth to her first child. The imposture is discovered after a kitchen boy, on two successive nights, has seen a duck swim in through the drain; has heard it inquire about its husband, its "guests" (meaning the stepmother and stepsister), and its little child; has watched it, transformed as the queen, go upstairs to nurse the baby and put it to bed; and has seen it, as a duck again, swim away then through the drain. On the third night the duck bids the boy to tell the king (her husband) to wave his sword over it three times at the threshold; and once this is done, the true bride is restored to human form and the stepmother and stepsister are put to death.

Under almost identical circumstances, the true beloved in "The White Bride and the Black Bride" (KHM 135) also returns to life as a duck. Her concern to expose the imposture, though, has more to do here with the devotion between her and her brother than with her desire to wed the king, who in this case is a widower, not a handsome young man. The girl is a fetching maiden only in the passive sense; and her yearning as the true bride is to serve as her brother's angel of rescue. In Basile's version of this story, "The Two Cakes" (IV, 7), the drowned bride returns as something like a mermaid, instead of a duck; and it is the erotically "fetching" vision of her rising (like Aphrodite) out of the sea that leads to the discovery of her stepsister's imposture and hence to the liberation of her devoted brother. Marziella's devotion to the brother, Ciommo, is emphasized by the fact that she emerges from the sea not to attract the king's attention but to feed the geese that her brother is forced to tend as his punishment for having promised to deliver a beautiful bride and then having arrived with an ugly one, as a result of the imposture engineered by their stepmother.

Just as the true brides in these stories focusing on maternal devotion to a newborn child or on sisterly attachment to a brother do not display qualities of the actively fetching female, in the Grimms' "The Goose Girl" (KHM 89) the maiden is preoccupied with thoughts not about the prospective husband of whom she has been cheated but about her mother. One reason is that the girl evidently grew up singularly attached to the widowed mother, she being an only child, as far as we hear, and there having been no man around to dote on her. Another reason is that we have the case here of an arranged marriage. Indeed it is the sort where the two young people have never met, and where the daughter, a princess, is sent off on her own to marry the intended. After the mother's chambermaid has bullied the princess into trading places on the bridal journey, the girl is reduced to herding geese at the castle of the intended's father. It is in this situation that she proves to be far more the "true" daughter than the loyal bride.[7]

The princess's self-pitying grief is projected in the lament, uttered by the severed head of her faithful horse Falada each time she mournfully greets it, that "if your mother knew . . ., her heart would burst in two." Yet despite her filial innocence, the daughter is not unaware of her erotic appeal, for when the goose boy Conrad, with whom she is constrained to serve, attempts to steal a lock of her hair as she is combing it, she enlists the wind's aid in sending him off after his hat each time, until she has managed to get her tresses safely braided again.[8] It is this teasing frustration of Conrad's boyish desire that results in bringing the girl once again to the attention of her intended's father, who already on her arrival was immediately struck by the beauty and charm that shone through her humble attire and who consequently arranged to have her stay on at the castle as goose herdess. Above all, though, it is the old king's subsequent discovery, in spying on the girl, of how she and the head of the slain horse join in lamenting their plight that renders him determined to discover her secret. Thus, in this case the girl's quality as a true daughter, together with her beauty and charm, results in exposing the imposture. Most important, in gaining a husband she wins for herself a devoted father, to fill the lack she had suffered and to compensate her for having had to leave her mother in order to go off to marry.[9]

As the story of the goose girl indicates, the true bride's virtue alone is not enough to insure that the false bride's imposture will be discovered. Since the folktale as love story belongs very much to the cult of Venus, it is the quality of beauty and erotic appeal that wins out. In some stories this comes right down to the matter of the wedding night. Thus, in Basile's "The Three Fairies," (III, 10) Cuosemo, an aristocratic young man, falls passionately in love with Caradonia's stepdaughter Cicella, whose beauty is evident despite her rags; but he is tricked into taking the woman's own, ugly daughter Grannizia with him for a night of love. Grannizia's ugliness so revolts him that he does not sleep with her, but spends the night yearning for the beautiful stepsister, whom he discovers the next day hidden in a barrel in which the envious stepmother was planning to boil her alive. (He puts the ugly daughter in the barrel in her place, where she then suffers the fate intended for the true bride.) Much the same happens in the Grimms' "Maid Maleen" (*KHM* 198). A prince is engaged to a princess so ashamed of her ugliness that she forces one of her kitchen maids to stand in for her at the wedding. The servant girl, however, is the prince's beautiful former beloved, whose father, wanting her to marry another suitor, had put her in a tower for seven years to break her defiant spirit. (After managing to escape, she, with her chambermaid, took service incognito at the beloved's palace.) On the way to the church, the prince notices the bride's resemblance to his former beloved. Then, in the bridal chamber with the girl to whom he is actually engaged, he discovers the trick just as the marriage is about to be consummated. He has the ugly, deceitful bride beheaded and takes Maleen, his true beloved, as his bride instead. And in "The Singing, Jumping Little Lark" (*KHM* 88), the heroine's husband, who is a lion by day and a man by night, is transformed into a dove (on the occasion of her elder sister's marriage) and flies off to the Red Sea. There he becomes captivated by the daughter of a sorceress, an enchanted princess who appears to him in the form of a dragon. The true beloved sets out to find and rescue the husband, which she does by bribing the false bride to let her spend the night with him. He thereby recognizes her and the evil spell is broken.

As in this last story, the true bride occasionally finds herself up against a rival possessed of magical powers. This circumstance poses a particularly difficult problem for the true bride, insofar as the rival may be capable of rendering herself most erotically attractive. In such cases, the true bride must depend heavily on the appealing quality of her deep and genuine devotion, which is, in the last analysis, the distinguishing characteristic of this type of romantic folktale heroine. In "The Water-Nymph in the Pond" (*KHM* 181), a wife rescues her husband, a hunter, from a mermaid's clutches by tempting her, successively, with a golden comb, a flute, and a spinning wheel. As the mermaid accepts each enticement, a bit more of the husband, from his head on down, is allowed to rise from the water. Only with the acceptance of the third gift, though, is his body below the waist released, suggesting perhaps that this is the part the mermaid cares most about. In view of the bedroom scenes just discussed, one can imagine, too, that the wife is determined, not least of all, to recover the husband's bottom third along with the rest of him. The husband, for his part, is quite happy about being rescued from his enchantment and about being reunited, in the end, with the devoted spouse.

As the example of "The Water Nymph in the Pond" shows once again, the Grimms' tales, in depicting the type of the fetching maiden or true bride, invariably employ magic to veil the role of desire. For the Grimms and their nineteenth-century German readers, pursuing men in answer to desire's call was unbecoming behavior for a young woman. By contrast, Basile, in accord with quite different literary tastes in Renaissance Italy, did not employ magical events to obscure desire's role in motivating his heroines' quests to captivate their beloveds, but did so if anything to call attention to their desire. The tale about "Spindle, Shuttle, and Needle" (*KHM* 188) was about as far as the Grimms were prepared to let their stories go toward depiction of erotic passion. It may be clear that the girl yearns to marry the prince, but she properly does not lift a finger toward that end herself. Wishing alone makes it happen, as the moral ideal of the Grimms' Germany required.

The type of the fetching maiden or true bride was depicted quite positively in Basile's stories, where desire's role is out in the open—and indeed celebrated—as it had been in the literary novella going back to Boccaccio. Basile's heroines of this type are clearly intent on getting the beloveds into the bedroom. This is not to say, though, that such behavior reflects the moral ideals or standards of Basile's seventeenth-century Naples. On the contrary, the Renaissance novella was an eminently comic genre, depending on incongruous, "unheard of" behavior for its effect. Neapolitan girls may actually have behaved as Basile depicted them, but they were not supposed to. That was the source of the fun for listeners or readers of tales like Basile's. Accordingly, our examples of fetching maidens were mostly from Basile, while the true brides are understandably more frequent in the Grimms' tales, since pursuit of a lost or wayward husband accorded far better with the sentimental poetic ideals of Biedermeier Germany.

Feminist critics understandably have tended to emphasize the passivity of fairy tale heroines, for their concern is with the very real and severe constraints that patriarchal society in early modern Europe placed on women's activities. The romantic heroines especially have been singled out as exemplifying the patriarchal ideal of feminine passivity. As one critic sharply put it, " 'Snow White' is an overt commercial for marriage, carrying with it the message that all that matters in a woman is her appearance. It is preferable that in all other aspects she be dead."[10] Snow White's role with the dwarfs, too, has been justifiably seen as "an important part of her education in submissive femininity, for in serving them she learns essential lessons of service, of selflessness, of domesticity.... The realm of domesticity is a miniaturized kingdom in which the best of women is not only like a dwarf but like a dwarf's servant."[11] Cinderella was similarly singled out for comment by another critic: "the message of the Cinderella story that seems most relevant for modern girls and women concerns the rewards one is supposed to receive for being pretty, polite, and passive.... In this ... interpretation, success for the female comes from being beautiful and sitting around and waiting."[12]

Other feminist critics, however, have called attention to contrary examples, in which the romantic heroine has a more active role. Thus, with reference to the type of the true brides, one critic argued that the Sleeping Beauty and Snow White stories, like many romantic tales, originally had

a second part in which the heroine loses her husband and finds and wins
him again: "If the loss of the second sequence always favors the role of
the man and diminishes the role of the women, that loss is certainly no
accident."[13]

The type of the fetching maiden has not been entirely ignored by feminist criticism either. Writing about the Grimms' "The Poor Miller's Boy
and the Cat," a critic pointed to the seductivity of the woman turned cat
who "invites Hans to the [sic] dance, and when he refuses . . . orders her
feline maidens-in-waiting to take him to bed."[14] Speaking broadly of the
magical powers of fairy tale heroines, this critic related such depictions to
a more general concept of women's ability to summon forth powerful natural forces: "The forms spells take and the conjurers apparently regarded
as licit in the Grimms' collection point toward a latent belief in the natural
powers of women, especially of virgins."[15]

What is certainly clear with the type of the fetching maidens and true
brides is that, with the aid of magic or not, they themselves are the prime
movers in overcoming the obstacles to their desire's fulfillment. Often this
is as an angel of rescue or magical helper; but one also finds teases and
flirts, like Cinderella and Thousandfurs (Allerleirauh), and boldly passionate girls like Rapunzel and others of the young heroines locked away
in towers. The underlying motive force in every case is erotic desire. In
this sense, the active roles assumed by fetching maidens and true brides
show them to be authentic daughters of Venus-Aphrodite, as the goddess
of erotic love; and these stories celebrate the "magical," all-conquering
power of desire as a compelling natural force.

NOTES

1. From a feminist perspective, Ruth Bottigheimer expressed the view that "the
many fairy tales involving the wooing and winning of a princess . . . are remnants
from . . . the ancient belief in the powers of women"; see "Transformed Queen,"
esp. p. 12.

2. For a discussion of the smallness of Cinderella's foot as an attribute of her
beauty, see Hermann Bausinger, " 'Aschenputtel': Zum Problem der Märchensym-
bolik," *Zeitschrift für Volkskunde,* 52 (1955), 144–55; reprinted in Laiblin, ed.,
Märchenforschung und Tiefenpsychologie, pp. 284–98.

3. Joseph Courtés pays some small attention to Cinderella's seductive qualities
in "Une lecture sémiotique de 'Cendrillon,' " in Courtés, ed., *Introduction à la
sémiotique narrative et discursive: méthodologie et application* (Paris: Hachette, 1976),
pp. 109–38. For an analysis based on the anthropological theories of Claude Lévi-
Strauss, see Timothy C. Murray, "A Marvelous Guide to Anamorphosis: 'Cendrillon
ou La Petite pantoufle de verre,' " *Modern Language Notes,* 91 (1976), 1276–95.

4. As Bruno Jöckel rightly observed, Allerleirauh "does not at all answer the paternal demand with a pure and simple 'no!'; her words are rather: 'Before I fulfill your wish I must first have three dresses . . . and an overcoat.' " Jöckel then goes on to claim, with some justification, "With that she means to say: Only when I possess the necessary maturity can I think about marrying. The overcoat, however, for which each animal had to relinquish a piece of its hide, symbolizes the transformation into an animal that unconditionally must precede maturity." See *Der Weg zum Märchen*, p. 136.

The version in the Grimms' manuscript of 1810 lacks the father-daughter relationship entirely. Instead, Allerley-Rauch, as she is called, has the role of true bride. In this version the girl's stepmother drives her from the house because a "foreign gentleman" preferred her to the woman's own daughter and put an engagement ring on her finger. The gentleman is a king, at whose castle the girl becomes a servant. The golden trinkets she uses, along with the ring, to attract the king's attention are presents he gave her as her bridegroom. She comes into rather intimate contact with him at the castle by virtue of her job of removing his boots at night in his bedroom. As he dances with her at the balls, he notices how much she resembles his beloved lost bride. Then, he recognizes her by her golden hair, the golden trinkets, and the golden ring. See Rölleke, *Die älteste Märchensammlung*, pp. 52–59. Rölleke identified the source of the Grimms' version in the manuscript as the "Allerley-Rauch" story told by a female character in the novel *Schilly* (1798) by Carl Nehrlich; see "Allerleirauch: Eine bisher unbekannte Fassung vor Grimm," *Fabula*, 13 (1972), 153–59.

5. It has been shown, by reference to the Grimms' printed source for "Spindel, Weberschiffchen und Nadel," that they themselves are responsible for the description of the girl's blushing, and for the roguish commentary and portrayal of her gazing after the prince, including her excuse to herself about why she went to the window. Moreover, in the source the incantation is different. The girl says, "Spindle fine, Spindle already, / Greet the prince for me!" which does not overtly express the wish to fetch him back, as do the verses in the Grimms' retelling. These changes suggest that the Grimms saw the girl to be very much the type referred to in the present discussion as a fetching maiden. See Hamann, *Die literarischen Vorlagen der Kinder- und Hausmärchen*, p. 97. The Grimms' source was "Die Patengeschenke," in Ludwig Aurbacher, *Büchlein für die Jugend* (Stuttgart, 1834), pp. 160–66.

6. A folkloristic study of the motif of the substituted bride was done by P. Arfert, *Das Motiv von der untergeschobenen Braut in der internationalen Erzählungsliteratur* (Diss., Rostock, 1897; Schwerin: Bärensprung, 1897).

7. Ruth Bottigheimer has commented on this mother-daughter relationship from a feminist perspective: "it appears to me that the young girl's queenship is related to her ability to conjure the elements and to the function of the three drops of blood, which were to be of service to her on her journey. The supernatural power of the old queen's blood is demonstrated by the girl's loss of dominance directly

following her loss of the handkerchief bearing the blood"; see Bottigheimer, "Transformed Queen," pp. 6–7.

8. Bruno Jöckel read this scene in "Die Gänsemagd" as showing a contrast between the princess's behavior as that of an adolescent and the boy's as that of a child:

> But that both poles, childhood and maturity, are still at war with one another in the girl is shown by her conversations with the horse, which each time succeed her actions on the meadow that are oriented toward her role as a woman: these conversations allow her to remind herself of home and parents.
>
> Kürdchen, by contrast, is still completely a child. This is shown by his interest in his little hat that is flying away, which he chases after with the complete delight of a child. If his game with the girl's hair had erotic origins, the little hat would never distract him from it.

See *Der Weg zum Märchen*, p. 151.

9. Jöckel interpreted the princess's feelings toward her prospective father-in-law similarly: "she is supposed, after all, to seek a husband; and she seeks him, too, not only at her mother's direction, but in accord with the direction of her own development. Yet the child in her is still so preponderant that she yearns for the parental, but not the erotic, component in a man"; see *Der Weg zum Märchen*, p. 150.

10. Jennifer Waelti-Walters, *Fairy Tales and the Female Imagination* (Montreal: Eden, 1982), p. 3.

11. Gilbert and Gubar, *Mad Woman in the Attic,* p. 40.

12. Kay F. Stone, "The Misuses of Enchantment: Controversies on the Significance of Fairy Tales," in Rosan A. Jordan and Susan J. Kalčik, eds., *Women's Folklore, Women's Culture,* Publications of the American Folklore Society, 8 (Philadelphia: Univ. of Pennsylvania Press, 1985), pp. 136–37.

13. Göttner-Abendroth, *Die Göttin und ihr Heros,* pp. 170–71.

14. Bottigheimer, *Grimms' Bad Girls and Bold Boys,* p. 157.

15. Ibid., p. 50.

6

Bridegrooms and Bachelors

n stories of romance such as those found in the collections of Basile, Perrault, and the Grimms, the central figure is often female. In these literary versions, the male's role is usually a secondary one of helping call attention to the beauty, appeal, and desirability of the heroine. He is not an interesting or intriguing figure in himself. It is his reaction to the beauty and appeal of the heroine that counts—which is the case, incidentally, with the role of the older woman as well. In tales of the brother and sister type, the sister's devotion to the brother is part of her appeal; and the brother's willingness to cohabit with her and her husband instead of marrying testifies to the degree of her charm. In the stories of beauties and beasts, the transformed male's role is to demonstrate that the girl's erotic appeal is such as to attract not only the human being in him but also the animal, as it were. The relationships depicted between fathers and daughters show that the maidens' charms are sufficient to cause the fathers to identify strongly with the daughters' suitors, whether present or only potential. And in the case of the fetching maidens and true brides, the intendeds' inevitable surrender celebrates the all-conquering power of the young beauty's charm and appeal.

There are, however, a number of instances in which male figures have the central role or something approaching it, albeit still in reaction to the fairer sex. These more central male roles are essentially of two types: the potential suitor or bridegroom and the confirmed bachelor. Where is the focus in such depictions? What hints are there about how men may react to the stirrings or tug of desire and to the prospect of marrying? How do these depictions of the heroes of fairy tale romance differ from the portrayals of the romantic heroines?

I. BRIDEGROOMS

Alongside the stories of beauties and beasts, there are tales in which an eligible young man is confronted with a magical seductress. The Grimms'

"The Water-Nymph in the Pond" (*KMH* 181) is a case in point, because the young hunter's abduction by the mermaid occurs not so very long after his wedding. The mermaid's power over him is the result of a bargain made with her by his father, a miller, who in despair over his poverty agreed to her demand that he give her "that which in your house has just become young." The miller imagined that the mermaid meant a little dog or cat, but when he got home he found that his wife had just given birth to a son: "he most surely recognized that the mermaid had known that and had deceived him." The youth's capture occurs as he is out hunting one day. In pursuing a deer, he passes too close to the fateful pond where the mermaid dwells and she embraces him and pulls him into the water. Thus, it is as he is engaged in his profession, which makes him eligible to marry, that the question poses itself whether he "rightfully" belongs to the mermaid, who is associated with his birth and hence his boyhood, or to the wife, who belongs to the period of his maturity.

A stronger hint regarding a youth's passage to manhood is given in "The Frog King" (*KHM* 1). The prince was transformed into a frog by a witch, quite possibly as punishment for his having rejected her advances. The result is to make it extremely difficult for him to court a woman's favor, a goal toward which his youth is strongly urging him on. Since playing with frogs is a traditional boyhood pastime, the curse may be viewed as having, in effect, turned him from a man back into a boy—a metamorphosis that a youth might at once dread and desire. Or the transformation might reflect a lovesick youth's fear that a beautiful girl could only find him repulsive, which is indeed the immediate result of the curse in this case. If the tale is read from this perspective, loyal Henry's rejoicing over his master's return to human form and his winning of a bride is that of a devoted valet who has watched his dear friend endure the psychic torment of awakening adolescent desire.

The passage from boyhood to manhood is indicated, too, in the "Tale of One Who Went Off to Learn Fear" (*KHM* 4), although this story concerns adventure rather than love and desire. In order to gain wealth, and the hand of a princess in the bargain, a youth must spend three nights in an enchanted castle. He is able to do so because he knows no fear, or at least cannot admit to experiencing that emotion. His involvement in this adventure stems from his preoccupation with learning what it feels like to shudder. This overriding concern with the matter may hint that the youth continues to think and feel as a boy. His problem, if it can be called that, may have its origin in the fact that his older brother, who possesses every other virtue, is extraordinarily fearful. The role as fearless fellow is thus the only one in which the younger brother has the opportunity to outshine the elder, favored sibling. This role as the brave son is one that a younger brother is likely to assume in any case, since in terms of age he is thought of, in boyhood, as being farther from becoming a man.[1]

Proving one's manhood by spending the night in an enchanted castle is a boyish way of doing so. The youth's marriage to the princess represents a truer test of his manhood, namely, accepting the role of husband. Here he fails, in the sense that his continued preoccupation with his quest to learn what it feels like to shudder renders his newlywed wife dissatisfied with him as a lover. His dream of learning to shudder leaves no room for dreams about love with her. Indeed, this preoccupation, once he has married, may serve him as a welcome escape from thoughts of desire, and represents in any case a clinging to the concerns of his boyhood. This avenue of escape or regression is cut off for him in the end by the wife's fulfilling of his yearning to shudder when she and her chambermaid pour a bucket of water and small fish over him as he lies sleeping in the marriage bed. His ensuing joy over having learned to shudder suggests that the wife's cure has worked and that his regressive compulsion has been overcome.[2]

Reluctance to part with one's boyhood role may also be involved in "The Little Donkey" (*KHM* 144), where it is not so much that a boy behaves like the proverbial jackass as that he has literally been born in that form. While all goes well on his wedding night as he sheds his donkey hide before joining the princess in bed, on the next night he is seized with panic when his father-in-law and the latter's servant contrive to burn the hide. With his accustomed boyhood identity now lost to him forever, "full of anxiety and grief" he tells himself he must "see to it that I escape." But as he tries to leave the bedroom the father-in-law stands in the doorway barring his path. In exchange for the son-in-law's agreeing to remain—that is, his acceptance of his loss of the right to appear outside the bridal chamber in his accustomed boyhood form as a jackass—the king accepts him fully as his kin, giving him half of his kingdom outright and willing him the other half on his death.

Another story, "The Two Royal Children" (*KHM* 113), calls particular attention to the passage from boyhood to manhood. In the horoscope of a king's young son it is found that he is supposed to be slain by a stag when he is sixteen years old. As it turns out, the peril does not concern the prince's proving himself a man at hunting but rather as a suitor, for the fateful stag is transformed before the youth's eyes into a man who takes him to the palace of a king who has three eligible daughters. The primary test that the youth must endure, in order to have one of the three daughters to wife, is to stand watch alone with her in her bedroom for nine hours, from nine in the evening to six in the morning. The implication is thus that it is the youth's loss of innocence regarding desire, not loss of his life,

that was destined to be at stake when he approached marriageable age.
Like spinning for the Sleeping Beauty, hunting connotes here the youth's
passage to sexual adulthood, which in the eyes of a father or soothsayer
may be seen to be fraught with something approaching mortal danger.

Under somewhat similar circumstances, in "The King of the Golden
Mountain" (*KHM* 92) the test involves redeeming an enchanted princess
at considerable risk to the youth's physical well-being. The youth's father,
when the boy is still a toddler, unwittingly promises him to the devil,
thinking that the latter is bargaining only for his dog. Since the devil is
intent on having the boy delivered to him twelve years hence, the implication is that he has designs on him once he is entering manhood. Or, if
one thinks of the devil as being a creature of fantasy, the father perhaps
envisions that period in the son's life as being perilous, or simply as the
time when he shall "lose" the son to a beloved. What happens, in any
case, is that in response to the youth's protestation that the devil had
seduced and tricked the father, the father and the devil agree that the son,
"since he did not belong to the hereditary enemy or any longer to the
father," should be cast adrift in a small boat. In doing so, the father and
the devil have, in effect, cast him upon the waves of desire, for the waters
carry him to an enchanted princess who is yearning for a redeemer. This
physical passage, bringing the youth from the role of son to that of lover,
is precisely the one appropriate to his age.

Dreams of involvement with magical beauties, or at least with women
possessing seemingly magical charms, are very much the stuff of adolescent
fantasy, of course. Generally, such association with magic is a desirable
quality in these dream beloveds, but it may also be the source, or projection,
of a degree of anxiety. Thus, in "Beloved Roland" (*KHM* 56) the title
figure's susceptibility to the seductions of another woman, when he goes
home to prepare for his wedding, may be related to the fact that his intended
has come into possession of a magic wand, which she stole from her evil
stepmother, a sorceress. The beloved has just demonstrated the wand's
power by using it to transform herself and Roland so that they might escape
the angry hag's pursuit. Perhaps, on some level of his being, Roland experiences aversion to, or anxiety at, becoming the bridegroom of a maiden
thus endowed. In the end, the true beloved does not win him back through
any exercise of her occult power "inherited" from the sorceress but through
the natural magic of her singing voice, which overcomes his temporary,
selective loss of memory and causes him to remember his love for her—a
love that antedated her coming into possession of the magic wand.

A boy's involvement with an enchanted princess has somewhat different,
though related, implications in "The Poor Miller's Boy and the Cat" (*KHM*
106). The youngest of a miller's three apprentices appears not yet to have

reached marriageable age, or at least not full physical maturity, when he makes a bargain to serve a little motley she-cat for seven years in exchange for her promise to give him a fine horse as his reward. Since it becomes clear, in the end, that the enchanted princess has set her cap on the youth, one may wonder why she does not reveal her identity to him until after the seven years have passed. Certainly the miller's son displays no aversion to marrying the cat turned princess when the time has come, though it must be admitted that she arranges everything so quickly that he is given no opportunity to object, or indeed even to express his assent. But the point may be that the princess contrived to bring the miller's son into her castle before he had reached the age to be attracted to women, much as an older woman might take a boy into her service in hopes of making him her lover once he has grown to manhood. That something of the sort happens here is indicated by the cat's attempt, after dinner that first night, to get the boy to dance with her, an invitation he declines by saying, in boyish fashion, "I won't dance with a pussycat, I've never done that." Seven years later, though, he has outgrown the clothes he was wearing when he first came to the castle; and, despite the lack of any intervening experience with women other than the enchanted cat and her feline chambermaids, he appears instinctively ready to prove his manhood on the wedding night.

Whereas the redemption of the pussycat princess by the miller's boy is done unwittingly, not having been part of his bargain with her, most youths in folktales involving enchanted beloveds are attracted precisely by the maidens' need for a rescuer to release them from a spell. A chief reason for this is of course that both maidens and youths experience the stirrings of desire as very like becoming enchanted. In some cases, this symbolic action is played out in the arena of romance as adventure, as in "The Raven" (*KHM* 93), where the hero redeems a maiden who, as a baby, was turned into a raven as the result of a careless oath uttered by her mother. In other cases, though, the opportunity to play the role of saving angel to a maiden in distress comes very much in answer to a young man's dreams of love. Thus, in "Little Briar-Rose" (*KHM* 50) the young prince's passion is enflamed merely by hearing about the young beauty slumbering behind the great thorny hedge; and the flowering of the hedge at his approach and its parting to let him through are very much the stuff of which erotic dreams of the more innocent or sublimated sort are made.

In some tales, the young man's discovery of his ideal beloved comes quite literally in answer to a dream. In Basile's "The Three Citrons" (V, 9), a king's son has so declared himself to be a sworn enemy of marriage and women that his father despairs of ever having grandchildren. Then one day as the prince is slicing a piece of cheese, he becomes possessed by the vision of an ideal beloved. The cheese evidently is associated in his mind with the flesh, all the more so once blood has fallen on it from his finger, which he inadvertently cut with the knife. He is overcome with desire for a woman who might be "just as white and red as the cheese colored by his blood" (cf. German *schön wie Milch und Blut*—and its equivalent in other European languages—for English "pretty as peaches and cream"). As the prince himself exclaims, in an odd manifestation of bachelorish narcissism, "Never has a woman set my blood astir, and now I want one who looks like my own blood."

The lovesick prince searches all over the world, vainly seeking the woman of his dreams, until finally on the Island of the Ogresses he finds the magical means for coming into the possession of such a beauty. Each of the three citrons given him by the third hag he encounters contains a fairy who will emerge when he slices the fruit with the knife the hag has provided, but the fairy will melt away like quicksilver if he does not immediately give her a drink to quench her thirst. The hags thus appear to represent the type of the older woman as potential go-between or matchmaker (the *ruffiana* of older comedy), all the more so because the first two hags warned him that their daughters are ogresses who, should they spy him, would eat him half-cooked, half still alive, and advised him that if he looked farther for his fortune, he would find it. It is the third hag, to whom the first two have evidently meant to steer him, who possesses the three citrons with the three beautiful fairies who will not hunger after his flesh but will languishingly desire that he give them a drink, albeit as a first step toward enjoying the pleasures of the flesh with him.

A suggestive association is established in this tale between the prince's having conceived his passion while slicing a piece of cheese and his coming into possession of the object of that passion by cutting open a piece of fruit. The humorous point is likely that in his earlier bachelor misogyny, the idea of cleaving flesh with his sexual member was secretly the object of some revulsion or inhibition. When the moment comes to wield the hag's knife to open the citron and release the fairy, he manages that well enough; but his awe at the beauty of the magical creature who emerges is such that he fails to perform the rest of the task, namely, to quench the beauty's thirst. Only with the third citron does he finally succeed in giving the fairy a drink before she dissolves. With that act he passes from bachelor admirer of female beauty to the role of lover, as it were.

The central figure's marriage to a supernatural creature, as opposed to a formerly enchanted human being, is relatively uncommon in the collections by the Grimms, Basile, and Perrault. As the case of the misogynistic prince in "The Three Citrons" suggests, this "unnatural" sort of passion occurs in connection with revulsion at, or resistance to, sexual relations with creatures of flesh and blood. A similar portrayal involving a bachelor is found in Basile's "The Myrtle" (I, 2), but with the difference that here the prince, far from having abstained from sexual relations, lives with seven concubines. The point in this case appears to be that familiarity breeds contempt, or revulsion, for the prince falls in love at first sight with a potted myrtle bough which he subsequently discovers to be, "in reality," a beautiful fairy, his ideal beloved. One can imagine that, with seven concubines, the prince may well be suffering from a surfeit of indulgence in the pleasures of the bed; but he proves quite thrilled to be joined at night by the mysterious, secret lover whose beauty, for a time, he can only guess at from having caressed her body during their lovemaking. While it is clear enough that the secret beloved's absolute devotion to the prince helps make her the fulfillment of his dream of love, in view of the concubines' vanity, envy, and perfidy, the fact remains that she is a creature of fantasy and his marriage to her not a real one in the usual sense. He has not married a woman, but an ideal of what a woman might be. Myrtle was a plant considered sacred in connection with the worship of Aphrodite, and as such came to be used with bridal attire. The prince's instinctive attraction to the plant thus would seem to bespeak, from the outset, a yearning for the ideal bride in an erotic sense, as one associated with the cult of the goddess of love.

In the Grimms' "The Drummer" (*KHM* 193), there is the circumstance, unusual in folktale, that the youth first sees the beloved, and hears her speak to him, in a dream. Though in this case the girl is real enough, being a maiden constrained by a witch to live on a glass mountain, she is a creature of fantasy on the part of the title figure insofar as her appearance in his dream offers him the opportunity to become her angel of rescue, an appealing role in erotic fantasies. Moreover, the dream is preceded—and in that sense, suggested—by his having found three little pieces of white linen by the edge of a lake. Unconsciously, he must have recognized the linen as garments such as maidens might have shed in order to go bathing. To no specific purpose, as far as he is able to admit to himself, he takes one of the pieces of linen home with him, thereby providing the immediate occasion for the girl's appearance to him in his dream to beg him to return the shift to her. And since the maiden explains that she needs the shift in order to be able to get back to the mountain, she must appear to him naked, thus further indicating the erotic nature of the dream. Evidently, the girl fears that she will be punished by the witch if she does not return, otherwise one would think that she might be glad to have an excuse not to do so. But the point is likely that, in terms of dreams as erotic wish fulfillment, the maiden must return to the mountain so that the youth may have the opportunity to rescue her and thereby prove his manhood.

That the young drummer here is something of the languishing suitor, given more to dreams of love than its consummation, may be indicated by the fact that the girl herself has to perform for him the magical tasks which are required for her rescue. Moreover, he then proves to be the all-too-dutiful and devoted son in returning home to ask his parents' consent to his marriage. When he kisses his parents on the right cheek, as the girl has warned him not to do, he forgets all about her and agrees to marry the bride his mother has chosen for him. By the same token, when the time for consummating this union has arrived, the young drummer's memory of the girl of his dreams is restored, through her efforts, and he chooses marriage to her instead, no doubt because she has demonstrated that she desires him so very much. The bachelorish "moral" of the story may be that, if one must marry, then it is preferable to marry one's dream beloved.

While it is not uncommon for the object of a youth's passion to be held captive by a witch, in some tales the girl is the daughter of a sorceress. This circumstance, of course, only increases the element of delicious peril in erotic adventure, and serves as an added, jestful indication that the passage from boyhood to manhood is fraught with danger regarding the awakening of desire. As we have seen in several stories already, the fateful moment for the youth often comes as he is out hunting. This is the case again in Basile's "The Dove" (II, 7). A prince, Nardaniello, after he has broken a poor hag's pot of beans with a stone in a wager with his hunting companions, is cursed by the hag with the fate of falling in love with the daughter of a witch. Hunting with one's fellows, or practicing the cult of the chaste goddess Artemis-Diana, is one way of avoiding paying tribute to the goddess of love. Thus, the hag's curse of the prince for his boyish prank may reflect the object of his unconscious anxiety, that is, nature's call to find a mate. The hag's association with the prospect of marrying is then further suggested at the end. She reappears at the prince's wedding with Filadora, the witch's daughter, to proclaim an additional curse, this time tailored to his new role as husband: that the spilled beans of hers he sowed upon the earth might come back to haunt him in fulfillment of the proverb that whoever sows beans shall grow horns.

In the Grimms' "The Herb Donkey" (*KHM* 122), a young hunter's encounter with a hag in the forest likewise sets in motion the events that lead to his marriage to a witch's daughter. In this case, however, the youth is aided, not cursed, by the hag, because he takes pity on her and provides her with money to enable her to satisfy her hunger and thirst. The magical items that he secures by following the hag's instructions allow him subsequently to gain entry to the castle of a witch, with whose daughter he has fallen in love at first sight. The witch covets the bird's heart he has swallowed, which makes him rich, and the cloak he wears, which enables him to wish himself transported wherever he desires. His passion for the witch's daughter is such that he continues to feel tenderly toward her even after she has obeyed her mother's command that she aid her in deceiving him. And once he has contrived to punish and destroy the witch, he not only marries the girl but allows her to remain in possession of the bird's heart, the magical source of his wealth. The point of this curious tale appears to be that falling in love with a girl whose mother happens to be a witch makes the experience of romance that much more thrilling and exciting, thereby easing the passage to manhood and the role of bridegroom.

II. YOUNG BACHELORS

While with most male characters in folktale the passage to manhood succeeds well enough, such is not always the case. One source of potential difficulty is a son's attachment to his mother, as we have seen (Chap. 3). A son's devotion or obedience may even result in his failure to marry. In "The Three Black Princesses" (*KHM* 137), for example, the youth's mother advises him not to redeem the princesses in the enchanted mountain but to sprinkle them instead with holy water. As a result, he fails to become their angel of rescue and the anticipated romantic ending does not come to pass.

Especially fascinating is the dependence of a son on his mother in "Clever Hans" (*KHM* 32). The mother appears very much to want her son, Hans, to marry his fiancée, Gretel, but his stupidity spoils her plan. Instead of showering his intended with presents, as a prospective bridegroom should, he goes each day to Gretel's house to demand a present from her. Worse, he shows himself to be incapable of taking proper care of the gifts as he brings them home to his mother. Each time he stupidly follows the instructions his mother gave him for handling the present the day before, after he had already spoiled it; and these admonishments of course prove entirely inappropriate to the new matter at hand. His behavior thus appears to be anything but clever, and he seems entirely undeserving of the epithet accorded him in the story's title. The result is that he loses his bride, for in the end Gretel quits him in anger, exasperation, and disgust.

If Hans's secret aim, however, is to avoid marriage, then he is quite clever after all. His continued begging for presents brings Gretel to the point where she has, or claims to have, nothing left to give but herself. In his seeming stupidity, Hans leads her home as though she were a calf, since that was her last present to him and just the previous evening his mother had instructed him as to the proper handling of such a beast. When his mother, on asking him what Gretel has given him this time, learns that he has put his bride-to-be in the stable, she tells him that he has acted stupidly and that he should, instead, have cast friendly eyes at her. Ever the simpleton, Hans follows his mother's advice literally, cutting out the eyes of all the calves and sheep in the stable and throwing them in Gretel's face (his mother used the expression *freundliche Augen zuwerfen*). This completely idiotic act on Hans's part is the last straw for the fiancée, who breaks loose from the rope with which he tethered her and runs home. Hans's misconstruction of his mother's advice in this matter shows, at the very least, that Hans is—or pretends to be—ignorant about love, and likely indicates that romance and marriage are a matter of indifference to him, if not an object of revulsion. Hans is thus surely happy to go on living with his—evidently widowed—mother and has no interest in disturbing this devoted relationship through the introduction of another woman into the house. This is perhaps secretly the reason why, when Gretel offered herself to him, he treated her so badly and led her to the stable, instead of the house (cf. German *eine Braut heimführen* 'bring home one's bride', referring simply to the bridegroom's entry into marriage).[3]

Devotion to one's sister, rather than one's mother, is a far more common reason why a young man in folktale remains a bachelor. Though the focus of interest in tales of the brother and sister type, as we have seen (Chap. 1), is usually on the sister's devotion, the brothers' attachment to the sister is indicated by the fact that they almost never marry but are content to live with the sister, even after she has married. The arrangement of living with the sister and her husband appears to be especially attractive, and most often forms the happy ending of these stories. This ending is particularly characteristic of the Grimms' collection, where it is found in at least a half-dozen stories: "The Twelve Brothers" (*KHM* 9); "Little Brother and Little Sister" (*KHM* 11); "The Six Swans" (*KHM* 49); "The Golden Bird" (*KHM* 57); "The White Bride and the Black Bride" (*KHM* 135); and "The Glass Coffin" (*KHM* 163).

The tendency toward remaining a bachelor may also be observed in stories depicting devotion between brothers, that is, in certain tales that may be termed the brother and brother type. A particularly striking example is Basile's "The Raven" (IV, 9), in which Gennariello loyally aids his brother, young king Milluccio, in finding and winning the girl of his dreams. The two brothers appear to have been leading a contented, uneventful life together until one day when Milluccio, pursuing his passion for the hunt, is seized by a yearning for a maiden as white as the marble stone on which a raven he has just slain has fallen, as red as the raven's blood that has flowed onto the marble, and as black as the dead raven itself. What has happened, in effect, is that a devotee of the chaste goddess of the hunt, Artemis-Diana, has surrendered to the contrary influence of the goddess of erotic desire, Aphrodite-Venus. Gennariello appears to identify mightily with his brother in his lovesick yearning for the unknown, perhaps unattainable beloved. In any case, out of brotherly devotion he succeeds in finding the fulfillment of Milluccio's dream in the beautiful Liviella and luring her onto their ship—an abduction which she proves quite willing to accept and excuse.

Of special interest is Gennariello's role once they are sailing homeward, for it is here that his bachelor identification with the brother in the role of the bridegroom is strongly indicated. On the ship Gennariello overhears a male dove telling its mate, during a storm, that the falcon Gennariello has bought for Milluccio will pluck out the latter's eyes when he hands it to him; that when Milluccio mounts the steed Gennariello has got for him as a present he will break his neck; and that when Milluccio lies the first night with the bride whom Gennariello has procured for him the pair will be eaten by a hideous dragon.

The first two envisioned perils concern presents having to do with Milluccio's bachelor passion for the hunt, before he conceived his lovesick yearning for the unknown beauty; and the third concerns the moment of consummation of that yearning. It is almost as though Gennariello himself, not Milluccio, were the prospective bridegroom, so intense is the implied vicarious identification. This impression is strengthened by the circumstance that Gennariello learns about these perils from doves, the bird associated with the goddess of love, and that the male dove—projecting a voice within Gennariello—tells the female that whoever tries to help Milluccio avoid these perils or to warn him about them will be turned into a marble statue. The point seems to be that Gennariello, as a young bachelor, inwardly looks upon marriage as a perilous, fateful step, and that he dreads his brother's wedding as putting an end to their former bachelor existence together.

Much as Gennariello may unconsciously wish that his brother would remain a bachelor, he is powerless to prevent the marriage. His loyal devotion, meanwhile, dictates that he must act to prevent the brother's suffering serious injury or death. The magical circumstance that his actions on the brother's behalf will be punished by his own transformation into a marble statue may be viewed as projecting his sense that with his brother's marriage their relationship will grow cold. To put it differently, his loving sacrifice for the brother, beginning with the procurement of the bride, will be immortalized in stone, even as part of him dies with the brother's marriage. Or Gennariello's vision of himself turning to stone on the brother's wedding night may express the hope, familiar from cases of suicide, that the brother will regret the betrayal of their former bachelor devotion that Milluccio's succumbing to desire represents in Gennariello's unconscious.

Gennariello's transformation before the brother's very eyes, as he explains the reason for his actions in beheading the falcon, cutting off the horse's legs, and hiding in the bridal chamber to ward off the dragon with his sword, does indeed have the effect of filling Milluccio with remorse over having doubted his brother's loyalty and devotion. The degree of this remorse is demonstrated, subsequently, by Milluccio's slaying of the twin sons born to him by Liviella. He does this in order to restore the brother to life, after this remedy has been suggested by a mysterious old man who appears to him as though in a vision. Although the thought does not occur to Milluccio, he has in effect chosen his love for the brother over that for his wife; for when Liviella learns what he has done, in her grief she attempts to throw herself from the window. She is prevented from doing so only by the arrival of her father, a sorcerer, through the same window. The father announces that he was responsible for Gennariello's transformation and all the other magic, to repay him for having abducted his daughter. His thirst for revenge satisfied, he restores his twin grandsons to life, so that they all may live happily together. Gennariello is described as being especially happy, no doubt because magical opportunity has been provided for Milluccio to prove his own brotherly devotion. In the end, Gennariello occupies an equal or greater place in his brother's affections than he enjoyed before Milluccio fell in love.

Substantially the same story is told in the Grimms' "Faithful John" (*KHM* 6). The depiction of bachelor fantasy here is, if anything, more obvious than in Basile's "The Raven." The young prince has grown up in a bachelor household with his father, evidently a widower, and the latter's valet, faithful John. That love of woman—the general object of bachelor panic—threatens the peace and contentment of the household is indicated at the outset by the king's dying words to his elderly valet that his son, the prince, must be prevented at all costs from entering the last room on the long hallway, in which there hangs the portrait of a beautiful princess: "If he spies the picture he will experience a violent love for her and will fall down and faint and will encounter great perils for her sake."

Although John is not the young king's brother but his servant, having become his valet after the old king's death, he enters upon the same role as Gennariello in Basile's version once the inevitable has happened and the young king has fallen in love with the maiden portrayed in the painting. Whereas Milluccio in that story became infatuated, as it were, with the carcass of a raven, here the dangerous nature of the young king's passion is reflected—especially as regards the bachelor valet's feelings in the matter—by the fact that it is three ravens, birds of ill omen, which faithful John overhears on the ship commenting on the perils that await the prospective bridegroom (remember that in Basile's version the birds are doves).

And the focus in these perils is even more completely on the erotic aspect of entering upon the role of bridegroom. When the young king mounts his horse to ride from the ship to his castle, it will fly off with him; when he puts on his wedding shirt (*Brauthemd*), it will burn him alive; and when the bride faints at the wedding ball, she will die unless someone picks her up, sucks three drops of blood from her right breast, and spits them out again. Understandably, it is John's attempt to satisfy this requirement for rescue of the bride, like Gennariello's concealing himself in the bridal chamber, that causes the young king, in jealous outrage, to denounce the friend as a traitor.

It is noteworthy that in both Basile's and the Grimms' versions, it is precisely the action on the loyal bachelor friend's part that involves saving the bride's life which directly leads to his being turned to stone. The ironic point is perhaps that, inwardly, the friend may be wishing that, on the contrary, the bride might be dispatched to Hades. That is to say, unconsciously the vision of the bride dying may project a secret wish on the friend's part, and is at the very least a reflection of resentment that, one way or another, she "will be the death of me," as the saying goes.

In the Grimms' version, the friend's role as procurer of the bride and guardian angel to the young couple is rendered the more comical, or sublimely ridiculous, by the fact that his identification with the prospective bridegroom is that of an older man. Moreover, faithful John's situation as the loyal manservant vicariously suffering through the perils of lovesickness and desire with his young master is reminiscent of the enigmatic role of Iron Henry at the end of "The Frog King" (*KHM* 1), who is depicted as having had to bind his heart with iron bands to prevent it from bursting, so great was his grief over the transformation of his master into a frog that set in motion the events leading to his union with the beautiful young princess.

If in the ending of Basile's "The Raven" the question that may secretly be posing itself to the young king is that of love *or* friendship, in "Faithful John" it is rather the possibility of love *and* friendship, that is, of conjugal bliss without the sacrifice of his relationship with the devoted servant, the relationship which characterized his earlier situation as a young bachelor. After faithful John's unswerving devotion has been demonstrated by his transformation, the young king has the statue placed next to the bed in the bridal chamber. And when he is lamenting John's loss one day, the statue speaks and reveals that if the king slays the twin sons he has sired with his bride and paints the statue with their blood, John will be restored to life. As in Basile's story, the king does not hesitate for a moment to act on this advice, but with the difference that here he knows that his bride shares his grief over the faithful servant's loss and that she likely will approve of his choice in the matter, as she then does. Unknown to the wife, however, John has been able to revive the slain sons, so that at the end nothing stands in the way of the blissful cohabitation of the husband, wife, and bachelor valet; and the king's yearning for love and friendship has thus been satisfied.[4]

In other stories depicting a brother's or friend's devotion to a youth of marriageable age, the act of rescue which proves that devotion occurs after the wedding night. The implications regarding the unmarried youth's identification with the friend or brother as bridegroom, and the bridegroom's ambivalence about that role, remain much the same, however. Thus, in Basile's "The Merchant's Two Sons" (I, 7) on the morning after the wedding night the bridegroom, Cienzo, succumbs to the charms of a beautiful sorceress who lives across the way and whom he spies as he is dressing at the window. Cienzo's younger brother Meo, who has come looking for him, is mistaken by the bride for her absent husband and goes to bed with her; but out of devoted loyalty to his brother he divides the bedclothes so as not to dishonor him. The next morning Meo spies the sorceress and is attracted by her, just as his brother was; and on learning that fact from the brother's bride, he manages to rescue him from the sorceress's clutches, so that the husband, his brother, and the bride live on happily together at the castle of the bride's father. The point of this portrayal appears to be that the younger brother, once he has spent a night—however innocently—in his brother's place as bridegroom, is as susceptible to the charms of another, magical beauty as his older brother was after he consummated his union with his bride. That is to say, what appears to be secretly depicted here is an unconscious ambivalence toward marriage which engenders an urge to flight by way of avoiding further sexual contact with the bride.

This same ambivalence about conjugal bliss is suggested in the Grimms' "The Children of Gold" (*KHM* 85). A brother marries, dreams on the wedding night of capturing a stag, and leaves his bride the next morning to go off to hunt, whereupon a witch turns him into stone. The bridegroom appears to find himself attracted to Artemis's pursuits, as an escape from those of Aphrodite. His plight is signaled to his brother back home by the collapse of a golden lily identified with his well-being. After he has been restored to life by the brother and returned to his conjugal role with his bride at her father's house, his father at home remarks that, meanwhile, "the golden lily stood up once again and continued to bloom"—a sly hint that if the son wilted as a bridegroom on the wedding night, through his brother's vicariously self-identifying act of rescue he has managed to rise again, in the erotic sense, to meet the challenge of his conjugal duties as husband?

The bridegroom in Basile's "The Charmed Hind" (I, 9) is seized by the same urge to hunt as is his counterpart in the Grimms' "The Children of Gold"; and his loyal friend learns of his fate at the hands of a sorceress the same way that the brother does in "The Merchant's Two Sons," that is, by replacing the ill-fated bridegroom in the marriage bed. After Canneloro has been married a month, he becomes sad at heart and yearns to go hunting. Despite his father-in-law's warnings, he is taken prisoner by a hind he pursues which is in reality an ogre. The loyal friend of his youth, Prince Fonzo, learns of his fate by the turbidity of a fountain and the withering of a myrtle tree which were appointed by Canneloro to alert the friend, should he come to be in need of his aid. When Fonzo arrives at the palace belonging to Canneloro's father-in-law, he is mistaken for Lady Fenizia's husband; and in order to be in a position to discover what has become of Canneloro, he sleeps with her, taking care to place his naked sword between himself and the bride so that his friend's honor will not be in jeopardy. The implication of this scene is thus, once again, that the bachelor, as rescuer, must put himself in the friend's place as bridegroom before he can discover the nature of this terrible magical thing that has befallen the friend in connection with relinquishing bachelorhood for marriage.

"The Charmed Hind" contains a further element suggesting that it is a veiled depiction of male ambivalence about conjugal involvement. The friends Canneloro and Fonzo have in common that neither of them was sired in the fashion nature prescribes. King Iannone, being childless and possessed of a great desire for offspring, followed the advice of a sage in having a beautiful virginal maid boil a sea dragon, from the steam of which both the maid and the king's wife became pregnant, the maid with Canneloro and the wife with Fonzo. The magical—and hilarious—circumstance that the steam from the dragon was so powerful that it caused even the furniture to reproduce reinforces the impression that the impregnations are wish fulfillments on the part of a male (the childless king) who is preoccupied with, or bothered by, the whole matter of potency and having sexual relations. Considering the circumstances of their conception, it is small wonder that the two "half-brothers" become involved in perilous adventures during their passage from youth to manhood. Nor do they make the passage all that completely, for in the end Fonzo returns to his putative father, and Canneloro, though he resumes his role as husband, bids the friend, on the latter's departure for home, to send his mother to live with him, his bride, and his father-in-law.

The story of a married brother's rescue from a transformation suffered while pursuing a hind is told at the end of the Grimms' "The Two Brothers" (*KHM* 60), but here the focus is on fraternal devotion, and there is little hint that vicarious bachelor identification with the brother as bridegroom is involved. Indeed, the circumstance that the unmarried brother spends a night in the bride's bed with a sword between them merely provides opportunity for the married brother to receive further proof of his sibling's complete loyalty.[5] Similarly, in "The Crystal Ball" (*KHM* 197) a youth's rescue of a princess and his marriage to her simply brings in its wake the restoration of his brothers to human form; and their earlier transformation has nothing whatever to do with the passage from youth to manhood, or with fraternal devotion for that matter. In "The Four Artful Brothers" (*KHM* 129), however, bachelor tendencies are indicated in the brothers' decision to renounce their claim to the princess they have rescued, in exchange for an offer of money, whereupon they go home to live with their father happily ever after. And in "The Three Brothers" (*KHM* 124), marriage does not even enter the picture, so content are the three male siblings to live together in the house inherited from their father until they are "all three laid in a grave together."

In "Ferdinand the Faithful and Ferdinand the Unfaithful" (*KHM* 126), though the young man does not have a brother, he enjoys a similarly devoted relationship with a talking horse. That relationship ultimately provides him refuge from an enchanting sorceress who has contrived to marry him. His preference for the horse's companionship is most understandable, because he has seen the sorceress rid herself of an unwanted bridegroom by first convincing him that she has it in her power to put a man's head back on after she has cut it off and then declining to do so after she had decapitated him. The enchantress's role as an object of bachelor anxiety about marrying is indicated all the more by the fact that she used Ferdinand, the youth on whom she has set her cap, as her experimental victim to demonstrate the power of her magic. It is small wonder, then, that the youth subsequently avoids her, since friendship with his faithful horse is far safer than involvement with a passionate woman who is wont to lop off heads to achieve the object of her whim or desire.

That the horse, however, has represented Ferdinand's unreadiness for marriage all along, even before his involvement with the sorceress, is indicated by the fact that the animal was promised him at the time of his birth, as a magical gift from his godfather. The horse's role as a substitute for the love of a woman is further suggested by the godfather's stipulation that Ferdinand shall not have the animal until he is fourteen, the age at which boys tend to form close relationships with members of their own gender in reaction to awakening desires that are urging them toward involvement with the opposite sex. Indeed, from all appearances, Ferdinand at the end of the story is still only fourteen, which would help explain his flight from the role as husband and the ensuing transformation of the talking horse into a prince, as a magical fulfillment of Ferdinand's need for a male friend as refuge from his passionate spouse.[6]

III. OLDER MEN

Bachelor panic and anxiety, in connection with misogynistic fears, are particularly typical of older men in folktale, as we have seen for example in the old king and the valet in the Grimms' "Faithful John" (*KHM* 6). A singularly intriguing instance of an older man's identification with a youth as potential bridegroom is found in "Iron Hans" (*KHM* 136). An eight-year-old prince is abducted by an ogre (a "wilder Mann") whom his father has held captive in a cage. The wild man raises the prince as his son; and the boy's passage to manhood is accompanied—that is, signaled—by his failing a magical test, with the result that he is sent out into the world. The wondrously golden hair with which the youth becomes endowed in failing the test renders him the object of a princess's passion. On the occasion of the youth's marriage to the princess, the wild man appears in his true identity as a proud king and reveals to the bridegroom that it was he, as the boy's devoted abductor Iron Hans, who "was transformed into an ogre, but you have redeemed me."

The youth's failure of the test, then, which sets in motion the events that lead to his marriage, proves to have been necessary in order to release his abductor from an evil spell. A possible, indeed likely, interpretation of this odd circumstance is that the youth's marriage represents a vicarious wish fulfillment for the older man. Iron Hans's metamorphosis thus would be a projection of the wild urges—that is, the erotic desire—which the evidently unmarried king does not himself have the courage to satisfy. A further indication that such urges are secretly involved here is that the occasion for the release of the ogre was the boy's desire to retrieve his ball, the toy associated with his childhood pleasure, which had rolled into the wild man's cage. Moreover, the reason for the youth's subsequent failing of the fateful test was his irresistible yearning to soothe the pain in the finger he injured in opening the cage by soaking it in the forbidden waters of the well the wild man ordered him to guard. The young prince is thus a male counterpart of the princess in "The Frog King" (*KHM* 1), who makes the passage from childhood to sexual adulthood in similar fashion. In this case, though, the magical helper is not the eventual lover but a member of the same sex for whom that "perilous" passage is evidently an object of vicarious identification (or, conversely, the role of the older man as a caged ogre is a projection of the boy's unconscious guilt about the wild urges attendant upon growing toward sexual maturity).

In "The House in the Woods" (*KHM* 169), another of the Grimms'
stories in which a king—here a handsome prince—suffers under his transformation into a forest dweller, it is not panic about the stirrings of desire
but misogynistic anxiety that appears to be involved. Three daughters of
a poor woodcutter and his wife are supposed, respectively and on successive
days, to bring lunch out to their father as he works. Unable to find the
way, and perhaps magically prevented from doing so, they come instead
to the house of an old man in the woods who lives alone with a rooster, a
chicken, and a cow. The two older daughters forget to feed the animals
and make supper only for themselves and the old man. Out of displeasure
with them on this account, he lowers their beds into the cellar as they are
sleeping and holds them prisoner there. When the youngest daughter
comes, on the third day, she thinks of the animals first. The result is that
as she and the old man are sleeping that night, in the same room but in
separate beds, the sylvan house is transformed into a castle and the old
man into a handsome prince. An evil witch had condemned the prince to
live in the forest as an old, gray-haired man alone with the three servants
turned into animals until a maiden came to them who was "so good-hearted
that she showed herself to be loving not only toward mankind, but also
toward animals." The point may be that the witch, in uttering her curse,
was speaking with a voice from within the prince, who inwardly yearned
to be assured that the girl he married was thoroughly loving, not moved
to kindness toward him out of a desire to marry a handsome prince. The
prince may also wish to be loved more as a father than as a husband, for
the girls who are led to his house as if by magic are on their way to carry
out their filial duty toward their father by bringing him his lunch. The
similar duty that awaits them at the house in the forest is to feed supper
to the enchanted prince, in his transformation as an old man.[7]

The older man whose attraction to a beautiful maiden is that of a father,
rather than of a lover, is depicted elsewhere in folktale. The old king in
"The Goose Girl" (*KHM* 89), as we have seen, conceives a fond, widower
passion for the presumed servant girl and, as a result, ends by discovering
that she is in reality a princess and by seeing to it that his son marries her.
She is, after all, the true bride, the one he had arranged for the son to
marry. But the impression is given that even if she were not, the old king
would be intent on having her join his widower household, so strong is the
devotion he harbors toward her. A comic, and not entirely so innocent,
portrayal of such passion on the part of an older man is found in Basile's
"Viola" (II, 3). There, we remember (Chap. 3), an ogre imagines that the
beautiful maiden he finds standing behind him in his garden has been born
full grown as a result of the thunderous gas he has just passed from his
bowels; and he takes her in as his daughter. The ogre's speech to the

maiden, as he passionately embraces her, is indicative of the degree of his rapture: "Daughter, daughter of mine, part of this body, breath of my soul, who could ever have told me that with an attack of flatulence I could have given shape to such a beautiful face? Who could ever have told me that a product of a cold could ever have generated this fire of love?" The ogre's joy is paternal, but with unmistakably erotic overtones, as is further evidenced by his showering her with gifts and attentions like a lover and by his having her sleep with him, however innocently, in the same bed. An equally comic revelation of his passion is his doting concern later to protect her from the fleas she imagines are biting her in the bed. (In reality, the imagined flea bites are pinches administered by her young admirer, who has slipped into the bedroom undetected either by her or her putative father.)

In Basile's collection one also encounters examples of passion for a maiden on the part of an older married man, with indications that this passion involves aversion to his wife and that it is colored by a bachelorish misogyny for which involvement with a beautiful girl is a magical wish fulfillment. As we have seen (Chap. 3), in "Sun, Moon, and Talia" (V, 5) the king's discovery of the presumably dead maiden alone in a castle in the forest ultimately enables him to escape from his barren marriage and to experience both the delights of passionate desire and the joys of paternity. The situation in "The Dragon" (IV, 5) is far more complicated, but the result is essentially the same. Pursuant to his encounter with a magically aided virgin, a king sires a child with her and thereby is eventually provided the opportunity of ridding himself of the wife to whom he was tied in barren wedlock. In this case, however, the king has been seized by a raging misogyny that moves him to set about raping and murdering all the women of a certain city. And it is this misogynistic rampage, reminiscent of King Shariar in the *Arabian Nights*, which brings him into contact with the virgin whose beauty captivates him and puts an end to his excesses.

The explanation of the king's mad compulsion is that a wooden oracle in the shape of a dragon has advised him that the only way to regain his kingdom from the sorceress who has robbed him of it is to deprive her of her sight. Yet this explanation is singularly unconvincing because there is no evident connection, rational or otherwise, between the aim and the means. How can raping the women result in blinding the sorceress? In view of the fact that it was the king's prior display of bad temper and cruelty that caused the inhabitants of his realm to welcome his being deposed, and that the loss of his kingdom occurred while he was away with his wife on a pleasure trip to a castle in the countryside, the secret explanation for both the earlier cruelty and the subsequent rampage may be unconscious aversion to the wife. This interpretation is supported, too, by the circumstance that, while it is a fairy who holds back his arm as he is about to kill the beautiful Porziella after he has raped her, the king imagines that it was the victim's beauty that prevented him from stabbing her. Granted, his mad plan for regaining his kingdom causes him to have Porziella walled into a gable room in his castle so that she might starve to death there. But in the end, on discovering that as a result of the rape he has sired a son with her, he is happy to have his wife out of the way and to marry the beautiful victim of his earlier mania.

An intriguing instance of misogyny is depicted in the Grimms' "Fitcher's Bird" (*KHM* 46). The bachelor sorcerer is evidently in the habit of abducting young girls, either to satisfy himself that there is not a woman in the world who would not betray a man out of curiosity or, more likely, in the desperate hope that such a woman could indeed be found. The test he sets for the girls involves giving them the keys to all the rooms in his house, as he is leaving on a trip, and warning them that great misfortune will befall them should they unlock the door to a certain room. The same test is posed, of course, in Perrault's Bluebeard story, where the villain, however, appears at least equally eager to have an excuse to butcher the maidens he marries as he is to find one who can resist the temptation to betrayal out of curiosity. The Grimms' figure, Fitcher, to be sure, is also a murderer of maidens, but appears to slay them less out of perverse lust than disappointment that he has failed once again to find one who can be trusted, that is, one he could marry.

Fitcher's bachelor fixation on the female sex is suggested by his use of eggs as the means of detecting whether the virgins have been unfaithful to his command. He rests assured that the egg will drop from the girl's hand in her horror at discovering the bloody corpses should she open the door to the forbidden room. His association of eggs with women is perhaps indicated as well by his mode of abducting the girls. He magically causes them to leap into the basket he carries on his back, as though they were just such an agricultural commodity to be carried to market. Moreover, when he is finally deceived by the youngest of the three sisters, it is because she takes the precaution of leaving the egg behind when she opens the door to the forbidden room—a ruse which Fitcher might easily have suspected if the association of eggs and the female sex had not been so fixed in his mind. The youngest daughter's taunting of Fitcher at the end with the vision of herself as his bird (hence the title) suggests a recognition on her part of his fixed notion of women as egg-laying creatures. It is also a final reference to his bachelor dream of caging a rare bird, that is, a woman devoid of curiosity.

Bachelorish feelings of both the misogynistic and avuncular sort are depicted in the Grimms' collection in relationships between gnomes and maidens. As earth spirits, these dwarfs are devoted rather to pursuit of subterranean treasures than to the pleasures of the marriage bed, so much so that preoccupation with gold and jewels and with mining may be said to be an escape from, or sublimation of, the stirrings and turmoils of desire. Gnomes of the avuncular type have the role, in folktale, of a maiden's adoring, doting, and devoted admirers, as for example in "The Three Little Men in the Forest" (*KHM* 13). Three magical gnomes insure that a mistreated stepdaughter who has proven herself kind, generous, and industrious will not be disappointed in love. They bless her with daily increasing beauty, the gift of producing a gold piece from her mouth with every word she speaks, and with the good fortune that a king will come and marry her. A far more touching depiction of gnomes as avuncular rescuers is found of course in "Little Snow White" (*KHM* 53), where the dwarfs are devoted to Snow White at least as much for her beauty as for her sweetness and domestic virtue. The dwarfs' devotion is a particular tribute, insofar as gnomes, by tradition, are imagined to be misogynistic.[8] Yet Snow White's dwarfs do remain true to their gnomic character. Though they are not indifferent to her erotic appeal, they are not the least bit inclined to attempt to enter upon the role of lover. They are content to be at once the object of her maternal devotion, as though they were her children, and her avuncular guardians as well. They wish only to enjoy her charming presence as their maiden housekeeper and the cherished adornment of their bachelor household.

A depiction of the darker side of gnomic cohabitation with a maiden is also found in the Grimms' collection. The gnomic lover may prove greedily possessive despite, or precisely because of, his disinterest in the pleasures of the bed. Thus, in "Old Rinkrank" (*KHM* 196) a maiden is forced, on pain of death, to become the housekeeper of an old man with a very long gray beard who lives beneath a glass mountain. That the old man is a gnome is suggested by his devotion to gold and silver. Every morning he goes off to work and returns each evening with a pile of the precious metals. His effectual imprisonment of the maiden reveals his gnomish character as a lover. He wants to have her as his housekeeper, and perhaps to enjoy the pleasure of her charming company, but he does not appear to want her as a spouse or concubine. As his prisoner, however, she is prevented from being united with her lover, which is surely a source of satisfaction to Old Rinkrank's greedy, gnomish heart. In particular, he appears to want to steal her maidenhood, as it were, by pretending that she is not eligible for marriage, since he takes special delight in calling her Frau Mansrot, as though she were a widow or beyond marriageable age.

While Old Rinkrank seems the type of the misogynistic old bachelor, the dwarf in "Snow-White and Rose-Red" (*KHM* 161) displays a regressive, boyish misogyny. He shuns the company of women altogether, and shows a special aversion to blossoming maidens. He is enraged by the necessity of his repeated rescue by the charming sisters Snow-White and Rose-Red; and he desires nothing more than to be left alone to admire his evidently ill-gotten treasure of jewels. When he finds himself in danger of being eaten by a bear, he is delighted to have the opportunity to offer the bear these "tender morsels, fat like young quail" in hopes that the beast will devour the girls instead.

If the dwarf's role is viewed another way, as either a projection of the prince's possible subterranean guilt about an element of greedy lust in his attraction to the girls (the dwarf's gnomish obsession with jewels) or a representation of the sisters' fantasies about misogynist reactions to their charms, then the prince's transformation and eventual restoration to human form appear in a different light. He has been constrained to show himself to the sisters in the form of an avuncular bear in order to suppress the gnomish urges within himself. With the arrival of springtime he has had to depart, out of fear that the stirrings of greedy desire within him will get the upper hand. As he darkly explains to the girls: "I have to go into the forest and protect my treasures from the evil dwarfs. In the winter, when the ground is frozen solid, they must assuredly remain below and can't work their way out, but now, when the sun has thawed and warmed up the earth, they break through, climb up, search, and steal; whatever once has gotten into their hands and lies in their caves never comes easily again into the light of day." When the bear reenters the girls' lives some weeks or months later, his reappearance comes at the fateful moment when they have encountered the dwarf in the forest a fourth time, now as he has just emptied a sack of jewels on the ground. That is to say, Snow-White and Rose-Red have come upon him as he is about to give himself over to the pleasures of lustful greed which, according to traditional lore about earth spirits, serves in place of desire and renders gnomes resistant to the obligations of marriage, especially intercourse. That this role of greed as a sublimation of desire is involved here is indicated perhaps by the dwarf's attempt to save himself by offering the bear the precious stones and the girls to boot: "Dear Sir Bear, spare me; I will give you all of my treasures; behold the beautiful jewels that are lying there. Spare my life; what good to you is a slim little fellow like me? You wouldn't even feel me between your teeth! There, grab the two wicked girls; they are nice delicate morsels for you, plump like young quail; eat *them,* for God's sake." The bear, of course, slays the dwarf instead. When the two sisters, who had run off in terror, halt upon recognizing the bear's voice as he calls to them and after he has managed to catch up with them, his bear-hide suddenly falls away. He stands before them as a handsome man dressed completely in gold.

The implication is perhaps that the prince not only has remained inwardly a man but that the "transformation" was hardly more than a disguise—one that may be discarded as soon as the prince has discovered, defeated, and slain the "gnome" within himself, that is, the ambivalently misogynous and lustful bachelor or little boy within him.

By far the most puzzling of the gnomes in the Grimms' collection is the dwarf in "Rumpelstiltskin" (*KHM* 55). He neither shuns the company of pretty maidens, like his counterpart in "Snow-White and Rose-Red," nor does he display a bachelor desire to have a pretty girl around his household, like Old Rinkrank. What Rumpelstiltskin proves to want, in the end, is a child. In particular, he covets the firstborn of the beautiful miller's daughter whom he has helped to avoid being slain and thereby aided in winning marriage to a king.[9] It remains unclear, though, just why the dwarf wants the child. Is he an ogre, who lusts after the tender flesh of a newborn infant? Or does he yearn, like the hag in "Rapunzel" (*KHM* 12), to acquire a child so that he may raise it and greedily appropriate its devotion entirely for himself? The latter possibility may be the more likely, for Rumpelstiltskin's approach to the miller's daughter somewhat resembles that of a suitor, albeit one of the childish, regressive type.

As Rumpelstiltskin bargains with the girl for his magical services in spinning flax into gold for her, he acts as though he were engaged in a game of forfeits or in extorting gifts from an older sister in exchange for doing her a favor. The erotic element in this game is indicated by the series of presents she accords him, each of which has symbolic import with regard to love and marriage. The first evening she offers him her necklace, an intimate part of a woman's attire of the sort to be especially coveted as a token of romantic favor. The second evening she pays him with a ring from her finger, which under other circumstances might serve as a token of engagement to marry. The third evening, it may be said, she indirectly offers him her body, as a bride does on the wedding night, when she exclaims that she has nothing left to give. Rumpelstiltskin, at least, is thinking of her body at this point, and in sexual terms, for he immediately demands that she give him her first child. Were he a lecher, or the type of the oversexed dwarf, he might indeed have asked for her body. The point, however, appears to be that, on the contrary, his desire is to become a father, without having to be a lover, much as a little boy might dream of becoming a parent, yet abhor the thought of doing what is required to achieve that end as nature dictates. Even if Rumpelstiltskin wants the child only to devour it, the fact that it will be the child of the miller's daughter appears to be important to him. Thus, his ogreish passion, too, would involve a perverse lust to possess flesh of her flesh.[10]

A final puzzle concerning Rumpelstiltskin's behavior with the miller's daughter is his subsequent offer, once the child has been born, to let her out of her part of the bargain if she can discover what his name is.[11] Perhaps he is only toying with her feelings, out of malevolent desire to witness her despair as she struggles to fulfill what he surely considers to be an impossible condition. Yet he is described as having been moved by compassion to offer her this chance. Thus, he may secretly wish, however ambivalently, that she will succeed after all. His challenge to her, in any case, is childish and is, at the same time, one that under other circumstances might be posed by a lover, as part of the mating game—just as the original bargaining had this same ambiguous character. Similarly, Rumpelstiltskin's infantile and suicidal rage over his subsequent loss of the game is partly that of a little boy who has been bested by a girl and partly that of a jealous lover who, though he did not covet a maiden's body, greedily yearned to possess the fruit of her womb. Thus, when Rumpelstiltskin shears himself in two, as he struggles to pull himself out of the hole he has dug for himself by childishly stamping his foot on the ground, one may be reminded again of his ambiguous physical appearance as half-man, half-boy and the emotional ambivalence about the male sexual role that appears to go with it.[12]

Our survey of the leading male roles in fairy tale romance has suggested that, unlike the fetching maidens and true brides, the men rarely exhibit forthright, or at least uncomplicated, desire for a woman. In this, they are more akin to the heroines in the tales of beauties and beasts, for whom the passage to sexual adulthood is attended by magical adventures that obscure the nature of the actual crisis at hand. At the same time, in contrast to the type of the haughty virgin, the bridegrooms and bachelors as central figures in the stories of the Grimms, Basile, and Perrault are not shown as attempting to sidestep the issue "to marry or not to marry" by declaring that they do not wish to or cannot find a bride who is sufficiently appealing. The reason for these differences may be that while maidens traditionally were supposed to experience reluctance to surrender their virginity, youths were expected to make this transition without trepidation, or any conflicting emotions, regrets, or second thoughts whatsoever. The type of the male sexual coward was—and perhaps still is—so unacceptable that it could not be portrayed directly at all, but only suggested in a veiled, indirect manner. Our study, though, has indicated that male flight from desire, as a ludicrous but sublimely comical subject, does indeed represent an object of depiction in certain fairy tales.

Already in the first chapter, "Brothers and Sisters," it emerged that devotion to a sibling of opposite sex, when it came time to marry, proved problematic not only in the case of the sister but for the brothers as well.

Indeed, while the sister married, the brothers typically did not. Moreover, the brothers appeared to welcome the sister's marriage, as is strikingly evident in those stories where the brother has the role of matchmaker, procuring a husband for the sister. In these stories, the brother's devotion—even attraction—to the sister seemed to be the main thing. Yet while the sister's love of the brothers might have prevented her from marrying, except that marrying enabled her to avoid losing the brothers' company, the brothers' devotion to the sister can be seen as hinting at a flight from desire, since it avoids direct confrontation of the issue of passage to sexual manhood and marriage. Living happily ever after for these young men typically means settling down to bachelorhood in the household of the married sister.

For the young men who do marry, as we have seen, the union rarely fails to be attended by a crisis arising from some form of magical intervention. In "The Water-Nymph in the Pond," this intervention comes after, not before, the marriage and consummation of the union, but results from a bargain struck by the hero's father at the time of the hero's birth, and thus because of the "magical star" under which he was born, so to speak. In "The Frog King," the prince was transformed even before he became attracted to the princess, and indeed is restored to human form as soon as he hits the wedding bed; but here, too, the magic may suggest an adolescent crisis about entering sexual manhood. There is something almost magical, as well, about the youth's obsession with wanting to experience a shudder in the "Tale of One Who Went Off to Learn Fear," an obsession that, while it does not prevent him from marrying, stands in the way of his fulfilling his husbandly role. Like the Frog King, the youth in "The Little Donkey" makes it to the wedding bed, but tries to escape when he discovers that he has been robbed of his premarital identity as a jackass. Other suitors, like the hero in "The Two Royal Children," set about hunting beasts of prey, but as a result of magical encounters find themselves courting women instead. Or courting a woman happens because of a pact with the devil, as in "The King of the Golden Mountain," or because the hero is courted himself by women with magical powers, as in "Beloved Roland" and more especially "The Poor Miller's Boy and the Cat," "The Raven," "The Drummer," and Basile's "The Three Citrons."

Contrary to the stereotype of the passive heroine but active hero, the heroes of fairy tale romance discussed here appear if anything less aggressive and forceful than their female counterparts. The heroines in these stories, indeed, come close to fitting the feminist ideal of the active woman in control of her destiny and possessed of symbolic supernatural powers. The heroines' object, though, remains that of the fetching maidens: to win a man; and the heroes' relative passivity suggests that in the type of story with the bridegroom as central figure, at least, the hero is the pursued, not the pursuer, and that he furthermore harbors some ambivalence or hesitation about entering that role. One way or another, Venus's power triumphs in the end, as the genre of romance requires; and Venus was, after all, a woman, the goddess, not the god, of love. The heroines of romance being daughters of Venus, the young men must willy-nilly succumb to their very considerable natural charms or, failing that, to the magical charms employed on the heroines' behalf.

As we have seen, some fairy tale heroes, to be sure, do not make it to the altar, despite encounters with potential brides. This was the case in "The Three Black Princesses" and "Clever Hans"; but those two stories cannot otherwise be said to belong to fairy tale romance either. As the stories about brothers and sisters showed, in tales about love and marriage the young men who do not marry are usually third parties who, if anything, only vicariously participate in marital bliss. In those stories, the brother's devotion to the sister and the taboo against incest provide the reason for the young men's willingness not to marry. For young bachelors in other fairy tale romances, this willingness is implicitly explained by devotion to a brother, as opposed to a sister, or to a friend. It is the case—as was said traditionally in early modern Europe—of 'friendship' as opposed to 'love', that is, devotion between members of the same rather than the opposite sex. Thus, in Basile's "The Raven" it is the suitor's brother, not the bridegroom himself, who experiences the magical adventures attendant upon the approach of matrimony; and in Basile's "Merchant's Two Sons" and "The Charmed Hind," as well as in the Grimms' "Children of Gold" and "The Two Brothers," the brother or friend, by putting himself in the bridegroom's place in the marriage bed, saves him from a magical predicament that befell him pursuant to the wedding night. Meanwhile, the hero in "Ferdinand the Faithful and Ferdinand the Unfaithful" takes refuge from his marriage to a sorceress by turning to his horse, who then turns into a friend, through magical recovery of his erstwhile human form.

As we observed in connection with the fairy tales of love and marriage that depict the relationship between fathers and daughters, the traditional role for the older men in the *commedia dell'arte* was that of lecherous and foolish pursuers of young women—maidens who were most often their daughters, nieces, or wards. In fairy tale, as we have seen, there are also examples of older bachelors as rather the opposite, as sexual cowards content only to identify vicariously with the role of lover. The old valet in "Faithful John" experiences a magical crisis in connection with his young master's entry upon the role of bridegroom. In "The House in the Woods," a handsome youth disguised as an elderly recluse lures girls to his forest hut to test their compassion, not their desire, apparently out of misogynistic anxiety. In "The Goose Girl" and Basile's "Viola," we likewise have the case of the older man taking in a sweet young maiden as surrogate daughter, not as lover. Other older men of this type, however, display their misogynistic anxiety more aggressively, like the king in Basile's "The Dragon," who finds irrational pretext for raping women and then murdering them, until the joy of fatherhood over the son he sired with a magical beauty puts an end to his mania; or the bachelor butchers in the Bluebeard story and in "Fitcher's Bird." Finally, we remember the dwarfs and gnomes, who vicariously play the role of admirer or spouse of a young maiden—avuncularly in "The Three Little Men in the Forest" and "Little Snow White," misogynistically in "Snow-White and Rose-Red," sinisterly in "Old Rinkrank," and enigmatically in "Rumpelstiltskin." This type of the vicarious gnomish lover appears to have been of special interest to the bachelorish Grimm brothers—Jacob never married, Wilhelm only relatively late. Their bachelorism, and especially their closeness as siblings, may also explain an apparent predilection for tales about an unmarried brother's or friend's involvement in his brother's marriage—such as Basile's "Raven" and their version of it as "Faithful John," Basile's "Merchant's Two Sons" and their "The Children of the Gold," Basile's "Charmed Hind" and their "The Two Brothers"—as well as their liking for the tales about devotion between brothers and sisters with which this study opened.

NOTES

1. A psychological approach to interpreting the frequently encountered role of the youngest sibling in various types of folktales was taken by Marianne Handschin-Ninck, "Ältester und Jüngster im Märchen," *Praxis der Kinderpsychologie und Kinderpsychiatrie*, 5 (1956), 167–73.

2. Bruno Jöckel interpreted the cure in "Märchen von einem, der auszog, das Fürchten zu lernen" as more directly related to sexuality: "so that he will for the first time experience his nakedness, that is, his sexuality, most profoundly, the young wife is to pull the covers off of her slumbering husband. When he then feels the fish, the emblem of the male reproductive role, and the water, symbol of the female, pressing in on him, the spell is finally broken"; see *Der Weg zum Märchen*, p. 76. G. Zillinger saw the tale as depicting the process of coming of age sexually and emotionally, and learning to love; see "Zur Frage der Angst und der Darstellung psychosexueller Reifungsstufen im 'Märchen vom Gruseln': Eine analytische Studie," *Praxis der Kinderpsychologie und Kinderpsychiatrie*, 12, nos. 2–4 (1963), 33–41, 107–12, 134–43. Like Zillinger, C. H. Mallet found certain scenes in the story to be symbolic of autoeroticism and masturbation, as a stage in the development toward sexual maturity and achievement of the capacity to love; see "Die zweite und dritte Nacht im Märchen 'Das Gruseln,'" *Praxis der Kinderpsychologie und Kinderpsychiatrie*, 14 (1965), 216–20. And Bruno Bettelheim commented,

"Whether or not the hearer of this story recognizes that it was sexual anxiety that led to the hero's inability to shudder, that which finally makes him shudder suggests the irrational nature of some of our most pervasive anxieties. Because it is a fear of which only his wife is able to cure him at night in bed, this is a sufficient hint of the underlying nature of the anxiety"; see *Uses of Enchantment*, p. 281.

Heinz Rölleke, however, viewed the youth's quest to learn to know fear as a process of learning to fear death; see "Märchen von einem, der auszog, das Fürchten zu lernen: Zu Überlieferung und Bedeutung des KHM 4," *Fabula*, 20 (1979), 193–204.

3. In a published version of the tale of Clever Hans from 1557, to which the Grimms refer in their notes, the mother is a rich widow with an only son. The youth, on spying a pretty young lady, begs the mother to get her for him to wife. The mother attempts to instruct him about how to court the girl. In this version, the youth is indeed purely the simpleton whose stupidity prevents him from getting the bride of his dreams. To be sure, he is a mother's boy in this version, too, but one who at least thinks he wants to marry. See Jacob Grimm and Wilhelm Grimm, *Kinder- und Hausmärchen*, ed. Rölleke, III, 60–63; and cf. Bolte and Polívka, *Anmerkungen zu den Kinder- und Hausmärchen*, I, 312–14.

4. The Grimms refer in their notes to a version of the Faithful John story in which the young man in love is Roland, the adopted son of a king, and the loyal friend is Joseph, the king's own son. In the scene on the ship, there are no birds; Joseph simply hears a voice tell of the three tasks that a faithful friend would have to perform to save the bridegroom: cut off the head of the horse when Roland is about to mount it; smash the glass with which he is about to toast his bride; and decapitate a seven-headed monster when it sticks one of its heads into the bridal chamber through a window. In this version it is the king, Joseph's father, who accuses him regarding his presumed disloyalty to the bridegroom—the accusation that leads then to the faithful friend's being turned to stone. And here the bride has a dream about how Joseph can be redeemed by being smeared with the blood of the son to whom she has just given birth. After Joseph's redemption, he takes the child's corpse with him on a successful quest to find the magical means to restore it to life. This version has in common with those used by Basile and by the Grimms that the three perils have to do with the young man's role as bridegroom, and that the perils are envisioned by his devoted bachelor friend. See Jacob Grimm and Wilhelm Grimm, *Kinder- und Hausmärchen*, ed. Rölleke, III, 16–19; and cf. Bolte and Polívka, *Anmerkungen zu den Kinder- und Hausmärchen*, I, 43–45.

For an investigation of certain narrative possibilities exploited by several oral tellers of this type of story, see Max Lüthi, "Von der Freiheit der Erzähler: Anmerkungen zu einigen Versionen des 'Treuen Johannes,' " in W. van Nespen, ed., *Miscellanea Prof. Em. Dr. K. C. Peeters: Door Vrienden en Collega's hem aangeboden ter gelegenheid van zijn emeritaat* (Antwerp: Govaerts, 1975), pp. 458–72. A folkloristic study of the type was done by Erich Rösch, *Der getreue Johannes: Eine vergleichende*

Märchenstudie, Folklore Fellows' Communications, 77 (Helsinki: Suomalainen Tiedeakatemia/Academia scientificarum fennica, 1928).

5. A study of the folktale motif of a youth's sacrifice for his brother, including the placing of a sword between himself and the brother's bride in bed, was done by Heino Gehrts, *Das Märchen und das Opfer: Untersuchungen zum europäischen Brüdermärchen* (Bonn: Bouvier, 1967). More reliable, however, is the earlier, standard study of this type by Kurt Ranke, *Die zwei Brüder: Eine Studie zur vergleichenden Märchenforschung,* Folklore Fellows' Communications, 114 (Helsinki: Suomalainen Tiedeakatemia/Academia scientificarum fennica, 1934).

The Grimms were acquainted with the motif of the magical conception not only because of their familiarity with Basile's stories but also from German versions that had come to their attention. In their first edition (1812), they included as No. 74 the tale "Johannes Wassersprung und Caspar Wassersprung." The names of the two title roles refer to the boys' having been conceived, as twins, by the daughter of a king who, having sworn that the princess shall never marry, banishes her to a lonely forest where she drinks from a spring. And in their notes, the Grimms also refer to a version in which a king has a daughter who is pursued by mice. Not knowing how to protect her otherwise, he has a tower built for her in the middle of a large river. But in this version, too, the procreative urge achieves its goal nonetheless. One day as the princess and her servant girl are sitting in the tower, alone as usual, a stream of water leaps in through the window. After the two of them have caught some of the water in a vessel and drunk from it, they both give birth to sons, whom they name Water-Peter and Water-Paul (*Wasserpeter* and *Wasserpaul*). See Bolte and Polívka, *Anmerkungen zu den Kinder- und Hausmärchen,* I, 529–33; and cf. Jacob Grimm and Wilhelm Grimm, *Kinder- und Hausmärchen,* ed. Rölleke, III, 105.

6. Ruth Bottigheimer, too, has voiced the suspicion that sexual passion is behind the queen's murder of her husband: "The queen takes the most direct route to eradicate the difficulties obstructing her union with the handsome man who saves her, and whom she fancies because her own husband, the king, has no nose. . . . The king is missing something important, perhaps central [i.e., potency], and the Queen can't say what it is"; see Bottigheimer, *Grimms' Bad Girls and Bold Boys,* p. 160.

7. Bottigheimer has seen the enchanted prince as, on the contrary, eager for the sexual attentions of young maidens: "What is raised in high relief here is the [first] girl's ignoring the old man, offending him because she has not waited for him, an insult that has nothing at all to do with the reason stated later for her imprisonment and subsequent punishment, that is, her lack of attention and compassion for his three animals. . . . the tale's sexuality shimmers palely and unmistakably through the veil behind which the unsatisfactory girls have been dumped"; see Bottigheimer, *Grimms' Bad Girls and Bold Boys,* pp. 160–61.

8. In their notes, the Grimms refer to a version of the Snow White story in which the girl's stepmother brings her to a cave in the forest where seven dwarfs live. These dwarfs, as the envious older woman knows, kill every girl who comes near them. They find the girl so beautiful, however, that they do not slay her; and the wicked stepmother's plan thereby is foiled. See Jacob Grimm and Wilhelm Grimm, *Kinder- und Hausmärchen*, ed. Rölleke, III, 87–90; and cf. Bolte and Polívka, *Anmerkungen zu den Kinder- und Hausmärchen*, I, 450–52.

9. In the Grimms' quite different version of the Rumpelstiltskin story in the manuscript of 1810, the dwarf's bargain is from the start that he will see to it that the girl marries a prince, in exchange for her giving him the firstborn child of that union. Here the girl's problem apparently is that she is ripe for marriage and dreams of wedding a prince, as symbolized by her inability to spin anything but gold. The dwarf does not do anything about the spinning problem itself. He simply promises to help her out of all of her difficulties; and what is needed for that, evidently, is just to marry a prince. The dwarf's problem, meanwhile, appears to be that he would like to have a child, but wants, needs, or must have someone else to sire it. In this version, the dwarf's excited anticipation of receiving the child expresses itself through his riding around his fire on a cooking spoon, much as witches are imagined to ride on broomsticks. When he learns that the princess has discovered his name, he does not tear himself apart but rides off through the window on the cooking spoon. The dwarf's riding on the magical spoon as though it were a hobbyhorse may suggest that he is still a little boy at heart, or impotent, or both. See Rölleke, *Die älteste Märchensammlung*, pp. 238–43.

10. Gonthier-Louis Fink observed that the symbolism of the forfeits the miller's daughter makes suggests that the sprite is after her body. Fink considers this element to have been introduced into the tale by the Grimms, but points also to the eroticism in the scene between the girl and the demon in some popular French versions of the story. See "Les avatars de Rumpelstilzchen: La Vie d'un Conte Populaire," in Ernst Kracht, ed., *Deutsch-französische Gespräche im Lichte der Märchen*, Schriften der Gesellschaft zur Pflege des Märchengutes der europäischen Völker, 2 (Münster: Aschendorff, 1964), pp. 46–72. Lutz Röhrich's view is that "Rumpelstilzchen longs for a human child just like the dwarfs in legends who foist their own ugly children upon humans as changlings and steal human children for themselves." He notes as well, though, that "In many variants Rumpelstilzchen does not demand the child, but the girl herself; and this too accords with central motifs found already in medieval dwarf legends: dwarfs abduct human women in order to enter a union with them"; see "Rumpelstilzchen: Vom Methodenpluralismus in der Erzählforschung," in Lutz Röhrich, *Sage und Märchen: Erzählforschung heute* (Freiburg im Breisgau: Herder, 1976), pp. 272–91.

11. For an older anthropological discussion of the belief that to know someone's name is to have power over him body and soul, with reference to the Rumpelstiltskin story, see Edward Clodd, "The Philosophy of Rumpelstiltskin," *Folk-Lore Journal*,

7 (1889), 135–63, and his *Tom Tit Tot: An Essay on Savage Philosophy in Folktale* (London: Duckworth, 1898; reprint, 1968). Fink, in "Les avatars de Rumpelstilzchen," sees the tale as belonging originally to the type of the stupid devil stories, especially as regards the exorcising of the devil through addressing him by name. In these stories, the devil's aid is accepted, but he is then cheated of his reward. As Röhrich noted, "The special condition for being freed from the contract . . . belongs to nearly all stories about pacts with the devil." Röhrich judges that the tale combines elements of the dwarf legends and the devil stories: "The connection between dwarf and devil must have been made relatively early. To be sure, one associates with the name 'Rumpelstilzchen' first of all the notion of a *Rumpelgeist,* a poltergeist, a goblin, that is, of a dwarf-like creature. Yet wherever a Martin Luther or Johannes Fischart [i.e., German authors of the sixteenth century] speak of a 'Rumpelgeist' they always already mean the devil." See "Rumpelstilzchen: Vom Methodenpluralismus in der Erzählforschung," pp. 290–91. Otto Kahn, meanwhile, argued—most speculatively—that the Rumpelstiltskin figure was originally a member of a prehistoric indigenous population in Europe; that his goal, as in some versions of the story, was to marry the girl in order to improve his social and legal status, in view of his membership in that repressed group; and that the girl is not bound by her promise if she finds out his name because she would then recognize that she had no legal or moral obligation to him since he is of that shunned indigenous population; see "Rumpelstilz hat wirklich gelebt: Textvergleichende Studie über das Märchen vom Rumpelstilzchen (AaTh 500) und eine Erklärung mit Hilfe der Rechtgeschichte: Ein Versuch," *Rheinisches Jahrbuch für Volkskunde,* 17/18 (1966–67), 143–84.

12. For an essentially structural approach to the story, see Max Lüthi, "Rumpelstilzchen: Thematik, Struktur und Stiltendenzen innerhalb eines Märchentypus," *Antaios,* 12 (1971), 419–36.

Conclusion

Our visit to the realm of fairy tale romance, as it exists in the collections of the Grimms, Basile, and Perrault, has shown that the authors of these literary stories—whoever they may have been—engaged in celebrating the experience of erotic desire and its effects. As we have seen, these sublimely humorous, gently ironic tributes to Venus's power tend to avoid direct description or portrayal of sexual passion. It must therefore even remain a matter of some doubt whether desire and the characters' reactions to it are indeed the veiled subject of many of these stories. Discussion of a rather large number of tales from these three collections, however, indicates not only that fairy tale romance definitely existed as a genre in the literary folktale but that its focus on desire and its effects was quite well understood by the authors of these versions themselves.

We return to literary classics to be enlightened through acquiring insight into human affairs or to be entertained with features of life long since familiar. Popular literature necessarily tends toward the latter. Little of what is depicted in fairy tale romance is wholly new to us, if it is unfamiliar at all. Only the mode of portrayal is novel, in its indirect depiction through the use of wonder and magic. The literary folktale shares with myth the function of providing a form of shorthand for describing well-known modes of human behavior. The gods of the Greek myths represent certain familiar human types, whose character is reflected especially through the situations in which they typically find themselves. And situations involving erotic passion are particularly common. Zeus is the philandering older man, ever conceiving a passion for a pretty woman, particularly sweet young things. Artemis is the maiden whose devotion to chastity only renders her more appealing. And Aphrodite is the irresistible beauty with a compelling urge to promiscuity. In the Greek myths, though, there is no mystery as to the sexual passions being depicted, whereas in fairy tale romance, especially as it came to be embodied in the Grimms' collection, these emotions tend to be relatively hidden and represented symbolically.

The stories about brothers and sisters remind us that special emotional bonds may exist between siblings, and that when the children are of opposite sex a crisis of incestuous desire may occur as marriageable age approaches. Devotion between siblings is encouraged, of course; but we view sexual involvement between brothers and sisters with horror. Fairy tale romance appears to have an especially strong tradition of depicting love between brothers and sisters, including symbolic allusion to the specter of illicit passion, as a threat to these relationships. Our revulsion at the thought of incestuous desire between siblings helps explain why Hansel and Gretel, not the siblings from some less innocent tale of this type, have become proverbial models of sibling devotion.

The folktales about beauties and beasts suggest a recognition that our sexual excitement may involve the feeling or fantasy that there is something animal about desire. The stories with animal suitors recall for us this aspect of sexual passion. We sympathize with the girl's fright or revulsion at the thought of going to bed with a beast; or—more often—we are amazed at her equanimity about entering the bridal chamber with an animal. In either case, the point remains that thinking of one's lover as a beast, or as beastly, may make the encounter all the more exciting. Not surprisingly, though, for us the proverbial fairy tale maiden confronted by a beast is not one of those with an actual animal suitor but Red Riding Hood, whose emotional situation is much more innocent in view of her tender age.

Fathers should love their daughters, we believe; and they understandably hope, as parents, that the daughters will marry and present them with grandchildren. The role of fathers in folktale, though, often goes beyond this legitimate paternal concern. Sometimes there is an unseemly involvement in the bride's choice of a husband or the reverse, a course of action undertaken for whatever reason that effectively prevents the daughter from falling in love or marrying. That is to say, fairy tale romance generally supports the traditional wisdom that fathers are sweet on their daughters, and shows indeed that this passion may grow to the point of incestuous desire. It is a mark of our abhorrence of any hint of such passion that no proverbial figure has emerged from this type of story. One does not, for example, call a girl whose father madly adores her an "Allerleirauh" or "Donkey-Skin," even if only in jest.

Older women generally, and mothers in particular, should help young girls understand what it is like to grow up as a woman. Fairy tale romance takes account of this ideal, but also of an almost inevitable identification with these blossoming maidens on the part of the older women. This identification may be positive, in the sense that the older woman relives the joys of young love through helping the girl to become a bride. As often as not, though, the identification is such that the older woman envies the girl her youth and beauty. The stories of hags and maidens, unlike those of brothers and sisters, beauties and beasts, and fathers and daughters, do not raise the specter of incest or bestiality. This may explain why two figures from these tales have become almost proverbial: Snow White's stepmother, as the ragingly envious older woman, and Rapunzel, as the prisoner of a jealously possessive hag.

Prospective brides and young wives have traditionally been expected to employ subtle arts in seeking to attract or keep a husband. Fairy tale romance very much reflects this ancient wisdom, yet equally delights in violating it. The heroines' modesty may prevent them from pursuing a prospective or wayward lover, but they are just as likely to contrive to get into his bedroom. Our resistance to the idea of aggressive pursuit of men by women may be reflected in our preference for the proverbial passive beloved, a Sleeping Beauty instead of an Allerleirauh, and in our failure to see Cinderella as a maiden engaged in skillfully fetching herself a prince.

Finally, the bachelor and bridegroom tales, as a group, have understandably failed, like those about fathers and daughters, to contribute any of the fairy tale figures that have become proverbial. This type of character is particularly foreign to our view of what is right and proper. Love may be everything for a woman, proverbially, and for a man a thing apart; but this is not to say that men are supposed to have any difficulty conceiving a passion for a woman or surrendering to desire. Today, if a young man refrains from involvement with women it is thought that his sexual preference must be for homosexual love. But in earlier centuries the matter was often put and viewed differently. There was much talk—among men— that a man had to choose between love, defined as sexual relations with a woman, and friendship, as a platonic relationship with another man. Bachelorism, as abstinence from sexual relations of any sort, was not an uncommon choice. While fairy tale heroes do mostly display great eagerness to enter the role of bridegroom and husband, there are yet occasional indications that some of them are inwardly on the run from desire. Small wonder, of course, that the type of the Prince Charming has become proverbial, and that no such status has been accorded fairy tale's cowardly bachelors. Indeed, when we speak of Rumpelstiltskin, we do not worry ourselves much about his curious desire for a child, but rejoice instead that the heroine manages to cheat him at his devilish game.

Assuming that we have managed here to identify and characterize a genre that may be called fairy tale romance, together with the spirit that animates it, are such stories typical of folktale as it exists outside literary collections like those of the Grimms, Basile, and Perrault? In other words, how prevalent is fairy tale romance in oral tradition? The answer to that question will have to be provided by folklorists. They have not yet shown much interest in focusing on tales of love and desire as a special type. We should like to know to what extent, in oral tradition, brothers and sisters are depicted as being devoted, and especially to a degree beyond what is considered proper. Do stories about animal bridegrooms carry hints that this—universally popular—situation is an ironic representation of an element in erotic fantasy? Do fathers tend to get overinvolved in the love lives of their nubile daughters? Do older women take a special interest, for better or for worse, in young maidens' dreams of love? Are young women in love often depicted as exceedingly modest or wondrously bold in their pursuit of a mate? And do the stories tell of bachelors, young or old, who may be suspected, however slightly, of having an aversion to sexual involvement with women, or who show a reluctance to sacrifice devotion to a friend or brother for love of a woman? In short, do folktales in oral tradition, like the literary collections discussed here, celebrate the power of desire and its effects?

As we have seen, there is little mystery about the erotic element in Basile's magical tales of love and marriage. His stories are far closer to the Boccaccian tradition of storytelling than are those of the Grimms two centuries later in a northern, puritanical, middle-class culture. One critic has recently called attention to this aspect of older narrative tradition and its relation to the Grimms' collection: "Easy eroticism, jocular sex, domestic trickery, and adultery run through the traditional European collections of tales of which the Grimms' tales form a part. Boccaccio's saucy maids and randy lads speak openly of sexual attraction and escapades, explicitly praising the pleasures of love, and in Chaucer's *Canterbury Tales* the stories run from the nun's priest's delicately phrased allusions to carnal pleasure in the miller's lewd and vulgar tavern stories. Straparola's naughty storytellers titillate their listeners with risqué double-entendres in the 'enigma' that closes each tale."[1] Another recent study likewise comments on the Grimms' own censorship of the erotic element in the stories as they had them from their sources:

> Sex and violence: these are the major thematic concerns of tales in the Grimms' collection, at least in their unedited form. . . . When it came to passages colored by sexual details or to plots based on Oedipal conflicts, Wilhelm Grimm exhibited extraordinary editorial zeal. Over the years, he systematically purged the collection of references to sexuality and masked depictions of incestuous desire. But lurid portrayals of child abuse, starvation, and exposure, like fastidious descriptions of cruel punishments, on the whole escaped censorship. The facts of life seemed to have been more disturbing to the Grimms than the harsh realities of life.[2]

Thus, the invisibility of the erotic aspect of love in the Grimms' stories is owing both to its relative absence already in their immediate eighteenth-

and nineteenth-century German sources and additionally to their own editorial censorship.

Attention has been called to the role of a process of "filtering" in eliminating such elements as eroticism. This critic outlines the process as follows, starting with the Grimms and working back through the contributors to the latters' sources:

> First of all, the Grimms were from the beginning only interested in texts that were well told, artistically appealing, and free of obscenity and class hatred. Therefore, they necessarily came into contact only with contributors who were eloquent, educated, and familiar with the extremely artistic French literary tradition.
>
> Second, these contributors, for their part, passed on to the Grimms only those texts that they considered appropriate in view of the brothers' criteria.
>
> Third, the servants, carters, and so on who confided their texts to the Grimms' contributors were undoubtedly very careful not to present to their masters texts that were obscene or expressed class hatred or resentment.[3]

The Grimms then submitted the tales to further editing, and typically also to some revision—major or minor—in the subsequent editions during their lifetime.

Despite so much "filtering" and downright censorship of the erotic, not only by the Grimms but already in most of their sources, we have seen that one still can speak of an erotic element in the tales of love and marriage in their collection. As was already happening in Perrault's late seventeenth-century French collection, the erotic element in its earthier aspects has gone underground, become veiled or only implicit, or has been romanticized or sublimated. By and large, the Grimms simply adapted the erotic elements to the literary tastes of their age, thereby lending mystery to the magical tales of love and marriage, as was being done in similar ways by those of their German Romantic contemporaries who invented their own stories. Where erotic love is depicted in German Romantic tales, it is almost always rendered ambiguous through its association with magic, thereby suggesting involvement of mysterious spiritual forces.

Knowing just how the Grimms themselves preferred to have erotic love depicted would be important for understanding the direction of the changes they made in the fairy tale romances they had from their sources. Unfortunately, in this we are almost wholly dependent on our knowledge of those changes themselves. There are, however, at least two possible exceptions.

As has recently been discovered, there is reason to believe that the part of the story "Snow-White and Rose-Red" that is about love and marriage may have been invented by Wilhelm Grimm.[4] That part tells of the tender relationship between a young prince, disguised as a bear, and two young maidens, and of the girls' marriage at the end to the prince and his brother. Thus, as we already noted in "Beauties and Beasts" (Chap. 2), the part presumably added by Wilhelm Grimm is modeled on the type of the animal groom. But whereas the traditional tale of this type has the suitor shed his animal disguise in the bedroom on the wedding night, the bear in "Snow-White and Rose-Red" is less suggestively restored to human form in the forest, and in broad daylight; and unlike the Beast with Beauty in that tale, this happens before, not after, he proposes marriage to the girls. Moreover, whereas the animal groom typically discloses his desire to wed the girl immediately upon meeting her, if not before, or at least makes no secret of it, the Grimms' bear adopts instead the role of avuncular family friend and wins the girls' devotion by romping with them in their widowed mother's living room. In other words, except for his bear costume—which is so thin a disguise that it tears on a doorknob—the suitor behaves for all the world like an eligible bachelor of the Grimms' own Biedermeier time, class, and culture.

In our second example of Wilhelm Grimm as putative author of a fairy tale, he shows himself similarly inclined to depict tender devotion between a young girl and an older man in the role of avuncular friend and protector. This tale is contained in a letter that he wrote in 1816 to a certain "Dear Mili"—presumably a young girl (Wilhelm Grimm was about thirty at the time, and not yet married). Attention was called to the letter's existence by a front-page article in the *New York Times* of 28 September 1983.[5] The *Times* reporter summarized the tale as follows:

> The story tells of a mother who sends her daughter into the woods to save her from impending war. The unnamed child, variously referred to as "the child," "the good child," "the poor child" and "dear Child," is led by her guardian angel to the hut of an old man who gives her shelter, and whose kindness she repays by serving him faithfully for what she thinks are three days but which are actually 30 years. When she finally leaves, he reveals himself to be St. Joseph and gives her a rosebud, saying that she will return when it is fully bloomed.
>
> The guardian angel returns the girl to her aged and still heartbroken mother. "They sat together the whole evening in great joy, then went to bed serenely and calmly," the story says, "but the next morning the neighbors found them both dead; they had blessedly departed this life, and between them lay the rose of St. Joseph in full bloom."

As the *Times* reporter then adds, the story "does not admit to easy interpretation or analysis."

Unlike "Snow-White and Rose-Red," this story does not belong to fairy tale romance. Indeed, love and marriage play no role whatsoever. Instead, Wilhelm Grimm—if he indeed was the story's inventor—quite consciously

modeled it on the type of pious children's tales, or "Kinderlegenden," as
he called the section of separately numbered stories at the end of the
collection. The genre, in any case, is clearly exemplified here.

While there is no romance, there is a long cohabitation of an old man
with a little girl alone in the forest. The length of the girl's sojourn with
the hermit can be explained, to be sure, by the assumption that it must
have been a long military conflict—indeed presumably the Thirty Years'
War itself—from which the girl's mother had acted to protect her by sending
her off into the woods. We can assume, too, that like Sleeping Beauty, the
girl is magically prevented from aging, so that when she returns to her
mother after the thirty years, she is not a forty-year-old woman in appearance but physically unchanged from the moment when she had left
home. And we understand, as well, that the girl's premature death the
following morning is a gift from heaven, because it means that the daughter
will not have to be separated again from the mother, who having not been
protected against aging has presumably grown quite old.

If we view the old hermit, alias St. Joseph, as the type of the doting
avuncular friend to a young girl, we find we have a different story, however.
Having a guardian angel bring a lovely young innocent creature to live with
him would be a magical wish fulfillment for this type of bachelor. A decidedly erotic element is indicated through St. Joseph's role as saving the
girl from the ravages of war—specifically, we imagine, the danger of sexual
abuse or rape—by taking her in. Moreover, the magical prevention of her
aging means that she does not blossom into a nubile maiden, which might
arouse powerful urges in the bachelor dreamer that he could not control.
Instead, he is allowed to spend a length of time almost exactly equivalent
to the average of a woman's childbearing period living with a little girl who
does not turn into every avuncular bachelor dreamer's stereotypical nightmare: a desirous woman. Yet as though the dreamer senses that Mother
Nature will prevail and he cannot hold back the hands of the clock in-
definitely, as a token of farewell at the end of the thirty years he gives her
a rosebud, which by the next morning has "miraculously" reached full
bloom. In answer to the avuncular dreamer's wish to be united forever with
the girl, the hour of her blossoming is also that of her death, so that "St.
Joseph" and the girl—not to forget her mother, of course—will be united
in heaven, where moth and rust do not corrupt, thieves do not break in
and steal, and mature young women no longer pose a threat to cowardly
bachelor hearts.

Was Wilhelm Grimm secretly conveying such a message to his presumably very young correspondent, as a sly confession of love and as a self-
ironic image of himself? Of course, we cannot know; but his evident creation
of the role of animal suitor as avuncular playmate of two innocent young

girls in "Snow-White and Rose-Red" lends plausibility to the suggestion. In any case, it likely is true enough, as one critic has maintained, that "Wilhelm Grimm was writing a letter to a little girl, and to please her, on the spur of the moment made up a story in which she figured as heroine." And for that very reason, one must disagree with the same critic when he maintains that this tale has no significance for the Grimm collection.[6] On the contrary, this story contained in the letter to "Dear Mili" is perhaps our most direct example of what sort of tales Wilhelm Grimm would have told if he had been inventing them himself, and sheds light therefore also on the direction of editorial changes and choices he was inclined to select, and the types of depictions he favored for inclusion in the collection.

This story about the little girl and St. Joseph is presumably only an imitation of a type of tale that existed in popular tradition, and is thus decidedly a case of what folklorists call "fakelore." The tales actually included in the Grimm collection—as well as most of those found in Basile and Perrault—can lay better claim to derivation from popular storytelling; but they, too, have been adapted to educated literary tastes. Folklorists are justified in objecting to any claim by critics that by interpreting tales in these and similar collections they are explaining the meaning of a tale as it existed in popular tradition. As a prominent folklorist put it, "When one analyzes fairy tales as written by Charles Perrault or by the Grimm brothers, one is *not* analyzing fairy tales as they were told by traditional storytellers. One is instead analyzing fairy tale plots as altered by men of letters."[7] The same scholar admits, however, that "the study of Kunst-märchen and literary versions of fairy tales is a legitimate academic enterprise," even while he goes on to add that "it is no substitute for and it ought not to be confused with the study of the oral fairy tale."[8] The latter point is well taken and important; this study has made every effort to respect that distinction.

The tales by the Grimms, Basile, and Perrault are of course not literary creations from thin air. With relatively few exceptions, they or stories very much like them had a prior existence in oral storytelling. Distinguishing which elements are literary in origin and which originated in oral tradition is largely impossible, however. One folklorist recently urged the following approach: "The impossibility and futility of separating oral and literary phases in folktale transmission is obvious. . . . [Folktale research] needs to recognize that the comparative study of direct or indirect literary influences and processual stages of retroaction between written and oral variants can offer new insights into the nature of creative process in storytelling. As a matter of fact, examples at our disposal indicate that most folklorists minimized the influence of the booktale and only very few experimented with comparing oral tales to their literary models."[9] It is hoped that the present study can prove useful to folklorists in such comparisons of folktale and so-called booktales by pointing to types of depiction that may, or may not, be encountered in oral fairy tales about love and marriage.

Whether the tales are from written or oral sources, simply comparing them according to their elements of plot is not enough. Scholarly critics, including present-day folklorists, increasingly insist on interpretation of the stories. The dissatisfaction with the limitations of the traditional folkloristic approach was expressed by one critic as follows:

> When folklorist and other critics discuss the *Kinder- und Hausmärchen*, it has become customary to type them according to the Aarne-Thompson motif index. That is, they are generally classified according to such motifs as animal helpers, the beastly bridegroom, the enchanted mountain, the test by fire, or the seven-league boots, so that parallels with other folktales and their origins can be traced. Such typification . . . may assist in the kind of work done by folklorists, ethnologists, and structural minded literary critics, but in the Grimms' collection it has detracted from the social and historical meaning of their work.[10]

The important point raised here is that one cannot ignore the cultural, historical, and social context in which a given type of tale is being narrated—and thereby necessarily adapted—if one is to understand why the story is told in exactly this certain way. The same complaint is legitimately raised against other critics who approach the tales as depicting universal psychic processes rather than reflecting the very concrete and specific situations of the particular tellers and their audiences. One scholar objected, "I . . . regard some of the psychoanalytic and pedagogic reverence for the fairy tale as a kind of idolatry, as a veneration of a false deity, as a denial of what the folk really recounted and what the actual psycho-social requirements of the lower classes were."[11]

Clearly, the mode of depicting erotic material is especially dependent on the audience. The erotic tastes of the lower classes will have been different—likely coarser and earthier—than those of the upper classes; and in the European Middle Ages and Renaissance sexuality was more openly depicted and discussed than it was in the bourgeois eighteenth and nineteenth centuries. Moreover, the oral teller can provide sexual innuendo through timing, tempo, inflection, and gesture, whereas the literary narrator is limited to words on a page, to the text. Most important, however, is that the tellers of oral and written folktales must communicate with their audiences by means of two quite different traditions, those of the tale as performance and as literature, respectively.[12] As we have seen, the versions of folktale offered by Basile, Perrault, and the Grimms strongly reflected in each case the literary culture of their respective periods and places, while at the same time being recognizably connected as belonging to European literary tradition stretching back to the Middle Ages and antiquity.

Among these three literary collections of folktale, that by the Grimms surely comes closest to oral tradition, at least as regards a majority of the texts gathered there. This, again, is owing to the specific literary culture of their time and place, because it was the Romantic generation of writers and scholars in Germany which was concerned to recover and preserve treasures of the European past and, in view of Napoleon's domination of the German-speaking lands, especially those treasures that could be considered expressive of the spirit of the German people, particularly the common folk. We have seen that the versions offered by the Grimms do not dwell upon or embellish erotic elements in their tales. This characteristic can be laid to the account of the literary taste of their Romantic age, especially in Germany, where such depiction was veiled or indirect, to the point where it can be overlooked, or interpreted as having some other reference. Quite possibly, too, the Grimms believed, justifiably, that since the tales' charm resided in the element of unexplained mystery and magic, the stories' power to entrance was increased by avoiding or eliminating any elaboration or hint that would remove the mystery.

An important element in this question of the cultural specificity of the given version is sexual gender, and all the more so in stories of love and marriage. As another critic observed, "Whenever and wherever psychological interpretations of *Grimm's Tales* use the deceptively generalizing *man, one,* or *the child,* we must look behind those formulations to the gender message implicit in the tales; there we find a consistent vision of gender-specific and gender-appropriate behavior that includes kindred values revived and incorporated from preceding centuries."[13] As the results of the present investigation have shown, the stories in the collections of the Grimms, Basile, and Perrault depict love and marriage specifically within the literary contexts of patriarchal European society. Granted, we have found that the heroines of fairy tale romance may be excessively attached to their brothers; secretly panicked or repelled by the thought of the wedding night; too devoted to or jealously adored by their fathers; envied or identified with by older women; and be pursuers of potential mates or true brides to those already captured. Yet the object is always plainly and simply marriage, and not even wealth—though most of the heroines attain it if they do not already have it—much less a career, power, or domination.

As culturally specific as the particular renditions by Basile, Perrault, and the Grimms may be, the fact remains that the motifs, and often even the cores of the stories themselves, were passed forward from still earlier times. The question of how such stories were understood by those who may have narrated them in oral tradition is of course impossible to answer. We must remember that even establishing how Basile, Perrault, and the Grimms understood their versions is an uncertain enterprise. As one scholar commented, "*Grimms' Fairy Tales* do not reflect the intentions of a single author, as literary masterworks otherwise do, but the highly divergent purposes of two imitative contributors, as well as thirty different published or manuscript sources spanning six centuries and almost all of the German-speaking areas."[14] Only implicit in this observation is the view that, on some level, every storyteller has an idea of his story's meaning. An explicit statement of that position was given by another scholar: "It is quite possible that a storyteller does not perceive the significance of his story. On the other hand, no storyteller wants to relate nonsense and so even the most contaminated version has an individual meaning for its narrator."[15] This critic indeed went so far as to embrace the extreme position that since any two people will have differing interpretations of a story, "The scholar analyzing the tale necessarily finds a different meaning from that of the storyteller."[16]

The interpreter can indeed never, in the end, lay claim to being in possession of the objective truth about the meaning of texts. As the scholar quoted above concludes, "Most interpretations are only assessments of probability. Nevertheless, the aim of the humanities is to arrive at valid interpretations. Yet certainty is not the same as validity, and recognition of ambiguity is not the same as uncertain knowledge."[17] The present interpretation of fairy tale romance has been made with this same understanding.

From the examples we have investigated in the collections by the Grimms, Basile, and Perrault, it has emerged that in these literized folktales we find a focus on certain patterns of relationships in stories about love and marriage. Sisters and brothers typically share a closeness that is undiminished by the sister's marriage. Young virgins are asked—or ask—to wed suitors who are beasts in either the literal or the figurative sense. Fathers become unseemly involved in their daughters' choice of a husband—and mothers occasionally in the sons' choice of a bride. Older women play bizarre roles in the lives of young girls arriving at marriageable age. Young women show themselves far from helpless and passive when it comes to winning and keeping the man they want. Bachelors, young and old, do not enter the role of bridegroom unproblematically.

These patterns suggest that tellers of these tales were not oblivious to the problematic nature of erotic desire. We appear to have here documentation and reflection of a popular wisdom about brothers and sisters being sweet on one another; virgins' fantasies about the wedding night; fathers' incestuous feelings toward their daughters and mothers toward their sons; older women's identification with younger women as objects of desire; women's instincts for winning and keeping a man; and the cold feet experienced by bridegrooms and bachelors over the prospect of marrying. Such observations surely belonged as well to the popular as to the literary culture. Since the depiction of these relationships, especially in their more incongruous aspects, is especially pronounced in these literized folktales, as contrasted with other contemporary literary genres, we may conclude that the folk wisdom about these effects of erotic desire reflected in these stories made the genre especially attractive to many or most of the tales' literary adapters as a welcome vehicle for depicting this realm of human emotional experience.

NOTES

1. Bottigheimer, *Grimms' Bad Girls and Bold Boys*, p. 156.

2. Tatar, *Hard Facts of the Grimms' Fairy Tales*, pp. 10–11.

3. Rölleke, "New Results of Research on Grimms' Fairy Tales," in McGlathery, ed., *Brothers Grimm and Folktale*, p. 107.

4. Rölleke, "Schneeweißchen und Rosenrot: Rätsel um ein Grimmsches Märchen," in his *'Wo das Wunschen noch geholfen hat'*, pp. 191–206.

5. Edwin McDowell, "A Fairy Tale by Grimm Comes to Light," *New York Times*, 28 Sept. 1983, 1, 21. The tale has since been published as Wilhelm Grimm, *Dear Mili*, illustrated by Maurice Sendak and translated by Ralph Manheim (New York: Farrar, Straus, Giroux, 1988).

6. John M. Ellis, "What Really Is the Value of the 'New' Grimm Discovery?" *German Quarterly*, 58 (1985), 87–90.

7. Dundes, "Fairy Tales from a Folkloristic Perspective," in Bottigheimer, ed., *Fairy Tales and Society*, p. 260.

8. Ibid., p. 265.

9. Dégh, "What Did the Grimm Brothers Give to and Take from the Folk?" in McGlathery, ed., *Brothers Grimm and Folktale*, p. 73.

10. Jack Zipes, "The Grimms and the German Obsession with Fairy Tales," in Bottigheimer, ed., *Fairy Tales and Society*, p. 275.

11. Schenda, "Telling Tales—Spreading Tales," p. 79.

12. See the studies by Bauman cited in the introduction: *Verbal Art as Performance* and *Story, Performance, and Event*.

13. Bottigheimer, *Grimms' Bad Girls and Bold Boys*, p. 168.

14. Rölleke, "New Results of Research on Grimms' Fairy Tales," p. 101.

15. Lutz Röhrich, "The Quest of Meaning in Folk Narrative Research," in McGlathery, ed., *Brothers Grimm and Folktale*, p. 12.

16. Ibid.

17. Ibid.

Appendix I

List of Tales Cited in This Study, by Collection

A. Grimms' *Kinder- und Hausmärchen*, by *KHM* number, with Aarne-Thompson index number in parentheses

1 (AT 440) "The Frog King"
3 (AT 710) "The Holy Virgin's Child"
4 (AT 326) "Tale of One Who Went Off to Learn Fear"
6 (AT 516) "Faithful John"
9 (AT 451) "The Twelve Brothers"
11 (AT 450) "Little Brother and Little Sister"
12 (AT 310) "Rapunzel"
13 (AT 403B) "The Three Little Men in the Forest"
14 (AT 501) "The Three Spinning Ladies"
15 (AT 327A) "Hansel and Gretel"
21 (AT 510A) "Cinderella"
22 (AT 851) "The Riddle"
24 (AT 480) "Frau Holle"
25 (AT 451) "The Seven Ravens"
26 (AT 333) "Little Red Cap"
31 (AT 706) "The Girl without Hands"
32 (AT 1387) "Clever Hans"
40 (AT 955) "The Robber Bridegroom"
46 (AT 311) "Fitcher's Bird"
47 (AT 720) "The Juniper Tree"
49 (AT 451) "The Six Swans"
50 (AT 410) "Little Briar-Rose"
51 (AT 313A) "Fundevogel"/"Fledgling"
52 (AT 900) "King Thrushbeard"

53 (AT 709) "Little Snow White"
55 (AT 500) "Rumpelstiltskin"
56 (AT 313C) "Beloved Roland"
57 (AT 550) "The Golden Bird"
60 (AT 303) "The Two Brothers"
65 (AT 510B) "Allerleirauh"/"Thousandfurs"
66 (AT 311) "The Hare's Bride"
67 (AT 884) "The Twelve Huntsmen"
69 (AT 405) "Jorinda and Joringel"
85 (AT 303) "The Children of Gold"
88 (AT 425C) "The Singing, Jumping Little Lark"
89 (AT 533) "The Goose Girl"
92 (AT 400) "The King of the Golden Mountain"
93 (AT 400) "The Raven"
96 (AT 707) "The Three Little Birds"
101 (AT 361) "The Sluggard"
105 (AT 285) "Little Tales about the Toad"
106 (AT 402) "The Poor Miller's Boy and the Cat"
108 (AT 441) "Hans My Hedgehog"
109 "The Little Shroud"
111 (AT 304) "The Skilled Huntsman"
113 (AT 313B) "The Two Royal Children"
122 (AT 566) "The Herb Donkey"
123 (AT 442) "The Old Woman in the Woods"
124 (AT 654) "The Three Brothers"
126 (AT 531) "Ferdinand the Faithful and Ferdinand the Unfaithful"
127 (AT 425A) "The Iron Stove"
129 (AT 653) "The Four Artful Brothers"
134 (AT 513A) "The Six Servants"
135 (AT 403A) "The White Bride and the Black Bride"
136 (AT 314) "Iron Hans"
137 (AT 425) "The Three Black Princesses"
141 (AT 450) "The Little Lamb and the Little Fish"
144 (AT 430) "The Little Donkey"
161 (AT 426) "Snow-White and Rose-Red"
163 (AT 410) "The Glass Coffin"
169 (AT 431) "The House in the Woods"
179 (AT 923) "The Goosegirl at the Spring"
181 (AT 316) "The Water-Nymph in the Pond"
186 (AT 313C) "The True Bride"
188 (AT 585) "Spindle, Shuttle, and Needle"

191 (AT 329) "The Little Rabbit"
193 (AT 313B) "The Drummer"
196 "Old Rinkrank"
197 (AT 302) "The Crystal Ball"
198 (AT 870) "Maid Maleen"

B. Basile's *Pentamerone*

I, 2 "The Myrtle"
I, 3 (AT 675) "Peruonto"
I, 5 (AT 311) "The Flea"
I, 6 (AT 510A) "The Cat Cinderella"
I, 7 (AT 303) "The Merchant's Two Sons"
I, 9 (AT 303) "The Charmed Hind"
I, 10 "The Flayed Hag"
II, 1 (AT 310) "Petrosinella"
II, 2 "Green Meadow"
II, 3 "Viola"
II, 5 (AT 433) "The Serpent"
II, 6 (AT 510B) "The She-Bear"
II, 7 (AT 313C) "The Dove"
II, 8 (AT 410) "The Little Slave Girl"
II, 9 (AT 425L) "The Padlock"
III, 1 "Cannetella"
III, 2 (AT 706) "Penta the Handless"
III, 3 "The Face"
III, 4 "Sapia Liccarda"
III, 5 "The Beetle, the Mouse, and the Cricket"
III, 6 "Belluccia"
III, 9 (AT 313C) "Rosella"
III, 10 (AT 403) "The Three Fairies"
IV, 3 "The Three Animal Kings"
IV, 4 (AT 501) "The Seven Skins of Lard"
IV, 5 "The Dragon"
IV, 6 "The Three Crowns"
IV, 7 (AT 403) "The Two Cakes"
IV, 8 (AT 451) "The Seven Doves"
IV, 9 (AT 516) "The Raven"
IV, 10 (AT 900) "Pride Punished"
V, 3 "Pinto Smalto"
V, 4 (AT 425A) "The Golden Tree Stump"
V, 5 (AT 410) "Sun, Moon, and Talia"

V, 8 (AT 450) "Ninnillo and Nennella"
V, 9 (AT 408) "The Three Citrons"
V, 10 "Ending"

C. Perrault's Tales

AT 312 "Bluebeard"
AT 510A "Cendrillon, or the Little Glass Slipper"
AT 510B "Donkey-Skin"
AT 333 "Little Red Riding Hood"
AT 410 "Sleeping Beauty"

Appendix II

List of Tales Cited, by Aarne-Thompson Index Number

(AT 285) "Little Tales about the Toad" *KHM* 105
(AT 302) "The Crystal Ball" *KHM* 197
(AT 303) "The Children of Gold" *KHM* 85
(AT 303) "The Two Brothers" *KHM* 60
(AT 303) "The Charmed Hind" Basile I, 9
(AT 303) "The Merchant's Two Sons" Basile I, 7
(AT 304) "The Skilled Huntsman" *KHM* 111
(AT 310) "Petrosinella" Basile II, 1
(AT 310) "Rapunzel" *KHM* 12
(AT 311) "Fitcher's Bird" *KHM* 46
(AT 311) "The Flea" Basile I, 5
(AT 311) "The Hare's Bride" *KHM* 66
(AT 312) "Bluebeard" Perrault
(AT 313A) "Fundevogel"/"Fledgling" *KHM* 51
(AT 313B) "The Drummer" *KHM* 193
(AT 313B) "The Two Royal Children" *KHM* 113
(AT 313C) "Beloved Roland" *KHM* 56
(AT 313C) "Rosella" Basile III, 9
(AT 313C) "The Dove" Basile II, 7
(AT 313C) "The True Bride" *KHM* 186
(AT 314) "Iron Hans" *KHM* 136
(AT 316) "The Water-Nymph in the Pond" *KHM* 181
(AT 326) "Tale of One Who Went Off to Learn Fear" *KHM* 4
(AT 327A) "Hansel and Gretel" *KHM* 15
(AT 329) "The Little Rabbit" *KHM* 191
(AT 333) "Little Red Cap" *KHM* 26
(AT 333) "Little Red Riding Hood" Perrault

(AT 361) "The Sluggard" *KHM* 101
(AT 400) "The King of the Golden Mountain" *KHM* 92
(AT 400) "The Raven" *KHM* 93
(AT 402) "The Poor Miller's Boy and the Cat" *KHM* 106
(AT 403) "The Three Fairies" Basile III, 10
(AT 403) "The Two Cakes" Basile IV, 7
(AT 403A) "The White Bride and the Black Bride" *KHM* 135
(AT 403B) "The Three Little Men in the Forest" *KHM* 13
(AT 405) "Jorinda and Joringel" *KHM* 69
(AT 408) "The Three Citrons" Basile V, 9
(AT 410) "Little Briar-Rose" *KHM* 50
(AT 410) "Sleeping Beauty" Perrault
(AT 410) "Sun, Moon, and Talia" Basile V, 5
(AT 410) "The Glass Coffin" *KHM* 163
(AT 410) "The Little Slave Girl" Basile II, 8
(AT 425) "The Three Black Princesses" *KHM* 137
(AT 425A) "The Golden Tree Stump" Basile V, 4
(AT 425A) "The Iron Stove" *KHM* 127
(AT 425C) "The Singing, Jumping Little Lark" *KHM* 88
(AT 425L) "The Padlock" Basile II, 9
(AT 426) "Snow-White and Rose-Red" *KHM* 161
(AT 430) "The Little Donkey" *KHM* 144
(AT 431) "The House in the Woods" *KHM* 169
(AT 433) "The Serpent" Basile II, 5
(AT 440) "The Frog King" *KHM* 1
(AT 441) "Hans My Hedgehog" *KHM* 108
(AT 442) "The Old Woman in the Woods" *KHM* 123
(AT 450) "Little Brother and Little Sister" *KHM* 11
(AT 450) "Ninnillo and Nennella" Basile V, 8
(AT 450) "The Little Lamb and the Little Fish" *KHM* 141
(AT 451) "The Seven Doves" Basile IV, 8
(AT 451) "The Seven Ravens" *KHM* 25
(AT 451) "The Six Swans" *KHM* 49
(AT 451) "The Twelve Brothers" *KHM* 9
(AT 480) "Frau Holle" *KHM* 24
(AT 500) "Rumpelstiltskin" *KHM* 55
(AT 501) "The Seven Skins of Lard" Basile IV, 4
(AT 501) "The Three Spinning Ladies" *KHM* 14
(AT 510A) "Cendrillon, or the Little Glass Slipper" Perrault
(AT 510A) "Cinderella" *KHM* 21
(AT 510A) "The Cat Cinderella" Basile I, 6
(AT 510B) "Allerleirauh"/"Thousandfurs" *KHM* 65

(AT 510B) "Donkey-Skin" Perrault
(AT 510B) "The She-Bear" Basile II, 6
(AT 513A) "The Six Servants" *KHM* 134
(AT 516) "Faithful John" *KHM* 6
(AT 516) "The Raven" Basile IV, 9
(AT 531) "Ferdinand the Faithful and Ferdinand the Unfaithful"
    KHM 126
(AT 533) "The Goose Girl" *KHM* 89
(AT 550) "The Golden Bird" *KHM* 57
(AT 566) "The Herb Donkey" *KHM* 122
(AT 585) "Spindle, Shuttle, and Needle" *KHM* 188
(AT 653) "The Four Artful Brothers" *KHM* 129
(AT 654) "The Three Brothers" *KHM* 124
(AT 675) "Peruonto" Basile I, 3
(AT 706) "The Girl without Hands" *KHM* 31
(AT 706) "Penta the Handless" Basile III, 2
(AT 707) "The Three Little Birds" *KHM* 96
(AT 709) "Little Snow White" *KHM* 53
(AT 710) "The Holy Virgin's Child" *KHM* 3
(AT 720) "The Juniper Tree" *KHM* 47
(AT 851) "The Riddle" *KHM* 22
(AT 870) "Maid Maleen" *KHM* 198
(AT 884) "The Twelve Huntsmen" *KHM* 67
(AT 900) "King Thrushbeard" *KHM* 52
(AT 900) "Pride Punished" Basile IV, 10
(AT 923) "The Goosegirl at the Spring" *KHM* 179
(AT 955) "The Robber Bridegroom" *KHM* 40
(AT 1387) "Clever Hans" *KHM* 32

Index

daughter in, 121; heroine's attraction of lover in, 136

"Pinto smalto" (V, 3): devotion between father and daughter in, 91; heroine's marriage to confectioner's doll in, 77–78, 88; yearning of heroine's father for grandchildren in, 89

"Pinto smauto." See "Pinto smalto"

"Pride Punished" (IV, 10): type of haughty virgin in, 76–77

"Raven, The" (IV, 9): brother's identification with brother as bridegroom in, 164–66; father's jealous passion in, 95; hero as bridegroom in, 167, 180, 181

"Rosella" (III, 9): heroine's winning of husband in, 143; mother's acting to prevent daughter's elopement in, 119–20

"Sapia Liccarda" (III, 4): father's acting to guard daughters' virtue in, 96; heroine's winning of husband in, 140

"Sapia the Glutton." See "Sapia Liccarda"

"Scompetura." See "Ending"

"Serpent, The" (II, 5): father's involvement in daughter's wedding night in, 96; hero's rejection of ogress's advances in, 116; heroine's rescue of bridegroom in, 136; maiden's reaction to animal groom in, 62

"Seven Doves, The" (IV, 8): devotion between brothers and sisters in, 37–38, 135

"Seven Pieces of Pork-Skin, The." See "Seven Skins of Lard, The"

"Seven Pigeons, The." See "Seven Doves, The"

"Seven Skins of Lard, The" (IV, 4): fairies helping maiden win a husband in, 126

"She-Bear, The" (II, 6): father's incestuous passion for daughter in, 102–4, 108; heroine's winning of husband in, 139; mother's involvement in son's choice of bride in, 109

"Sole, Luna e Talia." See "Sun, Moon, and Talia"

"Sun, Moon, and Talia" (V, 5): comparison with other versions, 130; erotic implications of prophecy in, 119; father's devotion to daughter in, 98–99, 108; Freudian interpretation of, 111; older woman envious of younger woman in, 114; passion of married man for maiden in, 173

"Three Animal Kings, The" (IV, 3): devotion between brothers and sisters in, 48–49

"Three Citrons, The" (V, 9): bachelor's passion for fairy in, 159–61, 179; fairy's winning of husband in, 147

"Three Crowns, The" (IV, 6): father's jealous passion for daughter in, 99–100; older woman's aiding a maiden win a lover in, 121

"Three Fairies, The" (III, 10): fairies' aiding maiden win husband in, 124; maiden's winning back of beloved in, 149

"Two Cakes, The" (IV, 7): devotion between brother and sister in, 47–48, 148; fairy's contributing to maiden's appeal in, 124

"Verde prato." See "Green Meadow"

"Viola" (II, 3): bachelor fantasy about siring a maiden in, 97, 172–73, 180; heroine's winning of a husband in, 141

"Wood of Garlic, The." See "Belluccia"

"Young Slave, The." See "Little Slave Girl, The"

Bauman, Richard, 17, 197

Bausinger, Hermann, 17, 24, 132, 152

Beastly bridegrooms, 66–73, 79–80; in contrast to animal suitors, 56

Beaumont, Marie Leprince de: her *La Belle et la Bête*, 15, 80

Beauties and Beasts, as tale type, 55–73, 80–85, 88, 155, 178, 187, 188, 191, 196. *See also* Beaumont

Enzyklopädie des Märchens, 6, 22

Eroticism: absence or elimination of, 17; in adolescent fantasy, 162; bridegroom's role and, 167; in dreams, 43; between father and daughter, 90, 97; in folktale, from historical perspective, 21; Grimms' rejection of, 109; handling of, in children's tales, 51; maidens' transformation as animal related to, 138; in Middle Ages and Renaissance, 189, 194; naked maidens and, 136; names' reference to, 64, 130; overtones of, 173; projection of, 171; prophecies indicative of, 119; relative absence in Grimms' immediate sources, 189–90; role of angel of rescue related to, 161; suppression of, 82–83; veiled, 17, 84, 108, 159, 168, 177, 183, 186, 190, 192, 195; in versions of Rumpelstiltskin, 184. *See also* Aprons; Fleas; Neckerchiefs

Ethnological approaches, 11, 23

European folktale: development during Middle Ages, 17; existence in Romance countries, 19; popularity of, ix

Eve: daughters of, 121; her eating of the apple with Adam, 123

Fairies, 106, 118–19, 174; absent in the Grimms' tales, 122; as objects of men's passion, 126, 160; old, 118; as type in folktale, 122–27; young, as objects of desire, 147. *See also* Godmothers

Fairy stories, vogue of, in France, 16

Fairy tale, as a term, 1, 2

"Fakelore," literary tales as, 193

False brides. *See* Substituted brides

Fantasizing. *See* Spinning

Fantasy: adolescent, 158; bachelors', 166; beloved as creature of, 161–62; devil as creature of, 158, element of, 115; marriage to creature of, 161; virginal, about males as predators, 55

Farrer, Claire R., 25

Fathers: daughter as mistress of their household, 70, 75; identification with daughter's suitor, 89, 109; indifference to daughters, 97–98; involvement in daughter's choice of husband, 187, 196; provision of fine clothes to daughters, 92, 103; wish for daughter to marry, 79; wishing to marry daughters, 111. *See also* Allerleirauh story; Fathers and daughters

Fathers and daughters, attachment between: as especially prevalent in Basile's tales, 107; as story element, 54, 78, 87–103, 107–8, 109–12, 128, 129, 132, 155, 180, 187, 188, 189, 195

Fathers-in-law, 154

Feeling, seeming lack of, in folktale, 4

Feminist approaches to folktale, 14–16, 25; fathers and daughters, attachment between, 79, 86, 110; mother-daughter relationships, 153; older women, role of, 128, 131; passivity of heroines vs. activity, 151, 179; position of women in society, 111; powers of women, ancient, 152; spinning as motif, 134; vulnerability of heroines, sexual, 53

Fetching maidens: as character type, 135–43, 150–52, 155, 178, 188, 195; frequency in Basile, 151; youngest daughter as, 96

Fetishism, 91

Film, fairy tales in, ix

Fink, Gonthier-Louis, 16, 184, 185

Finnish school of folktale studies. *See* Geographical-historical approach

Fleas, in relation to eroticism, 84, 100, 173

Flinders, Peter, 19

Flirts, maidens as, 137, 152

Folk humor, 2

Folkloristic approaches, 11; in combination with literary approaches, 24; interpretation, attitude toward, 193–94; lacking interest in romance as tale type, 188–89; studies of individual story types, 80, 81, 84, 85, 110, 132, 134, 153, 182–83

Folktale studies: as scholarly discipline, 21; since turn of the century, 21

A Note on the Author

JAMES M. McGLATHERY is professor of German and head of the Department of Germanic Languages and Literatures at the University of Illinois at Urbana-Champaign. He is the author of *Desire's Sway: The Plays and Stories of Heinrich von Kleist* and *Mysticism and Sexuality: E. T. A. Hoffmann,* and the editor of *The Brothers Grimm and Folktale.*